*How
to
Build
Your
Business
by
Telephone*

Telephone Marketing

Murray Roman

*Chairman, Campaign Communications Institute
of America, Inc.*

McGraw-Hill Book Company

*New York   St. Louis   San Francisco   Auckland   Düsseldorf
Johannesburg   Kuala Lumpur   London   Mexico
Montreal   New Delhi   Panama   Paris
São Paulo   Singapore   Sydney
Tokyo   Toronto*

Library of Congress Cataloging in Publication Data

Roman, Murray, date.

  Telephone marketing.

  Bibliography: p.
  1. Telephone selling. I. Title.
HF5438.3.R64 1976   658.8   76-9814
ISBN 0-07-053595-7

    890KPKP 8543

*The editors for this book were W. Hodson Mogan and Ruth Weine,
the designer was Naomi Auerbach, and the production supervisor
was Teresa F. Leaden. It was set in VIP Electra
by Monotype Composition Company, Inc.*

Printed and bound by The Kingsport Press.

*To our telephone communicators
who listened and learned
and made this book come true*

Contents

Foreword–Theodore Levitt   ix
Preface   xi
Introduction–Lester Wunderman   xv

1. *The Multimedia Sales Challenge*   *1*
2. *A Modern Approach to Today's Market*   *9*
3. *The Range of Applications*   *20*
4. *Identifying Your Market–Whom Do You Call?*   *33*
5. *Your Promotional Message–What Do You Say?*   *45*
6. *Get Ready, Get Set–Who Will Say It For You?*   *58*
7. *The Interdependency Factor*   *70*
8. *Telephone Economics*   *82*
9. *The "800" Route to Sales*   *93*
10. *Some Guidelines for the Independent Salesperson*   *105*
11. *The Eleven Commandmants*   *116*
12. *The Future State of the Art*   *124*

Appendix   132
Index   186
Endpaper   By James L. Hayes, Emerson Foote, Norman Cousins,
Robert Stone, Samuel Josefowitz, William T. Knox,
Blaine Cooke, William Hammond, Gordon Grossman,
Henry "Pete" Hoke, Lawrence G. Chait, A. Edward Miller,
J. Patrick Rooney, Putney Westerfield, Eugene Sollo,
Joan and Robert Blum, Richard Zeldin.   195

Foreword

*Theodore Levitt**

IT'S RARE WHEN NEW METHODS of doing business first get touted as being "revolutionary" that they actually ever produce revolutions. A lot of the world's work gets done by sheer inertia.

But things do change. Many revolutions in time get to be so casually taken for granted we don't recognize them as ever having occurred. The telephone certainly created a revolution in doing business. Think only what the business world would be like without it. How many of us come home from "work" at night and say, "I've been on the phone all day," and call that "work"?

Murray Roman has been a pioneer in using the telephone for a new kind of "work"—not simply the work of using that instrument to sell goods or services, or to get sales leads, or to foster political candidates, or to improve collection delinquencies—but the much more significant and exciting work of systematizing the work itself. He has pioneered the conversion of the telephone from an instrument for personal communication to a machine for production. He has converted a spade into a steam shovel, a tabulating machine into a computer. Or, more modestly, he has begun the transformation with some of the remarkable successes

* Professor of Business Administration, Harvard Business School.

this book describes. And in the process he has neither sacrificed the authenticity of the human interactions that are involved nor brutalized or vulgarized our lives by the required mechanization.

It is a rare individual, family, company, or country that would not rather get more results for less cost or effort. In a world where "service" seems increasingly to account for a larger proportion of the Gross National Product, it is these days a common plaint that this will inevitably reduce the rate at which our standards of living improve. The argument has some plausibility. "Service" cannot be mechanized like "Manufacturing." Hence there are fewer economies of scale, and certainly less productivity in the service worker than in the production worker. Thus, as we demand more service we increasingly buy more things that lend themselves less to cost-saving productivity improvements. So, we shall end up with higher "costs of living."

As I have pointed out elsewhere, this kind of reasoning may reflect more the preindustrial modes of behavior that have dominated our historic approach to service (service is personal, one-to-one, and besides, it's servile) than it reflects what needs to be and can be done. It is possible to apply production-line approaches to historic "service" activities that are as fully productivity-improving as the assembly line improved the work of the artisan carriage maker. And while we now view the carriage as having been nostalgically elegant, we forget it was also highly idiosyncratic and very expensive. It could be afforded only by the "carriage trade." The automobile, by contrast, is cheaper, more reliable, and remarkably customized to the special whims and needs of its mass-market owners and users.

This book describes how production-line approaches have been employed in the use of telephone selling and how these can be as effectively customized as the automobile, with similar reductions in relative costs and improvements in relative results. Whether they have the potential of making a revolution is not the point. The point is, they are here and cannot sensibly be ignored by anyone concerned with improving productivity in sales.

Preface

WHEN THE PHONE RINGS, we just reach out and pick it up; the telephone is such an unconsciously accepted part of our daily lives that we take it for granted. We misuse its "technology" because we don't truly understand McLuhan's concept—in the case of the phone, the medium really *is* the message. It's an electronic communications device with person-to-person voice contact, immediate response, and informational feedback.

Any machine has its limitations. Certainly the telephone has.

Actually, talking to a mass market is far more effective via television on a "cost-per-viewer" base; so it is with radio, newspapers, and consumer publications. Cost per inquiry is still cheaper when direct mail is responsive. And, of course, there's still no substitute for personal selling.

Are there some caveats or potential drawbacks in applying the techniques of telephone marketing? Of course there are. Because the Picturephone's use for mass marketers is 10 years off, you can't see "eyeball to eyeball" or sign a check or an order form over the phone. Though selectivity—made possible by the computer married to the Census—and select lists have opened new marketing horizons, a phone communicator still can't *see* the specific site or room being called: it could be a shack, mansion, trailer, or jail cell! Though credit card identification has improved control systems, it wasn't too long ago that one phone marketer made the grand mistake and supplied 10 credit cards to a well-rated mafioso! Sometimes a fourteen-year-old has a very mature voice and says "yes" to an order for a $300 hi-fi set. We can beam calls off the satellite, but you can still end up reaching the wrong number in Paris!

But these are small problems compared to the excitement and sense of progress involved in watching a new marketing medium evolve and take its place in the world of business. Its development is something I have been happy to observe and fortunate to have participated in for more than 25 years.

Understanding the telephone as a mass-marketing medium requires professional expertise. Because it is a labor- and equipment-intensive business, special systems and firm management controls for using it efficiently are necessary. There are proved methods and procedures that we at CCI have worked many years to perfect, and they can earn "plus profits" for you, too.

There's a challenge and an excitement in creating a new telephone marketing program. Each is different (I've never found two alike), each one takes its own thinking, its special custom design. *Reader's Digest*, *TV Guide*, and *Saturday Review* are as different from one another as night and day. Though the audience for one program may overlap another's, the specifications and telephone marketing strategies are always quite different. One audience responds to a tape message; another market approach doesn't need it.

Marginal account sales for U.S. Steel; group sales demonstrations for National Cash Register and for American Management Associations; Preferred Customer Service for A. B. Dick; maintenance agreements for IBM; customer cross-sell for Citibank; piggyback professional books for McGraw-Hill; motivating agency representatives with a message from the executive vice-president of Equitable; prospecting for leasing customers for Commercial Equipment Corporation; or signing on memberships for the Montgomery Ward Auto Club—the basic common denominator is the development of a marketing plan and approaches to fit the special need.

It takes a knowledgeable, creative team to produce results.

That's also true for the development and writing of this book. It represents a step-by-step collaboration of a dedicated group of marketing experts, learning from each new telephone marketing campaign, interrelating and feeding information to one another: planning, creative training, operations, fulfillment, customer service, and sales. The vast range and multiplicity of program experience is what makes us experts; each test teaches us something new to be applied to the next effort. Our major contribution to the development of telephone marketing as a specialized industry involves the constant search for new and improved approaches to some very old and rigid ways of business thinking.

It took the business crunch of the early 70s to start marketers thinking about alternatives—and many more years of learning from clients and associates. Mostly, telephone marketing's start-up momentum came in the 60s with a plunge into millions of calls for the Ford Motor Company. Then—thanks to his willingness to experiment, the tape messages created for a supportive, committed, and generous Norman Cousins signaled a huge leap forward into the 70s. Our systems were well ordered and operating, but it took the insight of Ted Levitt to give us a gestalt and philosophic rationale for our methods of telephoning.

Though my name is listed as author, these pages were produced by "our team," led by "the fastest copy chief in the East," Fred Borden, CCI's retired Vice President, Creative Services, who was most responsible for getting it all together and publishable. This book would not have been possible without him. Kudos go to him—critics come to me!

Rudy Oetting, CCI's president, the telephone marketing "expert of experts," spent countless hours poring over the manuscript and adding critical insight and experience to every leaf and chapter. Geri Gantman, Rosemary Bolgar, Mike Violanti, Robert Leiderman, Trudy Siegel, Helen White, Caroline Smith, my son, Ernan—all shared in providing valuable input. The contributions of a constructive editor, Bill Mogan; the critical evaluation of educator/researcher conceptualist, past client and friend, George Brown (now of the National Conference Board), who, as Director of Research for Ford, started it all; consultant Tom Parker, who was responsible for "pushing me into it"; and the late Gene Gilbert, who opened the door—the book is part theirs, too!

Pete Hoke, marketing conceptualist and innovative publisher, who was the first to "talk" about the use of telephone as a direct response medium . . . then, clients like the American Management Associations and the leading international direct marketer, Sam Josefowitz, who grasped the concept and never stopped seeking new and practical applications. The advice and counsel of Larry Chait, the "dean" of multimedia marketing; Gordon Grossman, client, partner, and consultant, whom we "leaned on" along the way; Murray Rosenberg who's adding to our knowledge every day—all have a share in bringing this text to you.

But in reality this book truly belongs to CCI's communicator staff. Our phone calls will always depend on honest, capable, and devoted human beings who work hard at what they do. Marketing by phone is most grueling for them; they also learn the most, and fastest! They know more about using the phone, what's happening, how to improve the technique and "what's wrong" than any of us. I'm grateful to them for making it all possible.

There's usually one person who stands alone in the preparation of a book—this case is no exception. A successful and exciting business can only have meaning if it's a shared experience. Eva Roman traveled this road with me. All new concepts first jingled in her mind; only later did I run with the ball! Partner, motivator, severest critic, and most patient loving wife, without her it just wouldn't have been nurtured along the way—or finally completed.

That's the story of this book—a shared experience. We hope it improves your use of a simple instrument, what is to me an almost magical electronic signal traveling through space, reaching out to colleagues, relatives and friends, and other friendly people who publicly list their phone numbers and expect the phone to ring.

New York, N.Y.   *Murray Roman*

Introduction

Lester Wunderman*

IN OUR SOCIETY, a medium is a communication form gone public. Print ads are handbills multiplied by the million. Radio and television commercials are either stand-up declamations, or small dramas of daily life, played in a nationwide theater where products rather than tickets are sold. The Avon ladies make neighborly visits as sales errands. Now the telephone is the latest of our basic communication forms to be converted to a medium of commercial persuasion. It retains its unique quality of long distance, person-to-person dialogue despite the new volume-media role it has begun to play.

Marketing has always been a process of bringing the buyer and the seller—or the prospect and the product—together. This seemingly simple process already occupies much of our human and physical resources. Our economic philosophers tell us that we are now entering the Post-Industrial Age—a time when as many as 70 percent of our working population will be employed in services rather than production. The objectives and styles of such an age will be vastly different from the Industrial Revolution, which has shaped our lives for the last several hundred years. If

---

* Executive Vice President, Young & Rubicam International; President, Wunderman, Ricotta & Kline.

revolutions are the overthrow of one social or political system in favor of another—then it might be fair to say that the Industrial Revolution over-threw humanism in favor of the machine and gave an equal or higher priority to industry than to man. This was done in the name of dominant new concepts such as the Standard of Living, Competition, Capitalism, Efficiency, Plenty, etc. While many have questioned whether the trade-off was worth it, the fact is that the Industrial Revolution controlled many of the calamities of nature as well as despoiling it—created plenty as well as need—developed wealth as well as poverty—and created new oppor-tunities as well as problems.

The Post-Industrial, service-oriented society suggests just such an opportunity: Machines in the service of man—machines as a connection between men—and men and networks of men in connection with each other.

The core of these new connections may well be the telephone—or the communications systems which will evolve from it. The telephone is a medium gone public—but it can never go so public that it ceases to be one human voice and human mind in dialogue with another. While other media strive for mass audiences at efficient costs per thousand, the tele-phone seeks to deliver a volume of messages—one at a time. While all other media have a voice but no hearing—there never was a telephone that had only a speaker and no receiver.

The telephone, therefore, must be better suited to a dialogue than a monologue. And this seems to be in keeping with the way the consumer increasingly perceives himself and his needs.

Identity may already be a more fundamental requirement than posses-sions. The famous line from Arthur Miller's play, *Death of a Salesman*, has become increasingly meaningful: "Attention must be paid!" Indeed, "Attention must be paid" by those of us in marketing not only as profes-sionals, but as citizens. We can no longer manufacture *at* people en masse, no matter how efficiently. We can no longer distribute *at* people en masse, no matter how conveniently. Attention must be paid or the piper will be—and his price will be an increasingly frustrated, resistant, rebellious, and cynical public and citizenry.

This book, in my opinion, is just the opening of what will begin to emerge as a whole new set of marketing systems aimed at creating a two-way process in our marketing communications. The telephone may be-come a video phone, laser beam network, satellite-based communication system, or the basis of a wired nation. Any one of these will revolutionize not only how we communicate, but what we communicate—or intercommunicate. We will sell by phone, see by phone, shop by phone, learn by phone, criticize by phone, praise by phone, communicate with business and government, and perhaps, one day, even vote by phone.

The telephone-computer connection is already controlling inventory, shipping orders, keeping accounts, providing banking and other financial services, and making it possible for people living anywhere to shop and order with the same or greater convenience than those living in the central cities.

The telephone-television connection is about to emerge as the newest entertainment and marketing miracle. Two-way cable television now being tested promises not only to provide entertainment of the viewer's choice, but to create shopping and learning dialogues. Television and telephone, T and T, could be the next marketing explosion.

Business and marketing executives, political leaders and citizens, producers and consumers will increasingly discover the telephone to be a basic and efficient tool. I know of no better way to begin to understand the new role of the telephone than to read, understand and apply the principles set forth in Murray Roman's *Telephone Marketing*.

Telephone Marketing

chapter one

The Multimedia Sales Challenge

MARCH 7, 1976, CAME AND WENT without the flying of colors or the flourish of trumpets. That day marked 100 years since Alexander Graham Bell was awarded a patent for the telephone. Sir William Thomson, Bell's contemporary and a renowned British scientist, called the telephone "the most wonderful thing in America."

What would he say now if he knew that 400 million telephone calls will be made today? That the telephone is today's fastest-growing medium in marketing goods and services? That before the lights go out tonight in United States households from Maine to Hawaii, some 7 million Americans will answer their phones, to listen while someone they've never seen or heard of tries to sell them something . . . that almost 3 million will hear a complete presentation . . . and that *fully 460,000 will buy what is being offered?* *

Can this familiar telephone instrument be—at one and the same time—an integral part of sophisticated electronic communications technology . . . and yet the most basic, most intimate person-to-person medium imaginable?

The answer is a resounding "Yes." And for business executives eyeing both the commercial community and the 95 percent of United States

---

* See item 29 in Bibliography, page 169.

households reachable by telephone, this channel of communication, properly exploited, has proved to be the most efficient, most flexible, most accountable medium available to marketers.

Direct-Response Marketing—
A Rigorous Discipline

Direct-response marketing, while not new, has exploded on the American business scene only in recent years. Because it offers accountability, traceability, and accurate measurement of results, it epitomizes hard-headed "bottom-line" marketing thinking. As direct marketers, many pragmatic aspects work in our favor:

■ Our promotional and product costs are precisely accountable so we can carefully limit our up-front investment.

■ We can thus establish our cost per inquiry or cost per sale.

■ We know exactly where our break-even point is.

■ We can identify and reach specific marketing segments, often based on a previous pattern of purchasing behavior.

■ By testing, we can control the variable—price, copy, graphics, offer, lists, etc. We can establish a direct relationship between each of these factors and response, sales, and profitability.

Every benefit listed above is common to all forms of direct marketing. The telephone adds a very special bonus, for it has demonstrated extraordinary potency, especially in an era where the business atmosphere is endangered by an uncertain economy.

No direct-response medium compares with the telephone for *immediacy* of impact. In the area of *costs*, the price of a telephone call has actually gone down while the costs of space media, direct mail, and, above all, personal sales visits have skyrocketed.

Whether the application is for direct sales, lead generation, subscription renewals, account cultivation, conversions, customer service, credit screening, or research, the telephone provides a cost-effective means of maximizing the results of such efforts.

The Role of the Telephone
in the Multimedia Mix

Now that direct-response marketing has entered the multimedia era, the telephone has taken its place as a vital component of the mix, essential to the synergism to which many elements contribute. It has been used to complement and support such diverse media efforts as newspaper and magazine campaigns, radio and television commercials, cable systems, outdoor advertising, direct mail, and the new Mailgram.

Telephone marketing programs, used in combination with direct mail, have proved 2 to 5 times as effective as direct mail alone. Another kind of cross-fertilization of media is demonstrated in the ability to pretest a direct-mail list by telephoning a relatively small segment of the list; the correlation has proved to be remarkably high.

The American Management Associations has become one of many "true believers" who are convinced that adding telephone follow-up to a direct-mail solicitation adds significantly to profit. The AMA finds that the phone produces up to a high of 18 percent in registration for specialized business seminars—and these are on calls made to lists that have *already* been covered by mail.

The Campbell Soup Company has used taped phone conversations as source material from which it uses excerpts for radio commercials.

Telephone conference calls are structured to sell and educate groups of executives, educators, or students.

The telephone can be used to upgrade the ticket on a sale initially achieved through other media—for instance, to make an "add-on" sale of related merchandise. The media combinations—and the uses to which these combinations can be put—are limited by the imagination of the advertiser.

In a marketing atmosphere in which media tend more and more to be highly selective in audience appeal (e.g., the development of special-interest magazines and regional editions for targeted geographical areas, the increasing tendency of radio stations to cater to highly specific tastes in program material, the availability of very sophisticated and highly qualified computerized mailing lists, etc.), the telephone—the most specific and most personal of all media—is playing a larger and larger role as an influential means of contact with today's alert, aware consumer, either alone or in combination with other media.

The Giant Awakens

It happened in the 1960s; not all at once, by a prearranged signal. Rather, it crept up before most marketers were aware of what was happening: the consumer, stirred from centuries of quiescence, insisted on his rights as a buyer of goods and services, and began to make increasingly loud noises reflecting the world and the times.

The revolt is well under way, and the consumer of the 70s is reaching out to express and maintain his identity as an individual. "I am not a number," he says, "nor a 'bit' for your computer. I have opinions and differences and anxieties and complaints. Boy, do I have complaints! I want to talk to someone . . . and you'd damn well better listen to me!"

Any marketer of goods and services who wants to maintain and increase his share of market must adapt his promotional and selling program to the demands of this new consumer.

Just to create products or services appropriate to rapidly changing tastes and times won't do any longer. The way in which that product or service is offered to the market is absolutely critical: it must be offered and made known in a way that is "in sync" with the new insistence on individuality and human dignity.

It is precisely in this sensitive area, by meeting the psychological needs of prospective customers on a one-by-one basis, that the telephone comes fully into its own as a powerful marketing medium.

A Century of Sell

The first telephone directory issued by the Bell Telephone Company of New York appeared in 1878. It consisted of a single sheet of paper, about 8½ in. wide by some 29 in. long, and it contained 272 listings. There were no telephone numbers in those days; one simply asked the operator to be connected with the called party.

Significantly, however, there were no telephones listed for individual residences, only for commercial firms. And, reflecting a very early awareness of the business potential of the new instrument and the service it could provide, they were grouped under business headings—some 38 of them, including "Segars," "Weighers," and "Passe Partouts."

Today there are more than a quarter of a billion telephones installed throughout the world. While the United States and Canada far outpace other countries in telephone use, the rest of the world is rapidly catching up. In 1960, there were 134.6 million telephones; 10 years later, the world total had very nearly doubled. A substantial portion of them are business-oriented.

On an unprecedented scale, telephones are used for sales and sales-related purposes. From the Ford Motor Company's pioneering 20-million-call mass-marketing program a decade ago to the widely heralded campaign undertaken 10 years later on behalf of Norman

Cousins' newly launched *Saturday Review/World* magazine, the use of the telephone as a marketing medium has run the full gamut of size, scope, objective, and approach. Now the phone is used to sell steel and seminars, candidates for office and supplies for the office, magazines and memberships, cosmetics and credit cards, travel packages and textbooks, footwear and furniture, real estate and reference works, insurance and idealism.

From that first single-sheet directory's business market segmentation approach—the great-granddaddy of today's Yellow Pages—to our current sophisticated crisscross directories, census tracts and zip-code groupings, the telephone's position as an effective sales tool has consistently been recognized and exploited.

Telephone Marketing
Sophistication Is
at Work TODAY

Although the showroom of tomorrow will be in each customer's living room, and even though the day may not be far off when the executive's office will be an electronic command post in his home, the inroads the telephone is making today on the nation's marketing operations are far from insignificant. The tiny percentage of United States households in the Continental United States without telephone service represent that portion of the nation which, for reasons that have to do with inadequate disposable income, are not likely prospects for any marketer. In the business world, the telephone is as much as a necessity for profitable survival as the typewriter, the ream of paper, or the postage stamp.

In fact, the telephone has become so inextricably a part of the life-style of America that in just one 7-week period early in 1974, no fewer than 3 million New Yorkers voluntarily made telephone calls—for which they paid regular rates—for no other purpose than to hear a favorite comedian tell them a few jokes! And they called, too, to learn about the weather, the condition of traffic patterns on major highways, racing results, and, during the appropriate season, to talk with Santa Claus.

Given this wide acceptance of the instrument, the marketing executive has at hand a medium enabling him to reach, on the most intimate kind of person-to-person basis, just about everyone and anyone who is a legitimate prospect for products and services of all kinds. And it can be done effectively, with minimum waste, maximum economy, and results that can be evaluated immediately. Today, properly planned and handled, the telephone can:

- Take an order for $15 or $5000
- Prospect for qualified leads
- Make marginal accounts profitable
- Motivate delinquent accounts
- Follow up and reinforce direct mail
- Receive direct-response inquiries to TV, radio, or print-media advertising
- Convert inquiries to sales
- Make an appointment for a sales visit
- Reactivate or upgrade old customers
- Promote special merchandising to generate store traffic
- Find and screen new business
- Solicit qualified credit applications
- Introduce a new product to a distribution network
- Deliver a tape message to a select audience
- Raise funds for institutions or public causes
- "Get out the vote" in key election districts
- Gain a reaction or develop information through survey techniques
- Determine campaign or brand penetration or price testing
- Cover distant customers economically
- Reach more customers in less time

Telephone–The Fastest-Growing Marketing Medium

About halfway through the 70s, the telephone was identified as the largest single sales and sales-related communication—surpassing, in dollars expended, advertising in newspapers, television, direct mail, radio, and magazines.

United States marketers were beginning to appreciate the points of superiority of the telephone over more traditional media. That learning process is continuing and broadening, as more and more businessmen realize that:

1. Through no other medium can a marketing message be delivered which can so thoroughly permeate the national fabric.

2. While all other media are beset by skyrocketing costs, telephone operations actually reflect variable but fairly stable prices.

3. Telephone is the most effective test medium, since it permits

judgment and evaluation to be made within a few hours of the launching of an offer, a copy approach, or a list being tested.

4. Telephone actually increases in effectiveness when used in combination with other media.

5. Telephone multiplies by 2 to 5 times the response generated by direct mail alone, and is a most effective pretesting tool for the mail medium.

6. It is the only medium that creates instant two-way dialogue between marketer and prospect.

7. It is the only medium that enables the marketer's communicator to evaluate the mood of the prospect at the moment of sales contact, enabling the marketer to implement his approach flexibly. The only other type of contact offering this luxury is the industrial direct sales call which now averages close to $75 per contact, as compared with about $3 for the telephone approach.

8. Again, with the exception of the high-priced personal sales visit, telephone is the only medium that permits the marketer to choose the time at which the contact will be made with the prospect.

Telephone calls are made daily in both directions—some originated by the marketing organization, others placed by the customer or prospect in response to a suggestion made through advertising in another medium. It is this interdependence of the various components of the multimedia mix that has resulted in the telephone's dramatic growth on the contemporary marketing scene. For alert marketers have learned that to consider all, and preclude none, of the media available to them is to exploit the best each has to offer.

And so millions of consumers and business people, today and every day, will call or be called, to buy or be sold a product or service. It may be an upholstery service from a department store. Perhaps an all-inclusive travel package to Hawaii . . . an insurance offer . . . the opportunity to buy securities . . . or a subscription to a magazine.

Their average purchase will come to more than $60, for a grand total nationally of $180 million—*every day!* That's just part of the impact of the telephone as a marketing tool.

Whether used independently or in combination with other media, the telephone today accounts for well in excess of $50 billion in completed sales transactions each year in the United States alone. While many forward-looking marketing executives have familiarized themselves with the approaches and techniques that are essential to success with the telephone, one thing is certain: far more will be catching on in the future.

The pages that follow are dedicated to a practical demonstration of the feasibility of telephone marketing as a sophisticated, powerful, and contemporarily oriented sales communication channel. They will help you determine whether and how your own sales efforts can be effectively enhanced through the use of the telephone medium.

They will carry you through the step-by-step procedures that must be undertaken if the full potential of telephone salesmanship as a contemporary marketing tool is to be realized. And they will demonstrate the broad scope of plans and preparation required to convert your telephone efforts into maximum sales results. We will be discussing such key program phases as:

1. Development of plans and strategy
2. Planning your budget
3. Setting target dates for starting your campaign
4. Developing collateral, supportive materials
5. Anticipating prospects' questions and establishing effective answers
6. Creating a communicator's script
7. Analyzing your market and selecting test lists
8. Designing record forms for noting results of each call
9. Working out coordinated efforts with your field sales staff
10. Writing and taping the special message
11. Training your calling staff
12. Initiating the calling operation
13. Setting a review cutoff point
14. Revising approaches, script and/or tape, as such action may be indicated by reactions to early calls
15. Carrying out calls to the balance of your test list
16. Analyzing and assessing reports of call results
17. Deciding upon the validity of continuation, either with additional test lists or with the complete balance of original lists
18. Analyzing and interpreting final results

This book is designed to demonstrate the practical value of the planned use of the telephone in making your sales operations more profitable.

How you use the phone is dependent upon your conception of its capabilities and your understanding of its capacity to produce qualifiable returns. The telephone can help you carry out the responsibilities of your job with greater efficiency and increased productivity when you recognize and correctly use its full potential.

chapter two/

A Modern Approach
to Today's Market

TO TELL PEOPLE WHO HAVE GROWN UP in our instant communication society that they may need some help in using the telephone is, quite often, to elicit a reaction of indignation—as though they were being accused of breathing incorrectly (after all, they've been doing it all of their lives).

That "who-are-you-to-tell-me" reaction is magnified many times, in our experience, when our partner in such a dialogue is the American business executive. For obviously business life would be impossible without the phone, and he has succeeded reasonably well in his commercial endeavors. His company's marketing effectiveness, his ability to pay the salaries of people dependent on him for their livelihoods, his own family's standard of living—these all bear an important relationship to that familiar instrument, the telephone, and how effectively it is used.

Paradoxically, therefore, one's very familiarity with the telephone may prove to be an obstacle in its creative exploitation as a marketing tool.

There is a second attribute shared by most decision-making marketing executives in the American business community: they know how to sell. They're past masters at matching a product's benefits to a customer's needs; they're experts at crystallizing the prospect's intent; they know how to turn objections to their advantage; they're superb closers; they're enthusiastic about the product; they're upbeat, flexible, sincere, and so on.

With the telephone's burgeoning growth and increasing impact on the business scene, it would seem that these two important qualities—familiarity with the telephone and an intimate knowledge of selling techniques—should enable almost all businesspersons to venture forth and joust successfully on the battleground of telephone marketing.

Yet only a relatively few major companies have "seized the time" and taken full advantage of the opportunities offered by the telephone. Why?

There have been two basic obstacles:

Obstacle Number 1: A Traditional Method of Doing Business versus A Changing Life-Style Many marketers have simply not taken the time to study the change in the life-style of today's consumer. While the consumer market has by virtue of sheer numbers become "mass," there has been simultaneous growth of a counter tendency—a desire *not* to be regarded as a number in a file. Significant numbers of people want consciously to be *unprogrammed*, to reach for personal, selective identity. The phenomenon is a key component of the consumer revolt discussed in the last chapter.

Obstacle Number 2: Bound by the "Service Approach" to Business This is a much more complex and serious barrier to mounting a unified, flexible telephone-marketing effort.

The heart of the problem can be most quickly grasped by following the cogent arguments to Theodore Levitt, professor of business administration at the Harvard Business School. It will repay any marketing executive to heed his incisive words.

Writing in the *Harvard Business Review*,* Professor Levitt makes it clear that a failure to adopt a new type of thinking has made it difficult to maintain the same rate of progress in a business's *service* operations as in its manufacturing processes. He notes that such firms "must think of themselves as performing manufacturing functions when it comes to their so-called 'service' functions." Then he proceeds to develop his argument as follows:

> Manufacturing looks for solutions inside the very tasks to be done. . . . By contrast, service looks for solutions in the *performer* of the task. . . . Manufacturing thinks technocratically, and that explains its successes . . . service thinks humanistically, and that explains its failures.

Now as you read the following concepts of Professor Levitt, try to relate them to your company's and your own telephone techniques:

* September-October 1972.

. . . thinking in humanistic rather than technocratic terms ensures that the service sector of the modern economy will be forever inefficient and that our satisfactions will be forever marginal. We see service as invariably and undeviatingly personal, as something performed by individuals directly for other individuals.

This humanistic conception of service diverts us from seeking alternatives to the use of people, especially to large organized groups of people. It does not allow us to reach out for new solutions and new definitions. It obstructs us from redesigning the tasks themselves; from creating new tools, processes and organizations; and, perhaps, even from eliminating the condition that created the problems.

In sum, to improve the quality and efficiency of service, companies must apply the kind of technocratic thinking which in other fields has replaced the high cost and erratic elegance of the artisan with the low-cost, predictable munificence of the manufacturer.

Substitute the words "telephone selling" for the word "service" wherever it appears in the paragraphs above, and you will quickly recognize what is wrong with most telephone-sales efforts in today's market.

Seminars, books, speeches, and articles devoted to the techniques of telephone selling have largely suffered from the failure to recognize the validity of what Professor Levitt means when he asks, "What technologies and systems are employable here? How can things be designed so we can use machines instead of people, systems instead of serendipity?"

Many of these guides to improved use of the telephone as a marketing tool have far too often been devoted to looking for "solutions in the performer of the task" rather than for "solutions inside the very tasks to be done." They have talked about the individual's telephone personality, his or her speech habits, the kinds of questions he or she should ask, the way to react to the prospect's responses. But far too infrequently have they considered the modernization of the overall technique of telephone marketing, the only real person-to-person mass-marketing medium that exists in today's society.

The Structured, Production-Line Approach

The first trap to avoid is that of regarding the telephone merely as a mechanical means of extending a sales territory. The next step along Professor Levitt's pragmatic road is to plan a basic marketing strategy through the use of supportive and integrated research efforts, professional creativity, logistical operations, careful personnel selection and training, and constant, prompt evaluation of cost-effectiveness.

The telephone is an electronic tool that is available to every marketer for use as a rigidly controlled, sophisticated, immediately measurable production-line base for a sales or sale-related operation that meets the requirements of the contemporary market.

Its unique person-to-person attributes, when carefully combined with manufacturing-type controls, provide for a productive and profitable marriage of uniform message presentation and alert reaction to the needs of an individual prospect. The telephone makes it possible to approach every potential customer with a prepared, predetermined, standard copy message while, at the same time, permitting reasonable flexibility in response to each individual prospect's requirements. In no other form of promotional communication does the medium so profoundly influence the message.

A Few Outstanding
Successes

Only in the past decade have a relatively small number of major companies devoted their marketing efforts to a basic renovation of the *techniques* required to achieve significantly improved results from telephone salesmanship. The outstanding successes they have scored amply validate the premise that selling by telephone represents a new and powerful approach to today's consumers and their requirements.

Having grasped the essence of these requirements—an obligation to respond in human terms to human needs—these firms have become aware of the expanding opportunities offered by appropriate technological employment of the telephone as a major sales tool to reach the mass market.

Because the marketing executives in these firms were personally involved in setting up telephone-centered programs shaped by a planned and scientifically directed approach to their companies' sales problems, they have learned the truth better than anyone else: that the telephone is indeed *the* person-to-person medium, the closest thing to eyeball-to-eyeball selling that is economically feasible.

Two Case Histories . . . Ten Years Apart What is generally regarded as being the very first mass-marketing campaign fully utilizing the telephone as a selling tool for business was the 20-million-call program undertaken by the Ford Motor Company over a decade ago.

Working through the J. Walter Thompson advertising agency and with

Communicator Network, Inc. (CNI), marketing executives of Ford decided to explore the potential of using production-line techniques—the "manufacturing approach"—in conducting a sales lead program, a goal that would normally be defined as "service-oriented."

Some 15,000 homemakers were hired and trained to make calls from their own homes in communities across the nation. With little or no previous selling experience, nor any particular proved selling talent, these people were nevertheless successful in generating an average of two sales leads every single day for each of 23,000 Ford salespersons.

The Ford communicator script. Working with the following carefully programmed script, the homemaker/callers contacted 20 million households—making as many as one million calls a week—to ascertain whether the plans of those called made them prospects for an automobile purchase; and, if so, how soon they expected to consider buying a new car:

Hello, Mr. (Mrs.) _____, this is _____ calling for the Sales Department of the Ford Motor Company, to find out about the car buying plans for the people in the (*your city*) area.

1. Are you or is anybody else in your household planning to buy a car within the next two years?
(IF NO, TERMINATE THE INTERVIEW) with "Thank You.")
2. When do you think you'll buy? Within three months, six months, one year, or when?
3. Will you buy it new or used?
4. Will it be regular size or compact?
5. Do you or anyone else in your household own a car?
(IF NO, SKIP TO QUESTION 8.)
6. Please tell me the make and year of each car you own.
7. (ASK FOR EACH CAR OWNED)
Did you buy it new or used?
(QUESTION 8 ASKED ONLY IN CITIES WITH POSTAL ZONES)
8. Could you tell me what your postal zone is?
(IF ASKED WHY YOU NEED THEIR POSTAL ZONE, SAY:) So that I will be able to determine which Ford Motor Company Dealer is closest to you. We can then send your name to him so that you can be contacted with information on his cars.
TERMINATE THE CONVERSATION WITH: Thank you very much for your help.

The simplicity of this completely structured and mechanized approach kept individual calling time to an absolute minimum, yet made it practical for the caller to forward the names of legitimate, qualified prospects, on the very day the call was completed, to an assigned Ford dealer. Names of those respondents who said they did plan to buy a new car within three months were in the hands of salespersons within 24 hours! Those prospects planning to purchase in at least six months were forwarded by mail to the Ford Division the day after the call has been made, for a series of follow-ups by mail and by direct sales contact. The two-month "planners" were also carefully nursed along by special brochures and letters through the mails.

What did this historic effort produce for the marketer? Here, in capsule form, is a dramatic summary of the results:

■ The calls generated more than 340,000 leads . . . of this total, 187,000 proved to be valid prospects in the market for a car within a six-month period.

■ Recorded sales on the first day that results were measurable came to a total of 444 cars . . . nine days later this figure had increased to 7,773.

■ The program produced sales for Ford Division at a cost of $65 per added unit, an incremental cost far below that incurred in other promotional programs.

■ Importantly, while 40 percent of the hot leads obtained during the telephone program were from Ford owners, the remaining 60 percent came from owners of competitive cars.

■ Normally, in Ford's experience, salespersons actually follow up about 20 to 30 percent of their leads . . . in this case, the figure jumped to 80 percent.

Evaluating the telephone marketing program, 75 percent of the participating Ford dealers considered it *excellent*, backing their assessments with such comments as "one of the best" and "the best program the Division has ever run."

All in all, from the point of view of profit, dealer enthusiasm, and salesperson participation, the program was characterized by marketing executives as showing "all the earmarks of a successful marketing endeavor."

. . . *And ten years later.* A full 10 years after this pioneering effort by Ford, a new campaign was developed that operated on an entirely different level in every significant respect—a unique sales effort conducted by Campaign Communications Institute (CCI)* on behalf of *World* magazine.

Here no leads were sought for ultimate conversion to sale of a well-known, standard product. The objective was to obtain firm subscription commitments for a publication that, at the time of the telephone solicitation, was not even in existence! Here no unknown homemakers were employed to make the calls; instead, the sales message was personally

---

* The author directed both the CNI and CCI programs.

conveyed to the "suspect" by a live communicator utilizing a prerecorded tape. The message was from a personality assumed to be well known to each call recipient. Here no vast market of 20 million was called, but only a highly selected group of some thousands of individuals, gleaned and carefully chosen on the basis of their life styles . . . their educational levels, social concerns, cultural interests, and higher economic scales. All names were pinpointed from specially rented lists of those most likely to want to subscribe to a new publication to be published and edited by Norman Cousins.

The technique was agreed upon because Mr. Cousins, a distinguished literary figure who had resigned after some 29 years as editor of the *Saturday Review*, was the only and best person to announce and discuss his personal plans for the new publication he was about to launch. The taped message ran a full two minutes, and was introduced by a live caller, whose script set forth the following: "My name is _____, and I am calling for Norman Cousins. I have a short, specially recorded message from Mr. Cousins that he has asked me to play for you, and I'm wondering, may I play it now and ask for your questions and reactions after you've heard it. It is about two minutes, Mr./Mrs. _____. Do you have the time right now?"

Since the names of those called had already been carefully screened and chosen for their known interests, there was virtually universal willingness to listen to Cousins' taped message. The tape was played only to those prospects who said, "Yes, I'll be happy to listen." If they did not respond to Cousins' name and said, "No," the call was short and efficient. "Thank you. Have a nice day. Goodbye." That "suspect" was not a good prospect in any case.

Sales results were astoundingly successful: on one test list of 5,000 persons, 40 percent agreed to subscribe immediately, with three out of four of those subscribing indicating they were ready to sign up at $25 for a special three-year charter subscription.

But one little twist added to this *World* magazine effort has brought a brand-new dimension to the use of the telephone as a reliable and resultful marketing tool: *the telephone proved itself to be an authoritative instrument for pretesting direct mail results*. Using rental lists in 2,000-name batches, 300 telephone calls were made to each batch against 1,700 pieces of mail. Throughout these tests, the sales achievements concluded via communicator-plus-tape came in at an average of about 2 to 5 times those attained by the mailman. Where telephone drew, for example, a 30 percent response in terms of committed subscriptions, the mail-approached portions of the same test list would draw perhaps some 10 percent; a 10 percent telephone return would be matched by 2 percent from the mail effort, and so on. And, if a list did not produce a profitable test result via telephone, no money was expended at all on it for direct mail.

A New Set of Conditions What had happened during the decade that elapsed between the Ford Motor Company's straightforward, relatively simple approach and the highly sophisticated effort represented by the *World* magazine campaign? A new set of conditions had emerged, requiring an alternative approach. Not only had the science of telephone salesmanship had 10 years in which to develop, but changing consumer attitudes and new economic realities had served to stimulate some very serious thinking in the direction of developing approaches and techniques leading to a lower cost per sale. And the telephone had demonstrated its ability to fill an important role between the increasing costs of direct mail and the unprogrammed efforts of the personal sales representative.

Yet despite the difference between the two programs in terms of such fundamentals as the nature of the offer, audience, and objectives, each served in its own way to demonstrate the validity of the structured, controlled production-line approach to the problems of meeting mass-marketing goals.

What the Naysayers Say

So new and unique is the application of the Levitt principles to the area of mass marketing by telephone that there are those who continue to denigrate it. Their arguments can be summed up as follows:

1. Material that is preprogrammed is "canned" and suitable only, therefore, for "boiler room" telephone sales operations.

Our rejoinder: The "canned pitch" argument is equally applicable (or inapplicable) to a print-media ad that repeats the identical wording over and over in every copy of the magazine. And who is more likely to use "boiler room" tactics: the communicator paid on the basis of time and general performance norms—or the commissioned salesperson spurred on by the desire to maximize sales results and thus increase commissioned earnings?

2. Mass-marketing telephone techniques are geared to a consumer audience. Commission selling, on the other hand, is appropriate for high-level business-to-business contacts.

Our rejoinder: This argument tends to ignore completely the vast scope and complexity of today's American business community. The fact is, of course, that the manufacturer of business equipment, the paper-mill owner, or the publisher of technical books, to name but a very few, faces the same kind of mass-marketing problem as does the cosmetic house, the fund-raising organization, or the distributor of children's encyclopedias.

3. The mass-marketing approach to phone selling removes from the communicator the basic responsibility for forcing sales, and assigns that responsibility to those who plan the strategy, develop the presentation, test and interpret the results, and set up the entire operation on a mass scale.

Our rejoinder: What better way is there to insure the integrity of any program than by assigning primary responsibility for its detailed implementation to management-level personnel, responsible for maintaining a company's public reputation in a highly competitive market? Application of the Levitt principle to telephone mass-marketing activities virtually ensures that no customer or prospect will be enticed with grandiose claims, false delivery promises, or exaggerated sales arguments, evoked by some individual salesperson's eager desire to increase his earnings.

4. Career selling, normally based on commissionable compensation, as opposed to mass-scale operation, does not impose a specific number of calls in a given time period. The communicator relies on interaction with the prospect—it may take him 2 minutes or 20 minutes to achieve his objective.

Our rejoinder: Today's marketing operations require procedures in which strict cost-per-inquiry or cost-per-sale accountability is an absolute requirement for planned profitability. With the production-line approach, cost-per-sale figures are always immediately on tap.

Special Marketing Situations

There are certainly some highly specialized situations in which the experienced salesperson's knowledge both of his firm's resources and his customer's needs are important factors in completing sales. These are, indeed, more responsive to career selling treatment than to mass-marketing techniques.

The experience of Valley Industries, a St. Louis-based fabricator and distributor of steel products, provides an example of this approach.*

* *Business Week*, Dec. 1, 1973.

Here is a company that simply sits its star salespeople down at the phone (no scripts, no tapes, no communicators) and moves about $85 million in pipe, mine roof bolts, and other steel products, aimed largely at the energy-related industries, including oil and gas producers. Valley officials estimate that this total phone volume represents some 85 percent of the company's entire annual volume of sales.

There are just 35 salespeople on the phone, each of whom makes 50 to 60 dialings a day. The company projects that it would require a personal-visit sales force of as many as 125 people to establish the same number of contacts. With travel costs rising markedly, there is thus recorded a net saving of about $2,000 per month per salesperson.

The continued presence of the entire sales staff in the company's headquarters area makes it possible to maintain continuous and immediate contact with Valley's credit department, top management, inventory data, and price information sections—as well as with a computer bank in which quickly retrievable data is stored, giving both past sales and known uses for each of the company's 3,000 products. This means that, in conversation with a prospect, a Valley Industries salesperson can negotiate an individual deal within a matter of a very few minutes, instead of taking up time writing a report and waiting for a response from some higher management level.

For the individual sales representative, too, this operation pays off handsomely: of the 35 salespeople on the telephone, 2 have earned more than $100,000 per year, 6 others have made over $60,000, and the balance average out well over $25,000 in annual earnings.

In still another aspect of its phone operations, Valley Industries successfully ignores a fundamental rule. Far from providing ideal physical working conditions in which the phone salespeople might function, the company allows them to be, in the words of one descriptive report, "huddled together in cramped bullpen areas—but for a reason."

Says a top Valley Industries executive: "Keeping them bunched together breeds excitement. What do you think happens when this guy sitting across from you lands a $100,000 order? You work harder to get one too."

An Overview

With such rare exceptions as the one just cited, the requirements of today's business climate call for the application of mass-marketing, direct-response approaches. The unique attributes of the telephone for responsive person-to-person communication—whether independently or as a component in multimedia operations—make it an important promotional and sales tool, geared ideally to the special conditions of today's economy, as well as to the newly emerging attitudes of the customer—business executive and consumer alike.

But the telephone must be seen as much more than merely a convenient electronically operated extension of the voice of the salesperson. In fact, like every other medium of sales and advertising, its use requires strict application of a very special set of rules, procedures, disciplines, judgments, acquired knowledge, and professional expertise. How well the telephone will serve a particular company in the area of sales and sales-related activity depends substantially upon the extent to which its management devotes itself to the supervised application of those highly specialized attributes.

It is within the framework of these concepts that the new techniques and competitive alternatives offered by the telephone must be understood and employed. That is the working premise of this book.

chapter three

The Range
of Applications

WHILE SOME INDICATION has already been given of the wide range of applications for which the telephone is ideally suited as a marketing medium, further study will serve to demonstrate that this unique and flexible tool—alone or in combination with other media—can attain marketing goals of a scope not reachable by any other normally employed means of mass communication.

With the use of two approaches (outgoing and incoming calls) across a range of several marketing areas, and employed in conjunction with a number of other media, it can achieve literally hundreds of primary and subordinate objectives.

To visualize graphically this concept, one might imagine a transparent cube (see Figure 1), across the top of whose face are listed the targets of the marketing program, while the applications and objectives are specified down its vertical dimension. The third and fourth surfaces represent the fact that, wherever an intersection of target and objective is marked, the goal can be approached either by outgoing or incoming calls.

The Targets

Within the scope of any marketing program two major categories exist, which can be subdivided and arranged by priority into a total of 10 probe-

worthy areas. These are the segments to be listed across the top of the face
of the prism:

1. Customers
    a. Present customers
        (1) Major
        (2) Marginal
    b. Past customers
        (1) Major
        (2) Marginal
2. Prospects
    a. Inquiries
        (1) New
        (2) Old

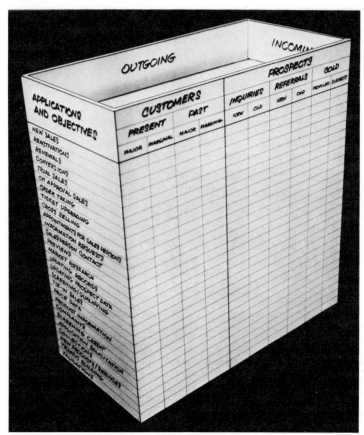

Fig. 1.   The "Range of Applications" Cube.

    b. Referrals
       (1) New
       (2) Old
    c. Cold prospects
       (1) Profiled
       (2) Suspects

Whatever the segments of the buying population your plans require you to reach, they will fall within the range of 1 or more of the 10 categories listed above.

The Third and Fourth Dimensions

The total of several hundred applications thus indicated through the combination of these categories with the goals to be attained is in itself an oversimplification, for in fact myriad combinations are available to the marketer.

In arriving at a recognition of the vast range of applications available to the telephone user, the marketer must take into account the fact that three additional factors must be applied to his considerations:

1. It is rare that a marketing program is limited to the attainment of but a single goal aimed at only one segment of the customer or prospect universe.

2. Some objectives can best be attained through the use of outgoing calls, some with incoming, and others through the combined employment of both.

3. In the achievement of marketing objectives, the telephone lends itself to combination use with a broad variety of additional conventional media.

Thus, the permutations available to the marketing executive, tied to the use of the telephone as a medium, become almost limitless in number. The broad potential at his or her command can be concentrated to a practical operation only upon serious consideration of the answers to these questions:

1. Which market segments are to be reached?

2. What is to be accomplished as the objective(s) of the specific marketing program?

3. What medium or combination of media can best be employed to attain those goals?

4. What resources—financial and professional—are available that can be cost-effectively applied to implementing such a program?

Applications and Objectives

Accordingly, the telephone can profitably be employed to achieve any normal objective of a marketing program, aimed at some or any of the targets indicated above. Here are the varied goals that might be listed vertically on the face of the "Range of Applications" cube.

1. Direct sales
    a. Closed sales
        (1) New sales
        (2) Reactivations
        (3) Renewals
        (4) Conversions
    b. Trial sales
    c. On-approval sales
    (It should be noted that in connection with some direct sales efforts follow-up or initial mail operations may be deemed desirable in order to obtain authorizing signatures or up-front payments.)
2. Order taking
    a. Ticket upgrading
    b. Cross-selling
3. Lead generation
    a. Appointments for salespersons
    b. Requests for further information
    c. Approval for salesperson contact
    d. Appointments for previews, general group demonstrations, or house calls
4. Surveying
    a. Market research
    b. Updating
        (1) Customer records
        (2) Prospect data
    c. Screening and qualifying
5. Customer service
    a. Upgrading
        (1) Tie-in sales
        (2) Conversion to higher ticket sales

      b. Educating and informing
        (1) Price data
        (2) Information re quality, style, etc.
        (3) New product announcements
      c. Complaint handling
    6. Credit handling
      a. Screening and checking of inquirers or prospects
      b. Application solicitation
      c. Collections
    7. Advertising and public image
      a. Announcing new products and services
      b. Building traffic
    8. Validations of previous orders

Examples of Applications

Telephone marketers have taken advantage of the broad scope of opportunity provided by this contemporary tool in perhaps every varied manner that is at their disposal. While it would be manifestly impractical to attempt to list them all, there are a number of major applications that can be cited to indicate the wide range of possibilities available, and to demonstrate how some leading marketers have made profitable use of them.

Validations. Aware that orders for high-ticket items may from time to time be placed by minor children or similarly unauthorized individuals, some major merchandisers have adopted the practice of telephoning an apparent purchaser just after receipt of order to make sure that the buyer is prepared to accept the item and is ready to assume responsibility for payment. The procedure can be used regardless of the medium through which the original order was placed.

A call of this nature can also be used to suggest a tie-in sale of merchandise related to the original item, when the purchase has been vertified and confirmed.

Renewals. Publishers of magazines such as *TV Guide, Time, Business Week,* and *Saturday Review* consistently earn increments of as much as 400 percent by telephoning expirations who have not renewed even after having received the full normal cycle of renewal notices—sometimes as many as 14—by mail.

New sales to present major customers. Nationally known mail-order houses regularly call customers who have already purchased from the pages of a catalog to suggest that they order additional related merchandise from that same catalog. In some cases, tie-in sales are induced through offering a special price on a catalog item, provided an additional specified item is ordered during the same call.

On-approval sales. The Dartnell Corporation telephones business-executive prospects to solicit their agreement to view specialized sales training films about which they have previously received announcement via another medium—through direct-mail letters and brochures.

Optional offers are proffered through which the prospect can agree, after viewing the film, either to purchase it outright or to rent it for a limited period of time.

Sales to marginal accounts. In some cases, a specialized target group is too small to justify the costs of preceding a call with a specialized mailing piece. On such occasions, a script (generally including a tape message from a recognized leader in the specialized field) is prepared and used. In many cases of this kind, the sale is closed immediately; in some instances, individually prepared letters are dispatched immediately following the completion of the call.

Sales appointments with cold prospects. Bell & Howell calls prospects in specific business fields—such as banking, for example—to obtain the agreement of executives to witness a demonstration of new equipment designed to streamline, modernize, and step up the efficiency of everyday operations. In this highly competitive field, both the efficacy and the economy of the new equipment are stressed during the telephone call, with the result that many unproductive prospects are screened out, effecting substantial savings in what would otherwise be fruitless sales visits.

New sales to prospects. Anyone who has ever watched television is aware that extensive use is made of this medium to encourage qualified segments of a broad public to screen themselves by calling in to an advertised "800" or local telephone number to place a direct order for such items as records and tape cassettes or popular or semiclassical music.

As a by-product of this type of operation, valuable mailing lists are amassed of actual purchasers, for future exploitation or for rental purposes to noncompetitive marketers.

Cross-selling to existing customers. Operating exclusively via telephone, many banks today call depositors, credit card holders, borrowers, and mortgage holders to acquaint them with available bank services other than those the individual customer is using. Calls of this type are normally well received because they originate with an organization with which the recipient already has an ongoing relationship.

Trial sales to inquiries. A national multimillion-dollar business is conducted through the combined media usage of print, return mail, and telephone for a home consumption item. Couponed advertising is run in selected magazines and Sunday supplements; respondents filling out and mailing the "soft" coupon merely ask for additional information and a brochure about the product. With only a small percentage of the inquiries responding to the brochure mailing, all nonrespondents are subsequently contacted by telephone, at which time a trial order is solicited.

The item is then shipped, subject to billing upon completion of a 30-day trial period if the merchandise is not returned to the marketer by that time. The telephone script serves not only as a straight sales message but also, since the item is directed mainly at young people, to obtain parental consent where required. Primarily, however, the telephone is utilized to produce incremental returns following the mail response.

Surveying for market data. The Sweet's Division of McGraw-Hill Information Systems Company binds catalogs of manufacturers and distributes them to architects, engineers, and others who are likely customers for those manufacturers' products. Sweet's has used the telephone in programs designed solely to identify and isolate those firms that are subsequently approached for the purpose of selling them on the concept of such participation.

Communicators are instructed to address their questions only to the marketing manager, the sales manager, the advertising manager, or the sales-promotion manager of each firm called. Says the script: "If none of the previously named executives are available, establish a definite call-back date and time. Do not speak to anyone else."

The purpose of the call is announced as an effort to determine whether Sweet's "important new information source will prove useful to companies like yours." After determining whether the called individual is familiar with the Sweet's operation (and briefly explaining it to him if he is not) the communicator then simply asks a series of questions about the company: if it manufactures, and if so, what kind of items it produces; whether or not it sells to the construction market; whether products are distributed nationally or regionally; the titles and functions of its customers' decision makers; the firm's advertising and selling procedures and the media it uses; the number of catalogs distributed annually; the name and title of the individual who makes the company's final advertising and sales-promotion decisions; and, finally, after a brief reiteration of the Sweet's Catalog Files operation: "Do you think a service like this would be helpful to your company?"

No attempt is made to sell anything at this juncture. But the telephone, quickly and economically, serves to pinpoint for Sweet's exactly which firms are likely to become logical participants in its files operations. Substantial savings are thus effected through the elimination of expensive cold calls on the part of the field sales staff.

Ten Out of Hundreds The 10 randomly selected telephone-marketing applications just cited provide but the barest insight into the many hundreds of possibilities that exist for its profitable use as an important and basic marketing medium. It should be noted that the potential that exists for the marketer within the broad scope of the "Range of Applications" cube encompasses not only market segment, objectives, and call direction, but also—as several of the examples have indicated—operations combined with the use of other media.

In this connection, the marketer should be aware that tools beyond the conventional print, broadcast, and direct-mail methods are available to him in pursuit of his objectives. Special-interest newsletters, business and industry directories, outdoor advertising, matchbooks, catalogs, field sales operations, and meetings and seminars all deserve consideration as legitimate promotional media whose attributes can be supported by—and can, in themselves, support—telephone-marketing operations. In fact, as fundamental a practice as the inclusion of a phone number on a letterhead can serve to stimulate incoming calls.

The widely varied combinations thus available offer a host of opportunities to the marketing executive to work out the details of the combined program operation best suited to the achievement of his or her goals.

The tables on the following pages summarize various telephone marketing programs and their measurable results.

Establishing Your Own Program

Faced with the scope and the complexities of telephone-marketing possibilities, it is an essential fundamental prelude to launching any operations that the marketing executive definitively analyze his own sales objectives and pinpoint those areas in which telephone marketing can possibly play an effective or maximum role.

One way to achieve this is to do so in writing, creating (and, of course, completely answering) a basic questionnaire the detailed study of which

RESULTS OF TELEPHONE MARKETING FOR
VARIOUS CONSUMER PROGRAMS

Product service	Dollar value	Program goal	Target	Percent response
Exerciser	$41.00	Sales from inquiries	Youth aged 18–25	Increased lead conversion by 35%
Magazine subscription	Average $16.00	Prospecting and renewals	Intellectual elite	Prospecting—18% Renewals—25%
Sewing and fabric kit	$5.00 per subscription, plus average $50.00 or more annual purchase	Renewals	Homemakers	No mail—57% After three mailings—21%
Automobile	$2,500.00+	Prospecting and dealer traffic	Auto households	Peak periods: 2 leads per day for 26,000 Sales reps—3% "hot leads" plan to buy in 3 months
Public broadcasting		Fund-raising	Viewers and Select Lists	25% at average $15.00 per pledge

RESULTS OF TELEPHONE MARKETING PROGRAM FOR
VARIOUS INDUSTRIAL PROGRAMS

Product service	Dollar value	Program goal	Target	Percent response
Business equipment	$19,000	Prospecting sales appts.	Bankers	27%
Copier supplies and equipment	$10.00 to $1,000	Continuing sales from marginal accts.	Office managers	15%*
Maintenance agreement for office typewriters	$49 to $400 annually	Signed contract	Customers with 7 or less machines	11%
Leasing services	+$50,000	Sales appts.	CEO/CFO	20%**

 * Plus Incremental Equipment Sales
** 100% Qualified Sales Appointments

RESULTS OF TELEPHONE MARKETING FOR FUND-RAISING PROGRAMS

Name	Percent pledged	Average pledge	Will contribute no definite amount	Have contributed	Unsure	Will not contribute	Misc.
Ashbrook for President	13.4	27.54	9.6	7.3	7.7	52.3	9.7
McGovern for President (1)	31.8*	31.67	18.9	20.4	6.6	13.5	8.7
(2)	2.9	Over $500	2.5	9.1	16.4	69.0	—
(3)	1.8	Over $500	7.4	25.9	18.5	46.3	—
Republican National Committee	40.0	20.00–105%	20.0	7.9	—	20.7	9.3
Nat'l. Womens' Political Caucus	39.7	11.24	1.6	11.1**	11.1	39.7	6.3
National Organization for Women	40.0	11.62	.07	.01**	22.0	20.0	8.0
Center for the Study of $25—39.0		26.31	—	—	—	—	—
Democratic Institutions $50/100—17.4		49.00	—	—	—	—	—
Expires—26.0		18.78	—	—	—	—	—
32.6		25.13					
Red Cross Past Contr. 25.0		5.00	—	9.0	3.0	47.0	16.0
(New York) Prospects—13.0		8.40	11.0	8.0**	2.0	56.0	11.0
Public Broadcasting Systems	28.75	13.99	9.77	12.50	10.56	30.04	8.34
Planned Parenthood							
Previous Donors	24.5	20.72	6.8	—	36.4	17.8	14.5

* Expense to income ratio 21.3% cost per $20.00 pledge $4.26
** Requested more information.

RESULTS OF TELEPHONE MARKETING PROGRAM FOR
VARIOUS INSTITUTIONAL PROGRAMS

Product service	Dollar value	Program goal	Target	Percent response
Book set	Set = $895.00 Individual books: $65 to $185.00	Sales: follow-up to ad leads	Libraries, businesses, and individuals	25% lead conversion to sales
Self-instructional business course	$750.00	Lead follow-up for sales	Business executives	3% lead conversion to sales—incremental to mail follow-up
Textbooks	Average sale: $700.00	Class adoption	Professors	14%
Dictionaries	Average sale: $300.00	Special offer— 100 minimum order	Store managers	19.5%

will suggest some possible answers. Among the queries you should pose to yourself, the following are suggested:

1. *What is the product or service involved?* A full description of the item should be entered, including price range, average sale normally recorded, and the allowable cost range per order. List here, too, any related products or services that might be added to maximize each phone contact made.

2. *What is the nature of the market to be solicited?* Is it consumer or business? . . . and within each, what kind of individuals constitute the decision makers you must reach? This segment will include one or more of such varied categories of target as head of household, young married, executive-level businessperson, educational department head, home owner, wheat farmer, librarian, credit card holder, needlework buyer, police chief, purchasing agent, teacher, car owner . . . in fact, whatever classifications of individuals constitute the market for your goods or services.

3. *What is the size and location of market to be reached?* Estimate how many persons are logical targets for your offer, and how many are located where: regionally, locally, nationally.

4. *What are your current marketing methods?* List the media you are now using to market this particular item, including the reach of each individual medium, inquiry response normally generated, and your experi-

ence relative to the sales attributable to each. Make sure you include your field sales staff operation in this category, since the numbers here may very well provide you with further insight as to the desirability of using the telephone to cut down on cost-per-appointment figures.

5. *What are the objectives of your telephone marketing program?* Out of the many approaches already indicated that a telephone marketing operation can attain, it is likely that only a relatively limited number will be practical within your own framework of marketing plans and goals. Listing them here will serve to sharpen your focus in arriving at a decision as to how best to use the telephone as a marketing medium for your own needs.

With the answers to these questions determined, you may more quickly visualize the overall needs of your operation, and come to a practical and correct conclusion as to the optimum approach. This summary-questionnaire technique should make it possible for you to eliminate the many telephone marketing applications that may not apply to your own situation. In short, it will help you narrow to your own pragmatic dimensions the wide area encompassed by the "Range of Applications" cube.

Preparing for Operations

Once a determination has been made as to the nature of the telephone operation to be undertaken—its goals, its audience, its relationship to other media usage—consideration must then be given to the application of the many professionally oriented facets of the telephone marketing world:

1. How will you find the individuals comprising the market segments you want to reach?
2. What will you say to them?
3. What is the most effective way of saying it?
4. Who will say it for you?
5. When should you say it—before or after mail, print, or broadcast campaigns?
6. What equipment and facilities will you need to attain maximum results?
7. Where will you find able or experienced communicators and their supervisors?
8. How will you establish and implement a training program?
9. How will you motivate your staff?
10. Where and how will you design and construct a telephone workshop?

11. What will the direct and indirect cost factors be?

12. What results can you realistically anticipate achieving?

You can project answers to these and related practical questions through reference to and study of the experiences of major marketers who have learned how to use the telephone as an integral part of their direct-response mass-marketing multimedia mix . . . experiences which are distilled and analyzed in the pages that follow.

chapter four/

Identifying Your Market—
Whom Do You Call?

IN ONE OF MANY IMPORTANT RESPECTS, the world of telephone marketing bears a striking resemblance to that of direct-mail merchandising operations: regardless of the validity of your offer, irrespective of the professional skills that go into its presentation, your program can achieve success *only* to the extent that it is directed at its proper and logical market.

Your telephone-marketing campaign will prove only as good as the universe to which it is directed, and that universe is determined by the list of names you use.

Selecting the Right List

In going after valid prospects, the first thing you must determine is the answer to a basic question: *whom are you trying to reach?* If you're sure it's business executives: what kinds of companies are they connected with? . . . by industry . . . by annual volume . . . by title within company . . . by distribution and marketing mechanism for their products . . . by number of employees. If consumers: where do they live? income brackets . . . number of children . . . owners or renters of their domiciles . . . drivers of cars . . . ethnic backgrounds or affiliations.

Those are just a few of the demographic* criteria you might apply. And with an estimated 220,000 lists available from many sources throughout the industry and the information bank provided by the U.S. Census Bureau, you may be sure that once you've properly determined the characteristics of the list you need, it will be available to you by rental, purchase, or compilation from some dependable source.

Start out by making up your own list—not of names, but of the ideal qualifications you would like to find in your "perfect" prospect. Here are just a few of the classifications into which you might want to place those you're trying to reach:

Business

By occupation or profession. Top-level executive, purchasing agent, contractor, police officer, doctor, office manager, garage owner, librarian, used-car dealer, teacher, hospital administrator, pharmacist, editor, insurance agent, etc.

By characteristics. Type of business (SIC code),† annual dollar volume, number of employees, product or service offered, area of operations (international, national, regional, local), type of equipment used, etc.

*By psychographics.** Reputation in specific field, attitude toward new concepts, history of relationships with your company or with your competition, etc.

Consumer

By description. Homemaker, head of family, teenager, senior citizen, car owner, home owner or home renter, student, holder of bank account, etc.

By characteristics. Income bracket, ethnic background, magazine subscriber, book buyer, purchaser of craft materials and/or courses, credit card holder, delinquent credit risk, record or tape purchaser, previous customer of your company, age, social and cultural interests, education, value of home, etc.

Thus, by selecting the descriptions, qualifications, and characteristics of the *kind of prospects* you want to reach, you can arrive at a determination of the *kind of lists* you will require. In turn, the next question must be answered: Where and how do you locate and obtain those lists?

* See App. 2 and 3 for definitions of terms.
† See App. 3 for definitions of terms.

List Sources

One of the most frequently overlooked sources of a valuable list that can produce sales results on a high-return percentage basis is <u>stored up right within your own files.</u> It is surprising how many major—and otherwise alert—marketers fail to make use of the vast amount of information conveniently at hand that is readily convertible for promotional and sales purposes.

Your own records of the history and activities of customers and prospects, properly analyzed and recorded, can give you immediate access to your very best prospects for your new offer. Let's assume that your earlier sales records indicate the existence of individuals who have purchased a specialized kind of high-ticket item from your firm—for example, a $250 stereo set.

That knowledge can lead you to a pinpointed attempt to find other prospective customers for the same or a similar item, since "birds of a feather flock together," it is in the nature of our society that people of related income levels also group together geographically and tend to reflect somewhat similar cultural and social interests.

Zoning regulations, the costs of property, rental-price standards and similar economic considerations lead almost inevitably to the existence of a neighborhood structure as a feature of American life. Thus, if one family is known to have been able to indulge in the purchase of a $250 stereo set, it is a fairly safe bet that most of the immediate neighbors are also *financially able* to make that kind of purchase; it is equally valid statistically to assume that a substantial number of the families living in that vicinity will not be culturally averse to owning and using such an item of home entertainment.

With this set of principles in mind, a marketer can target his or her efforts to sell such a piece of equipment to prospects most likely to purchase; at the very least, he or she can avoid the expensive operation of directing sales efforts toward those who cannot possibly afford to buy such an item. In the specific case of this example, what remains to be done is to identify and "cluster" the addresses—by census tract* and/or by zip code—of previous buyers of your high-ticket item, and to obtain lists of families resident in those identical areas. They will prove to be your most test-worthy prospects.

Similarly, your own sales records should prove to be the source of varied data leading to logical conclusions about new customers and repeat

* See App. 3 for definitions of terms.

sales to old customers. Such factors as seasonal buying habits, credit limitations, nature of items previously purchased (such as sporting goods, children's books, automobile-related equipment or supplies, insurance policies, etc.), travel and vacation habits, household items, and other indications of primary interest can lead you to conclusions regarding the nature of additional lists to be obtained and tested—conclusions that can result in a high percentage of conversion to sales at lowest possible cost per contact.

But your organization's list of previous customers by no means exhausts your own files' potential as a source of leads for further sales efforts. Individuals or businesses to whom you have never actually completed a sale but who in one way or another have shown some interest in your operation in the past, and to whom your name will thus be familiar, are also logical prospects for telephone marketing efforts. These would include respondents to previous advertising who might have sent you coupons of inquiry regarding an earlier offer, prospects who have written to your company for some type of information, and possible leads suggested by members of your sales force based on their knowledge of the field.

Before you attempt to obtain lists with which to launch a telephone marketing effort, search your own records for guidance as to what kinds of lists will prove best for you.

Related Trade Sources   Having established the characteristics of the prospects you want to approach, and having examined your own records to see what specific names and general direction they can offer you, the next step is to obtain the actual lists you require for your program. Basically, there are three fundamental sources available to you.

Depending upon the nature of your project, its extent, and the parameters of your own budget, you may elect to use one, or two, or of course all three. The primary concern is your evaluation of which combination will lead to maximum results for you.

1. *The specialized press.* In a nation that supports something more than 5,000 magazines, there is at least one that covers virtually every area of contemporary human interest.

Consumers buy and avidly digest the contents of publications devoted to their interests in such diversified fields as photography, needlework, hunting, household electronics, racing cars, motorcycles, fashions, sports, travel, finance, politics, food, social activities of the elite, mores, motion pictures, music, art—there is probably no field of personal concern that is not reported, discussed, and analyzed by some publication.

Businessmen find it essential to their interests to follow the pages of dailies, weeklies, and monthlies in such areas as building construction, aviation, paper, management, personnel selection and training, lumber, insurance, advertising, materials handling, marketing, petroleum, investments, corporate finances, design engineering—once again, where there exists a valid, functioning area of commercial activity, there certainly exists a publication reporting upon its developments.

The circulations of these periodicals are achieved in one of two ways: either the readers are sufficiently interested in the subject matter involved *to pay an annual subscription fee* or, as is significantly true in the business publication field, the publisher has gone to the trouble and expense of amassing an unpaid subscribers' list of individuals he has ascertained are sufficiently concerned about developments in their areas of interest to warrant maintaining them on his *controlled circulation* list. In either case, the validity of reader involvement is attested to by the supervisory activity of a disinterested auditing organization which periodically examines publisher records for accuracy of circulation claims.

From your point of view as a telephone marketer, the essential fact is that, by and large, such lists of specialized reader interest are broadly available for your use.

In some cases, a magazine seeking to increase its circulation base might agree to *exchange* a sampling of its list for an equal number of names in your files; in other cases, subscription lists are available for rental either directly from the publisher or through a local list broker (the nature of whose activities is more fully discussed below). Some publications will rent circulation lists only to advertisers, either on a one-time basis or in return for a minimum annual space commitment.

The scope of editorial coverage and the nature of the individuals making up the circulation base of each publication are generally set forth fairly concisely in promotional material issued by each publisher. Often these can be located for your study and analysis in the pages of the Standard Rate & Data Service reference books used extensively by those in the advertising profession. As a rule, copies of these SRDS books can be found in the public libraries of most major communities, so it is possible for you to do some basic research into the desirability of specific magazine lists for your purposes without first contacting any specific publisher.

The nation's thousands of periodicals, because they are so clearly delineated by the nature and interests of their readerships, constitute a good source of possible lists for your telephone marketing efforts.

2. *Noncompetitive operations.* Exchange with or rental from other business organizations of a noncompetitive nature represents a second general source of list acquisition.

It is axiomatic in the promotional and sales field that individuals who habitually buy products and services offered through direct-marketing media will continue to do so. Reasons ranging from convenience of that method of purchase through the difficulty of getting to a retail outlet in person tend to make many people better mail or telephone buyers. It will prove valuable to you, therefore, when you are investigating list availabilities for your own operations, to check out the feasibility of obtaining the names and addresses of potential customers from organizations whose major area of profitability is in the direct-marketing field.

Although businessperson leads sought in this manner should be considered in the light of a valid relationship between what they've already purchased from someone else and what you want them to buy from you, there is no need for such close correlation in the area of consumer sales. The mere fact that an individual has shown a tendency to buy direct is sufficient indication that he or she might prove a viable prospect for you; however, it would be well to analyze the previous purchase or purchases in the light of some generalized relation to your own offer—price range, for example, would serve as a practicable guide to your decision.

In this connection, there are a number of large mail-order houses which, over the years, have amassed mailing lists of both actual and potential customers numbering in some cases in the millions of names. In fact, their advertising—examples of which you have regularly seen in popular magazines and in Sunday newspapers—is often aimed at gathering names as much as it is geared to selling the advertised merchandise. Firms like Jay Norris, Fingerhut, Ambassador, American Express, and others realize significant profits through making their lists available to other advertisers.

3. *List brokers.* While it is sometimes possible to negotiate directly with such organizations, most frequently they turn over the rental details to a recognized *list broker.* These organizations, which can be easily located through reference to your local Yellow Pages (under the heading "Mailing Lists") or through the DM/MA, do not charge you for their services, but are paid a commission on each transaction by the list owner. Staffed by experts who can help you to obtain the best lists for your own specific purposes, list brokers are likely to prove your main and most reliable source for the names and addresses of those you want to approach via the telephone.

One major advantage to you of dealing with one or more local list brokers is that you will be working with knowledgeable professionals whose interests lie in helping you attain your goals. If they recommend test lists that prove successful for you, they obviously stand a good chance of renting many of the total names on those lists when your tests prove out—and, of course, the more names they rent, the larger their own income.

Thus, in calling in a list broker, you will find yourself consulting with an entrepreneur whose interests coincide with your own, and whose judgment will be tempered by a conscientious desire to have you succeed in your efforts. So it will pay you to take the brokers completely into your confidence and to regard them as trusted advisers.

To provide the broker with a direction in which to operate, start off by discussing the nature of your project's objectives and show the profile of the "perfect prospect" you have already created. The broker will know the full gamut of available lists and, with this information furnished by you, can intelligently go about fulfilling the assignment.

In all probability, after a few days the broker will supply you with a number of list cards (Figure 2). These are in standardized format, and each

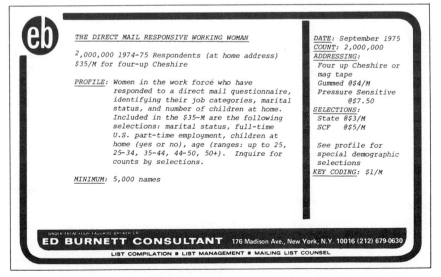

Fig. 2.   A typical list card, furnished by a broker.

will contain a pertinent summary of what you want to know about each recommended list: total number of names available, most recent updating, percentage of men and women, method by which list was acquired, minimum number of names you are required to rent for testing purposes, whether available by zip code, whether available by states and/or individual communities, etc.

In addition, he or she will tell you—or the list card will show—if the list owner has placed any limitations on its usage, such as requiring his approval of the material you intend to expose to the prospects, or perhaps some restrictions as to time availability. In some cases, for example, list owners will not rent at certain periods of the year because they want to use their own lists at that time for their own sales purposes; often, too, the owner will insist on the lapse of a prescribed period of time—perhaps three weeks or a month—between a scheduled rental of the list by someone else and your own use of it, as a means of protecting "their people" from what might be considered overexposure.

The cards will also probably indicate—or in any event the list broker can tell you—the form in which the list can be made available to you, whether on labels, cards, or on a series of typewritten sheets. For telephone marketing purposes labels are preferable, since each individual label that you receive can reasily be detached and mounted directly on the call-record sheet you expect your communicator to work from and fill out, showing the results of each call.

From time to time, a situation may arise in which you will find it desirable to obtain a very specific market segment list which is not available through normal rental or exchange sources. In such a case, the services of a list compiler should be sought. Most regularly established list broker operations are also fully equipped to carry out this function for you, putting together from a variety of sources the very special kind of list you might need. Compiled lists, of course, are considerably more expensive than rental lists, but on the other hand, a list put together especially for your own purposes and to your own order becomes your property to use and reuse as frequently as you may elect to employ it.

Make use of the expertise of your local list brokers. They can help you avoid expensive, time-consuming false starts.

4. *Other sources.* Available from your local telephone company or special directory publishers,* are the crisscross directories—specialized books

---

* See App. 4 for sample listings.

listing telephone subscribers by address rather than by the more usual alphabetical method. They provide an invaluable means of locating potential customers by residential areas, as outlined above in the case of seeking out neighbors of previous purchasers of the high-ticket stereo set.

Yellow Pages, too, provide the means for easy isolation of business and professional prospects, as do local city directories. Club membership lists, records of real estate or car-buying transactions, lists of apartment lease signers—all these are typical of specialized prospects whose names normally can be obtained without great difficulty. Special lists of that type are often highly profitable when used for calls relating to sales of goods or services that tie in with the activity that put the individual on such a list originally. Insurance, sporting goods, gardening tools, furniture—such items can be profitably offered to people who have just bought a house, rented an apartment, or purchased a car, or who are members of the local golf club or garden club.

Cost Factors

Rental fees for lists to be used in telephone-marketing programs vary with the nature of the list, but it can be safely projected that the average commercially available list you might consider testing will run at the rate of about $25 to $30 per each 1,000 names. They can, and do, run higher for certain specialized lists that have consumed excessive time and effort to put together; in fact, an occasional list might be rented for as high as $150 per 1,000 names.

But the cost factor associated with the use of a rented list often relates to facets of its *use*, not to the basic rental fee alone. For one thing, it is important that you check on the manner in which the list has been maintained, and find out how recently it has been revised and updated. Americans are a mobile lot, both in their residential habits and their business relationships: it is an established fact, for example, that 50 percent of the names on any business list you may obtain will be invalid if the list is even one year old, and that an additional 30 percent of the remaining valid half will be incorrect after the passage of another 12 months. People change jobs and titles; companies merge, change their corporate names, go out of business. Consumer lists, too, reflect a fairly high transiency factor with about 20 percent of the country's population moving just about every year.

Any attempt on your part, therefore, to conduct a telephone marketing campaign using an inadequately cleaned list will result in wasted phone calls, in time unproductively spent by communicators finding out the correct name of the executive who has succeeded the individual you thought you were calling, in interceptions by operators to tell your communicator that the called number is no longer in service. Every such deviation from your normal production schedule means fewer productive calls per hour by your communicators, hence reduced sales results per hour, as well. This can be expensive and, in fact, can serve to provide you with an inaccurate picture of the efficiency of telephone operations as an effective marketing medium.

Although a few organizations, such as Metromail, Dun & Bradstreet, and Standard & Poor's Corporation, can furnish lists that include telephone numbers, most lists you will obtain from other sources will not. This means you must budget for the added expense of clerical operational time taken up with phone "look-up" procedures. To minimize this drain on your staff's costly time, you should obtain your lists in alphabetical zip-code sequence fashion. With addresses thus bunched together in "alpha" and homogeneous groupings, telephone number look-ups can be made with the aid of a local phone book or cross-reference directory.

Zip sequence listings also provide the means for bunching operator-assisted searches for telephone numbers, once again minimizing the time your clerical staff must spend on this important operation. Look-up operations can be projected as costing you anywhere from 4 to 25 cents per name, depending on labor cost, directory availability, volume, and geographical spread of names. For example, calling information operations for widely scattered phone numbers with only rural post office boxes as addresses can be a frustrating as well as a time-consuming experience.

As an average, approximately 40 to 50 numbers can be found per hour by consulting a local directory, as against perhaps 30 per hour through calling and asking a directory operator for the required numbers. Utilizing the services of a phone company information operator in your own city may involve direct costs as high as 10 cents per name, based on new tariff filings.

But, regardless of how your list is organized when it is furnished to you, it is rare ever to obtain a list on which more than 85 percent of the names are immediately usable for telephone purposes. Often up to 25 percent will have unlisted or unpublished numbers which cannot be made available to you, so this factor should be considered in calculating your list costs.

Controlling Effective List Usage

The acquisition *and the preparation* of your test lists are primary factors in the total costs of your telephone operations. They are an integral part of the overall cost figures that you must take into account when evaluating the results of your tests in terms of sales and dollar achievement. For that reason, and since telephone provides you with a means of immediate reaction to whatever your operations reveal, it is always a sound procedure to launch your campaign with a test of the list you consider to be the best possible source of profitable returns.

If that kind of list does not quickly pay off for you—and remember that often you can tell within as few as 200 calls in any select business market, or 500 calls to a consumer audience—then it follows your list-building work has just begun. List testing thus gives you an opportunity to probe your market scientifically without risking significantly large investment capital.

But care must always be taken to impose effective management controls over list usage. How failure to effectuate this vital aspect of administration can result in dollars needlessly spent is illustrated by the example of a publishing organization seeking to obtain bulk subscriptions to a specialized magazine circulating among personnel active in the field of communications.

The original test list, correctly chosen, consisted of senior ranking newspaper editors, selected broadcasting organization executives, and top-level individuals connected with specialized publications. Encouraged by the success of this telephone test, the sponsors of the program permitted calls to be continued among lower-echelon personnel—special section and departmental editors—and made the offer also to limited-circulation media that held no possibility for bulk subscription sales.

Ineffective management control of the calling operation permitted this secondary phase to continue well beyond the 200 calls that would have quickly indicated the unproductivity of this market segment, had anyone stopped to analyze the figures. As a result, the continued test ran on until, after needless dollars had been spent, someone spotted the unfortunate trend and halted the entire call operation.

A parallel situation, with happier results, involved the use of a carefully structured professional telephone-marketing program of only 100 calls. It was quickly revealed that on the prospect list being called 50 were already subscribers to the publications for which new customers were being solicited. The list was bad, because the computer that furnished it had not been correctly programmed. But thanks to the test and careful supervision of its progress, the program was stopped at a minimum-cost disbursement level.

Lists must not only be carefully specified and correctly selected—their use must be closely watched, and the continuing record of results achieved from them must be analyzed and evaluated by a decision-making executive on the management level.

chapter five/

Your Promotional Message—
What Do You Say?

IN ANY FORM OF PROMOTIONAL EFFORT, the basic sales thrust is the message that is conveyed to the prospect. Whether in print media, broadcast, or direct mail, once the attention of the possible customer has been attracted by format, it is the copy that has to do the primary sales job; it must maintain interest in your offer, evoke involvement, and stimulate positive action.

In every conventional form of promotional effort, your basic message is conveyed in a predetermined, fixed manner to a significant number of individuals. Your newspaper or magazine advertisement appears in exactly the same wording (even if you use a split-run test), no matter how large the circulation of the publication in which it appears . . . your radio or television commercial reaches every viewer's or listener's consciousness with the same wording . . . your direct-mail piece carries the identical syntax to everyone at whom you aim a particular package.

But with telephone—by the very nature of the medium—communication is through a variety of voices and personalities. To subject your sales message to the same kind of unity of approach to the marketplace that benefits all other kinds of advertising, your telephone sales effort should employ a fixed, pretested *script*.

Most of the elementary standards that influence the preparation of copy in other media also guide you in the preparation of your script, a written piece of copy that is furnished to every member of your communicator staff: its language must suit the needs and the cultural level of your chosen audience, it must make immediately clear the benefits of your offer to the prospect, it must be short enough so that he or she does not lose interest, it must be long enough to tell your story accurately, completely, and convincingly.

But in a number of significant ways, it differs from the conventional copy block that is provided for other kinds of media:

1. Since it will be used in a person-to-person communication, it must be worded without too much formality; that is, it must sound *natural*. Under no circumstances should it be so worded as to make your communicators sound as if they are reading it, even though they may actually be doing so in the early testing.

2. It cannot make vague "advertising language" claims, because the prospect is in a "responsive" position at the other end of the line, reserving the right to break in and interrupt with what might prove to be an embarrassing question. Integrity of information is critical. It is important that your script and communicators state only that which is factually accurate and true. Innuendos, tricky offers, half-truths, concealed facts, and the old-fashioned "hard-sell" pressure approach have no place in today's telephone-marketing operations.

3. It must provide your communicators with material beyond its own original basic wording, so that they can refer to additional data that will help them answer specific questions or objections that might be raised.

4. Precisely because it is used as a tool in a person-to-person medium, the telephone script should be geared to take maximum advantage of that unique facet of its existence. It should be designed to *elicit* and *encourage* response from the prospect, to make him or her feel at home with the communicator, to convey a sense of confidence and intimacy.

In short, you should approach the creation of your script conscious that it will be used essentially as a key portion of an important personal conversation; its content must be informative without sounding "canned."

To set the proper stage for this, the first four steps of any script (regardless of the offer or the reason for the call) should always follow this format:

1. Ask for the prospect by name, and verify that he or she in person is actually on the telephone.

2. Announce the name of the communicator.

3. Announce the name of the organization (or person) for whom the communicator is calling.

4. State the general nature of the call.

By following these four proved steps you can obtain your prospect's undivided attention in a matter of about 20 seconds:

> Hello, may I speak with Helen Morgan, please? . . . (called party will then respond) . . . Mrs. Morgan? . . . this is Sally Wilson calling for Hart's Department Store. I'm calling today to let you know early about a store sale on linens next week that we thought you might like to know about. You'll probably see an advertisement in the Globe or the Courier on Wednesday, but since you are a special charge customer, we wanted to let you know well in advance that this sale really starts *Tuesday* for you. Tell me, Mrs. Morgan, . . . etc.

You will note that, in that example, the benefit to the customer or prospect is hit upon almost immediately. In that respect, script openings can be flexible insofar as the benefit to be offered might vary as it affects different levels of prospects. "Thank you for having been such a good customer," or "Did you receive the special sample packet of cosmetics we mailed to you a few days ago?" or "I know you benefited from your attendance at last year's seminar" are all introductory remarks that imply a new prospect advantage in your upcoming offer.

Since your communicator is operating without the benefit of layout, illustration, or color printing, your copy may have to prove more graphic in its description than would be true for printed materials. You certainly can honestly tell the prospect that the product you are offering is 10 in. by 6 in. and cylindrical, but how much more effective it is to describe it as "about the size and shape of an ice bucket." A product is not just "red"; it is "the color of a raspberry."

Another marked difference in the presentation of your message between traditional print- or mail-media advertising and the telephoned sales message lies in the area of multibenefit offers. In a printed advertisement or in a direct-mail letter or brochure, dramatic impact can be achieved by displaying a series of benefits, in bulleted, machine-gun fashion, followed by copy blocks listing each benefit again and qualifying it with details. But to attempt to enlist the interest of a telephone listener by assailing him with a series of staccato sales points will leave him not only bewildered, but suspicious of your motives and skeptical about your integrity. This, for example, might look pretty impressive in print, but imagine hearing someone telling it to you over the telephone:

- Available in all sizes!
- Your choice of red, green, white, beige, or blue!
- Delivery guaranteed within one week of receipt of order!
- A free gift included if you send cash with your order!
- Money-back guarantee if you're not satisfied!
- Exclusive with Brown's . . . you won't find it anywhere else!

To overcome this unique telephone problem, testing is essential. Properly handled (as discussed in greater detail later in this chapter), it will serve to indicate which of the several benefits you might be offering is most effective in moving your prospects into the action stage.

Maximizing Your Use of Tape

Marketing professionals are turning increasingly to the use of taped telephone messages as a technique that achieves controlled, effective sales presentations.

Such notables as Alistair Cooke, Doris Day, Gloria Steinem, Charlton Heston, Betty Furness, Norman Cousins, and Wall Street's Gustave Levy—among many others*—all have become voices on tape in support of either commercial products they endorsed or worthwhile social causes.

Tape is increasing the effectiveness and accountability of telephone. The use of famous people can provide added dimension to a wide range of telephone programs, by reinforcing product credibility through third-person endorsement.

The burgeoning use of taped messages started in 1972 with the telephone program developed by CCI to launch Norman Cousins' *World Magazine*, as noted earlier.

Today this program, which exceeded 500,000 calls, stands as a milestone in telephone marketing. While tape had been used previously in political campaigns, the program for Norman Cousins marked the first sophisticated commercial project using cost-effective methods and accountability. Since that initial effort, hundreds of telephone programs using taped personal messages have been implemented. For example:

Dr. Franklyn Barry, president of the American Management Associations' Extension Institute, went on to reach business executives, while J. Oppenheimer, publisher of Standard & Poor's *Outlook*, found the medium an effective way to reach subscribers.

---

* See App. 6 for examples of "voices on tape."

Gustave Levy, senior partner at Goldman, Sachs and Company, provided his endorsement on tape to *New York Affairs* Magazine. At the other end of the publishing spectrum, fashion czar John Fairchild extolled through taped telephone messages the virtues of subscribing to *Women's Wear Daily*, which he publishes.

Educator Robert Hutchins raised funds for the Center for the Study of Democratic Institutions, which he heads; and for National Organization for Women (NOW), the voice of Betty Furness effectively raised money.

Mickey Mantle's taped voice has been instrumental in selling a body-building exerciser product to young men. Doris Day's recorded message convinced many homemakers that they can add to family income by becoming representatives for a cosmetic house.

The tape can be advantageously used by correlating the identity of the name personality with the indicated interests of those on the prospect list. When WNET, New York's Public Broadcasting Service educational television station, sought public financial support through a telephone campaign, it built its operation around thousands of names of viewers who had previously written to the station about specific programs they watched. A number of different tapes were made so that those who had written about their interest in "Masterpiece Theater" heard the voice of its urbane host, Alistair Cooke, whereas viewers whose major interest was a popular cooking and food show heard from its dominant personality, Julia Child. WCBB, the Channel 10 PBS station at Lewiston, Maine, benefited from a tape made by then-Senator Margaret Chase Smith, in calls directed to her constituency. Tapes for specialized audiences who normally viewed specific PBS shows were also made by William F. Buckley and David Suskind, hosts of those particular programs.

The individualized treatment, reflecting both the personality of the special speaker and the particular interest of the specialized audience segment, is demonstrated by this script, taped by Alistair Cooke:

> I'm Alistair Cooke. For some time now, I've been introducing you to the plays that you see on Masterpiece Theater. It's been more than a pleasure. It's been the happy continuation in this country of a lifetime's work in a public broadcasting system, that doesn't have to bow to an advertiser, or an administration, and doesn't ask you to shut your eyes and ears in the middle of some fine play or great piece of music while a total stranger makes a pitch for a soap or a refrigerator or some probably useless drug. I believe the airwaves belong to you, the public, and to nobody else. But if you want to keep the best in broadcasting, you are going to have to help. Look across this country and you will see that the public broadcasting stations are in trouble. They are in trouble for the oldest reason. They're short of money. They don't receive any com-

mercial or advertising money. The main reason, in fact, why they're great to watch and listen to—and perform on. It seems to me it will be a tragedy for America if public broadcasting is allowed to die. Not only shall we lose fine, imaginative programs; we'll lose a precious relation between the broadcaster and the people which is uncluttered by third parties whose main aim is to make money.

I have worked for nearly forty years for the BBC in England. It is not, as many people strangely think, a government system. It's a public corporation, kept going by the contributions of the people. It has maintained a standard of news, and entertainment, and quality unmatched by systems that are at the mercy of salesmen. We can match it here. But the awkward thing is that when you show an advertiser the door, he takes his money with him.

Somebody has to fill in. In other words, we need more than your goodwill. We need your contribution. Money. Not much, enough to make you a member of your local broadcasting station. It will be enough to save the system, to keep up the good work, and save you from the constant artillery fire of the advertiser. Our telephone communicator will take your membership pledge and answer any questions. Thank you very much for listening. I'm Alistair Cooke simply asking you to invest a dollar or two in your own pleasure—and—your own peace of mind.

The tape message, combined with a "production-oriented" communicator, produced as high as 40 percent response—4 of every 10 completed calls pledging a contribution of $15; as many as 86 percent actually sent in their checks!

Taping the Business Executive   A combined tape-plus-live-communicator call can be especially effective for industrial marketers. Here, the combination serves as a "personal" sales presentation and is well suited to any effort; cost-effectiveness is especially possible when the effort is targeted to marginal prospects and accounts, or to offers too low-priced to support a salesperson's visit.

The technique has proved to be an important new tool for industrial marketers like Bell & Howell, U.S. Steel, Xerox, IBM, A.B. Dick, and NCR, as well as business-oriented organizations such as the American Management Associations. Here, as an example, is the text of a tape recorded by a corporate vice president and divisional sales manager, used as part of a telephone-marketing program designed to obtain appointments for sales personnel:

Hello. This is David Jones, of the Bell & Howell Business Equipment Group. I'm using this special telephone message approach because I'd like to bring to your attention, as directly as I can, an important new breakthrough in automated banking systems.

Over the years, we at Bell & Howell have been concerned with the needs of many banks that cannot justify the cost of large and elaborate equipment to handle statement rendering and mailing efficiently, accurately and economically. I believe, based on our sales to banks of smaller or similar size, that our new Matchmaker 2, specially designed to handle your volume of demand deposit accounts, can provide just this type of streamlined statement handling at a cost that may well be significantly lower than what you incur in your present manual system. Here's how it works:

The new Matchmaker 2 and one operator is all that you need to automate your statement rendering and mailing system. In a fraction of the time that the costly hand method takes, the Matchmaker 2 automatically counts the number of transactions and matches checks, deposit slips, statements and special inserts, then stuffs and seals envelopes, ready for mailing. Designed to handle an average of three to four hundred statements per hour, the Matchmaker 2 gets statements in the mail on time every month. And because it's from Bell & Howell, any user is assured of continuous, efficient performance and dependable service.

So that you may judge its value and application for your bank's special requirements, our telephone communicator will be happy to arrange to have one of our representatives call on you at a time that is convenient. I hope you'll take this opportunity to consider the new Matchmaker 2 but, in any case, thank you for taking the time to listen.

This tape, together with its communicator opening and close, resulted in immediate appointments being set up with 35 percent of the prospects called, while an additional 19 percent expressed sufficient interest to request added information.

The cost ran at about $5 per phone contact, so that the actual cost-per-appointment was something under $15. Within two months after the completion of this program, a total of $190,000 in equipment had been sold.

Attributes of the Tape   Use of the taped message accomplishes two important results simultaneously: it ensures the use of a controlled advertising message without deviation, and it brings to bear the weight of an implied or stated endorsement from a known personality, business executive, or satisfied customer, in whom the recipient of that message feels complete confidence.

How do people respond to the announcement of a telephone message from Gloria Steinem or Betty Furness, Senator George McGovern or Alistair Cooke, only to find they are getting the voice and not the person?

Surprisingly, people understand that well-known personalities or business executives can't spend their whole day calling people personally, and they respond well to a famous person or a believable company executive with whom they can often identify in a peer relationship, who tells a totally authentic sales story, rather than a communicator whose voice and name are unfamiliar and who doesn't know the product or service as well as the decision maker who produces it.

The taped message should provide important leverage for the acceptance of your sales message by establishing an intimate level of personal contact between the prospect and an individual with whom the potential customer can easily relate. Thus it exploits, to a maximum degree, the built-in person-to-person relationship factor that so uniquely characterizes the telephone. The most effective "tape voices" for your product or service will generally prove to be those who fall into either one of two categories: for the business prospect, it will be the industry leader toward whom the prospect feels both a peer relationship and a marked degree of professional respect; for the customer, it will be the famous personality whom he or she idolizes from afar—the baseball player, the glamorous movie star, the big-name band leader—or the publisher, or perhaps the well-known author.

The critical ingredient of all tape programs has been the use of live telephone communicators to first determine if a person is willing to listen to a taped message.

"Hang-ups" are a rarity. Screening questions, posed by the communicator following a script, serve to qualify the listener and determine his or her readiness to listen to the taped message from the prominent personality. The communicator must always return to the line, directly, upon the final words of the tape, to answer the prospect's questions, request the order, and record the response.

Success Is Not Automatic The use of a prestigious individual as the deliverer of a taped message is a decision that must be related to other facets of the marketing effort. When a home-movie-via-cable television promoter decided to test-market a small rural town, he engaged the services of one of America's best-known, most popular motion picture stars to tape his basic sales message, using it as the keystone of the call to every single telephone subscriber in the tiny community.

However, for weeks prior to the launching of this effort, subscriptions to the service had been solicited by every possible method: local publications, radio and television commercials broadcast from a nearby city, saturation via direct mail, and even house-to-house visits by sales representatives. By the time the telephone program was initiated, the small market had already been completely creamed, with the result that the taped message from the movie star attained virtually no sales results at all.

It proved to be not only an unnecessary tape, but a completely unneeded telephone effort as well—a classic case of "overkill" that served only to boost significantly the ultimate cost per sale.

A More Successful Use of Tape   In contrast to this unhappy experience, a publisher catering to the educational market found success by calling legitimate, carefully selected prospects, a logical audience for the playing of a tape.

The College Division of Prentice-Hall, Inc., marketed WNWD (*Webster's New World Dictionary* of the American Language, Second College Edition) to bookstores serving all colleges and universities. The dictionary was produced, published, and marketed by Collins + World, who selected Prentice-Hall to distribute it to all educational markets. One reason for the selection of Prentice-Hall was its superior marketing capabilities, which included the largest staff of sales representatives calling on college faculty and bookstores. The largest college advertising department prepared direct-mail ads. Prentice-Hall had used personal selling by representatives and direct-mail ads to establish WNWD as a leading dictionary in the college market, especially the adoption segment (required use in a basic English course).

For a reprinting of the second edition of WNWD in the summer of 1974, Collins + World prepared an updating of the content, redesigned the cover, and increased the retail price. They announced the 1974 printing to all the nonschool markets with an offer of 1 free dictionary for every 11 ordered between June 1 and September 30.

The Prentice-Hall marketing campaign for the new printing included the same 1 for 11 offer made by Collins + World. The primary sales channel for this campaign was the Prentice-Hall field staff, who made personal calls on major dictionary accounts, especially where WNWD was adopted. A Prentice-Hall direct-mail ad brochure announcing the special offer was mailed to every college bookstore the first week of August.

Prentice-Hall discussed telephone marketing early in the planning of the college campaign. An outside telephone marketing organization was contacted for a program to supplement the representatives and direct mail. Telephone sales offered complete coverage of key market segments in a short period of time. Important accounts where personal selling and direct mail were not productive in the early weeks of the promotion could be contacted before the special offer expired.

Selecting test lists. The initial list tested in the telephone campaign included accounts that had purchased large quantities in past years, but that had not ordered the new printing by mid-August. The field staff was notified in advance of the test and identified several key accounts where telephone contact closed sales begun by personal visits. With encouraging results from the 10 test calls, the initial list of previous large-volume customers was contacted within several days. At the same time, a second list was made of previous medium-sized purchasers who had not placed an order by mid-August. The second list, 4 times larger than the initial list, was contacted within a few days.

The first two lists, covering previous customers who had as yet to respond to the special 1974 offer, produced effective sales results. A third list was prepared from internal records of the largest textbook accounts that had never purchased WNWD in significant quantity. Over 100 calls were made to this list before the end of August, when the telephone campaign was concluded because delivery couldn't be made in time for college openings in early September.

Using the tapescript. The key to the telephone campaign was a two-minute tape-recorded message. Two separate appeals were directed to the individual in the bookstore initially identified by the telephone communicator as responsible for ordering dictionaries. The first appeal was from Prentice-Hall, and was presented by Dave Amerman, director of college marketing. He first introduced the editor in chief of WNWD, David Guralnik, who talked about the content changes he and his editorial staff had made in the new printing. Amerman returned with news of the price increase, announced the 1 free for 11 offer, and asked for an order, to be taken by the telephone communicator who also answered questions on the two appeals by Amerman and Guralnik. No negative responses or reactions were reported on the message, or the use of the telephone to take orders.

An effective response. A total of 19.5 percent of the dictionary purchasers contacted in the telephone marketing campaign placed orders immediately with the telephone communicators. Very few of those who promised to order later through the field representatives or by direct mail actually did. The response rate and average order varied on the three lists used. The telephone campaign was effective within the total market program for WNWD. It provided almost complete coverage of the small percentage of key accounts that had not responded during the first half of the special offer period. Timely coverage of key segments by telephone marketing supplemented Prentice-Hall's campaign by personal sales calls and direct mail.

Another reason for the success of this telephone marketing campaign is the content and presentation of the basic sales message. Dictionary buyers in college bookstores identified with the dual presentation of the editor's new product and the supplier's special marketing offer. The persuasive tape made by Amerman and Guralnik had a receptive peer-group audience, and motivated listeners to action.

Testing Your Script

A careful record-keeping procedure, plus an analysis of prospect reactions, should generally provide you with a sound basis for determining the effectiveness of your test script within the first few hundred calls. Questions like these will be answered for you:

What are the respective percentages of positive responses and of those who show no interest?

How many refused to listen to the tape? . . . Why?

How many have asked questions? . . . and what questions were asked?

How many raised objections to your offer? . . . and what kind of objections?

How many asked for additional information? (In this connection, does your script offer literature, and if so, should you cut down on that offer?)

Which of several sales points made was the best received?

Is your call running too long? . . . are you getting closings before each call has run its planned course?

You can test the effectiveness of your script within panels of 200 to 500 calls, making necessary modifications as you go along. Remember that small test runs via telephone are much more feasible and certainly much more reasonable financially than similar test operations in other media. That fact alone means you have almost unlimited opportunity to test and modify, and to continue to test and change, until your call reports indicate that you have reached maximum effectiveness with your approach.

The split-run testing technique, so commonly used in other media, is of course available to you in your telephone marketing operations, too, and at much less cost, because preparatory costs are so much cheaper. Given, for example, an offer with five important customer benefits, it is easily practicable to select a random grouping of five panels of 200 names each from a single list, and prepare as many separate scripts, each highlighting one of those benefits and subordinating the other four. Once again, within a few hours, you will know which benefit has the most effective impact on your prospects.

In precisely the same manner, you can test all kinds of approaches, offers, prices, payment methods, direct call versus salesperson's appointment, and other variants, coming up with definitive answers sometimes within the very first day of testing. If several individuals connected with your company, product, or service seem to you to be equally promising as influential and effective presenters of tape messages, there are situations (such as a marketing plan envisioning the eventual calling of a broad and large universe of prospects) in which it will be highly practical to tape them all, and to test their relative degrees of impact on your prospective market.

Your Final Script

Your total script—including call introduction, identifications, statement of offer, tape message, reintroduction of the live communicator, and the closing effort—should be put together in a physical format easily handled by your communicators.

One highly recommended method is that each separate step, with its preset wording, be typed or printed on a small card, with a key identifying word at its bottom margin. Then the cards are stapled or otherwise bound in such a manner that the keyword on each card is always visible, enabling the communicator to respond immediately to the question or objection raised by the prospect. All the communicator need do is to flip out of the way quickly all the cards covering the one that bears the key word (see Figure 3).

The Script is Your Selling Tool

The key to the success of your telephone marketing efforts will often prove to be the nature, content, and informational feedback of your script.

It provides your communicators with a complete calling structure: everything they need to accomplish the results you expect of them. It enables you to control the exact wording with which every single prospect will be approached. It allows you to use the endorsement technique in the true voice of the actual endorser.

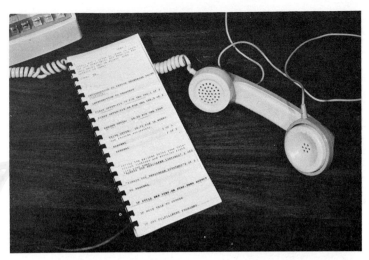

Fig. 3.   Communicator's flip-chart.

And it provides you with a method of testing your approach at low cost, giving you virtually immediate flexibility and a prompt method of evolving your most effective sales approach.

It will do all these things for you if you keep in mind the *Four C's* that should guide its preparation: your scripts must be *clear, concise, conversational*, and *convincing*. If your offer has any validity at all, a script prepared with these facets in mind will do the job for you.

chapter six/

Get Ready, Get Set—
Who Will Say It for You?

THERE ARE THREE fundamental considerations you must take into account before you even begin to plan the launching of a sales program via telephone. Failure to accomplish each step adequately and thoroughly can have a marked effect upon the results you will ultimately achieve; a shortfall in any one of them can conceivably lead to bewildering disaster.

But an adequate and thorough operation in each of these three basic areas of preparation will provide you with a crew of communicators properly equipped—psychologically, physically, and mentally—to do the job you expect of them . . . a job whose results will warrant the close attention to detail and the time-consuming preparations that the steps of necessity entail. Before you have anyone make even the first telephone call you must:

1. Select personnel properly geared, by attitude and personality, to function as communicators.

2. Provide for them a complete and authoritative training course, directed by competent and experienced instructors.

3. Set up a physical environment specifically designed to enable your communicators to function at a top level of efficiency.

Each of these basic steps requires concentrated and serious consideration. Each necessitates the use of a considerable amount of precious time.

But each is an investment that, properly and thoughtfully made, will ultimately pay off handsomely for you.

What Kind of Person Do You Need?

Training begins with personnel selection, because even the best training program you can possibly create will not adequately prepare an individual for this exacting, specialized kind of task if he or she is not temperamentally suited for it in the first place.

To guard against the possibility of staffing up with communicators who may not produce properly for you, it is highly advisable that you take the time initially to set down, in writing, your concept of the varied functions you will want them to carry out. Will they make outgoing calls or serve by answering incoming inquiries? . . . will they be required to repeat the words of a prepared script, without significant deviation, upwards of eight or ten times each hour all day long? . . . will they be expected to have the tact and flexibility to enable them to adjust their messages to varied kinds of antici-pated responses?. . . will they be limited to essentially vocal tasks, or be required to carry out some amount of detailed clerical record keeping or follow-up assignments?

These—and other considerations germane to your own particular objectives—provide you with a basis for analyzing the personality and skill requirements of the kind of persons you should seek to make up your communicator staff. Ask yourself, What kind of person does it take to carry out the specific tasks you have listed? You will have to give mature consid-eration to such factors as skills, education, business experience, communi-cation experience, physical attributes and limitations, dexterity in han-dling whatever type of equipment is to be employed, personal attitude and approach to the continually repetitive nature of this type of work, clerical abilities and experience, and similar personal attributes.

Having satisfied yourself as to the qualities you will require in those you decide to employ, create next an interview form that will, in each case, remind you of the individual, detailed qualifications you are seeking. As you talk to each prospective communicator, make careful notes, and then rate each person against each other individual interviewed on a relative scale for each and every specific qualification.

Sources of likely candidates for communicator operations may vary from time to time, depending to some degree upon general economic condi-tions. Obviously, in a soft economy in which unemployment and trends toward "moonlighting" are labor availability factors, a greater number of potentially effective communicators will be available to choose from. Persons whose normal pursuits have accustomed them to deal with the public are logical candidates: actors and actresses, airline clerks, hotel personnel, stock or security sales representatives. But equally important as sources are homemakers—whose children no longer require their continued presence and attention—seeking part-time employment on schedules adjustable to their own needs, older persons wanting to supplement retirement incomes, students looking for a means of underwriting tuition costs, or a "mobile" handicapped person. Anyone who can learn to "smile as they dial" can be taught how to dial profitably for most normal phone marketing programs.

Some of the most successful communicators have developed out of the ranks of individuals who, for whatever reasons of personal psychology, wish to work with the public but want to do so in what is essentially an anonymous fashion. Self-generated doubts about personal appearance, for example, can lead an individual in some cases to assume the responsibilities of telephone communication—and to do so enthusiastically and successfully—secure in the knowledge that he or she remains invisible during the entire process.

The sources for your interviewees might well be the traditional ones: newspaper advertising and employment agency referrals. However, if you use an agency, make sure that it's one that is interested in something beyond merely collecting its fees. Discuss your problems thoroughly and in depth with an agency principal, and furnish him or her with a copy of the qualifications list or the interviewing form you have already prepared. In that way you can expect that only persons with the qualities you are seeking will be sent in to talk to you.

Above all, remember that interviewing is a two-way process. While you want to use it as a means of selecting those best qualified to serve your pragmatic needs, it is important that you supply to those you interview full details of what those needs are and what you expect to have done for you. Failure to provide such information can lead to communicator staff turnover, with its resultant loss of time and money. For example, you may discover—as others already have—that the "ideal" female communicator you have hired will walk off the job almost immediately because of her reluctance to make "sales" calls as opposed to the survey calls she's comfortable doing. Finding the right people can frequently mean matching them to the right program. For example, college students generally enjoy calling educators, art students like to sell art books, and so forth.

Remember too, in selecting your communicators, that an entirely different set of skills is required for telephonic selling than for person-to-person contact. The $60,000-a-year "supersalesman" can't be taught much about telephone communicating; by exeperience, training, and temperament, he's probably great on the phone—or won't listen. But the average $3- to $4-per-hour intelligent, ambitious, perceptive communicator can usually be trained to become effective on the phone and is often eager to prove an ability to sell well.

Your phone communicators must know how to listen. Listening skills are as important as "talking" skills, sometimes even more vital. Communicators must be able to determine and interpret voice and phone nuances, recognize the significance of pauses or hesitations in the responses of those to whom they are talking. And, of course, they must be able to operate efficiently without recourse to the traditional salesperson's reliance on charts, tables, and similar visual aids.

Men and women are equally effective on this type of sales assignment, but you should give due consideration to the nature of both your offer and your potential audience, and come to a decision as to whether either or both may profit more from the use of male or female communicators. Clearly, for example, if you were soliciting memberships in the National Organization for Women (NOW), you would have women communicators calling your female prospects.

Whether or not your procedure calls for the inclusion of a taped message should also be a factor in your determination of the characteristics that will mark your "ideal" communicator. The communicator who will be called upon to do the total selling job alone and the one who will supplement the message that's been taped by a prominent person can frequently represent two entirely different kinds of individual, and should be chosen accordingly.

In your interviews, and particularly in your training program (details of which follow), stress the fact that you do not expect anything even approaching universal acceptance of your offer, that the communicator's job is a *professional* operation, and that a negative response must not be interpreted as a personal rejection of the communicator. Your use of a programmed script and certainly of a taped message will help your communicators accept and adjust to this nonpersonalized role.

In summary, you should seek to employ communicator personnel with personality, native intelligence, objectivity, a sense of responsibility, an ability to listen and to react in flexible fashion within the framework of your needs and instructions, and with a voice that reflects both warmth and maturity.

Now that you've selected and hired the right people to make up the best possible communicator crew available to you, you're just about ready to embark on the next vitally important step—training them to do the job.

Training Your Communicators

The nature, the time span, and degree of intensity of your training course will depend, of course, on such factors as the relative complexity or simplicity of your offer, the parameters of your objectives, the kind of audience your people will be calling, and the results you seek to achieve. But in any case it should be designed to be deep and complete, and at its conclusion every one of your trainees must feel fully equipped and completely confident to move into carrying out his or her assignment.

To achieve these goals, the training procedure must encompass two fundamental operations:

1. Theoretical training and instruction in all necessary procedures, attitudes, and operations

2. Simulated practice sessions, using actual equipment to imitate the kind of practical experiences that will be met when the training program is completed and calls to prospects or customers are undertaken

As a prelude to actual instruction and practice in the use of the telephone, it is of primary importance that your group of new communicators be thoroughly briefed about your company, the product or service you expect them to offer, and the nature of the kinds of responses they might expect to receive from various listeners. Your training sessions should be conducted with limited numbers of personnel, so that each trainee can be treated by the instructor in human, compassionate fashion. More than five or six individuals per trainer is hardly recommended, since varying learning speeds must be taken into account on a highly individualized basis.

Above all, make sure that your trainers are themselves adequately trained to do their important instructional job!

The Course of Instruction   Since, as has already been pointed out, different skills are required for telephone-sales efforts than for the traditional person-to-person operations, it is important that you do not allow yourself to fall into the easy trap of starting off by distributing to your classes the sales aids materials you use for your outside salespeople. Whatever printed or otherwise-reproduced materials you employ should therefore be specially prepared for the edification of telephonic communicators, and angled to stress the qualities they will require to carry out their assignments successfully: their ability to listen, the need to interpret nuances and inflections and pauses, the flexibility of response.

Your instructors should be supplied with clear, easily understood tapes of "ideal" sales communications between salesperson and prospect, and these should be used in interrupted fashion, allowing the instructor opportunity to break in from time to time to explain what is going on, why the communicator gives a particular response, what the prospect's reaction can be interpreted to indicate, etc.

The Pragmatic Approach   To back up this kind of instruction, ample opportunity should be furnished for trainees to utilize the lessons they have learned, through the application of carefully supervised practice sessions. In this connection, role playing should be extensively employed, with the trainer or some other knowledgeable person acting as customer or prospect.

Each such exercise should be fully taped and, at its conclusion, not only the trainee-participant, but all of the other trainees in that unit as well, should take part in a trainer-led critique. In this manner, under competent guidance, all trainees can gain a significant understanding of where their individual strong points, as well as weaknesses, lie and can thus improve their performances in session after session.

Through this practical demonstration procedure, trainees can most readily be brought through the stages of development required to enable them to master such key areas of telephone selling as getting through to the decision maker, handling objections in a flexible and tactful manner, proposing package offers, and projecting various types of closings.

A typical tape-with-comment exercise will carry trainees through the following six fundamental steps of the traditional sales process:

1. Introduction and initial benefit statement
2. Probing for the prospect's needs
3. Recommendations to meet those needs
4. Paraphrasing objections in order to clarify them
5. Meeting objections soundly and logically
6. Moving into a direct or an assumptive closing

When employed in a role-playing framework, the critique should always be taken step by step; that is, in the first instance the tape should be stopped after point number one, with trainer's comments and group discussion ensuing. When point number two is reached, the critique should not only discuss what has happened in that area, but should return to the first point again, and relate the new development to the previously developed evaluation. Step-by-step role-playing exercises ideally should always restart from the very beginning of the operation, thus continually strengthening the trainees' understanding of the ongoing relationship between the various steps of the selling process.

Training Principles   In setting up and assessing the efficiency of your training operation, you can be well guided by the standard principles that leading educational consultants apply in evaluating the validity of the learning process. Your training course should ideally include these eight elements:

1. Adequate *input*, both written and oral, to enable your trainees to understand the basis of your operations

2. Consistent and repetitive *questioning* at all stages of the training procedure, but particularly in relation to the input

3. Sufficient opportunity for each trainee to supply *responses* to those questions

4. *Reinforcement* of awareness of material taught, through the use of practical examples and actual experiences

5. Constant *repetition* of all major points made by your trainers, even at the possible risk of boring some of the more alert and advanced trainees

6. Use of *simulation* techniques, so that the trainee is made to feel thoroughly at home with procedures and equipment before he or she undertakes even an initial sales call

7. Provision of adequate *motivation* to encourage the trainee to extend his or her efforts to the utmost

8. Clear presentation of *performance objectives* to enable each trainee to understand without question exactly what level of accomplishment is expected

Organize your training courses so that maximum student involvement is encouraged. Make sure, too, that there is constant testing at all stages, in order that both trainer and trainee will have an opportunity to measure the individual trainee's absorption of what he or she is being taught; and clearly establish in your own mind exactly how you will handle those who fall below average levels of achievement, as revealed by such testing procedures.

Remember that in many cases—perhaps in most—your newly organized communicator team will consist of people who know little or nothing either about selling or about the specifics of telephone marketing techniques and procedures—so don't let your trainers assume too much, and don't let them overlook what might appear to you and them to be obvious basics and fundamentals.

The Training Objective The fundamental purpose of your training program, obviously, is to develop a communicator crew thoroughly capable of fulfilling the task you set for them: obtaining maximum cost-effective results from your telephone marketing program.

But at all times you should keep in mind that optimum employment of the telephone as a marketing tool in a direct-response, mass-market operation can be achieved only through the application of the basic principles enunciated by Professor Levitt (already fully discussed in Chapter 2). In brief, they call for using manufacturing operational techniques as an integral part of the service function of selling and marketing—for looking for solutions "inside the tasks to be done," rather than seeking improvements in "the performer of the task."

Successful telephone marketing operations depend upon using *mechanized production- and labor-control techniques* to achieve maximum results. In short, a good telephone marketer is in the manufacturing business. He makes this transition—so essential to success—by management's application of a manufacturing discipline and style of thinking to a people-oriented service situation.

This point of view must be kept prominently in mind when you develop your communicator training program and during each of the steps of its implementation. If "you view machinery as a piece of equipment with the capability of producing a predictably standardized customer-satisfying output while minimizing the operating discretion of its attendant, . . ." then you will perceive the essential quality of the mass-marketing telephone operation: "It is a telephone machine that produces, with the help of unskilled machine tenders, a highly polished product."* Through painstaking attention to total design, creative effort, facilities planning, control and systems, everything is built into the machine itself, into the technology of the system. *The only choice available to the communicator is to operate on the telephone exactly as management intended.*

While, of necessity, some portion of your training program will be devoted to improving the personal skills of those you have chosen to serve as your communicators, all of the theory and practice of your training course, as well as all of the role-playing and feedback sessions must be

* Theodore Levitt, *Harvard Business Review*, September–October 1972.

projected within the framework of this fundamental concept. For telephone marketing based on pretested communicator scripts, taped personal messages, completely structured answers to questions, and hourly response norms is the only correct "production line approach to service" inherent in the Levitt approach, and has been demonstrably successful for many companies.

Choosing communicator candidates whose personalities lend themselves to this operational level, and imbuing them with a thorough understanding of the nature of the role they will play in your operation thus becomes an absolute essential for success.

"Phone-Power." Attendance at local "Phone-Power" sessions is suggested as a means whereby the potential communicators might benefit from the application of the skills and knowledge of experienced professionals.

"Phone-Power" is a service of the Bell System, operative in virtually all of this country's major cities; in the New York area alone, for example, it is staffed by 32 specialists and trainers. Its educational services are available in two ways: your local telephone company will set up free classes within the headquarters of any company to train a staff of potential communicators, or, if you have a small staff or are working on your own, you can join a class conducted by the telephone company, consisting of individuals in various business enterprises who, like yourself, are seeking training that will lead to improved sales operations to business prospects via telephone.

To support and supplement its teaching services, "Phone-Power" will make available to you any or all of a series of self-help booklets designed to function as workbooks that carry the learner logically from step to step in the sales process. Specific booklets can be obtained to cover such varied operations as handling inquiries, opening new accounts, collecting overdue accounts, reactivating inactive accounts, introducing new products or services, selling on the service call, selling existing customers, and qualifying prospects and making appointments.

Each booklet is accompanied by two summary cards—one of desk reference size, the other in convenient pocket-sized dimensions—that can be used by the new telephone marketer as reference documents when he or she first begins to approach the market. The booklets and their related reference cards are intended for self-help use as a segment of the "Phone-Power" training courses. There is ample space provided for written comments or answers to the many questions posed in the pages of the little booklets, so that involvement on your part becomes an integral part of the learning process.

If you are an independent salesperson who is seeking to improve the results of your telephone marketing efforts, or if you are handling marketing operations for your firm, the Bell System's "Phone-Power" service is worthy of investigation, and can provide a real help in getting you started.

Salary and Incentive versus Commissions   While detailed facets of telephone economics are discussed fully later in these pages, it should be noted here that the method of compensation you elect to use for your communicator staff (and a presentation of which must be an integral part of an employment interview) related directly to the philosophy of the Levitt approach.

Starting with the concept that to get maximum results you must offer your communicators a basic living wage, many successful telephone marketers use additional bonus or incentive devices to stimulate call activity. You might, then, want to reserve some portion of your budget for some types of incentive programs: anything from annual overseas trip awards through "Rep of the Month" luncheons, quota clubs, and recognition by top management, on to cash bonuses for achievement over and above an established and announced sales figure.

"You can give away a package of jelly beans if you do it right, and still get motivation out of it," one telephone marketer has said. But while incentives can help make your communicators enthusiastic and stimulate them into increased activity, the question of paying *commissions* as a basic means of remuneration must be carefully examined in an entirely different light.

As we have seen, the communicator functioning as part of a successful telephone marketing program represents a standardized unit in a highly structured, production-line operation. Every facet of that project is geared to the attainment of established performance goals, through the sophisticated and disciplined administration of a planned program. The commission system, on the other hand, is built around the concept that some individuals, acting on their own initiative and applying their own self-developed techniques, can produce more effectively than others.

The commission system, therefore, must be seen as the very antithesis of the structured program concept that marks the controlled, result-projectable telephone marketing program. Any communicator might understandably welcome incentives as added boosts to the needed consciousness of personal involvement, but paying total remuneration as a percentage of achieved sales can serve only to contravene the organized and controlled ability of the modern telephone marketing program to deliver maximum results.

As a basis for establishing an aura of cooperative, smooth, and well-integrated operations, your communicators should be made fully aware of this important principle.

Mass Marketing versus Career Operations   If you're marketing one product, one line of products, one service or a group of related services, you can support a continued "on-premises" call program for 12 months a year. Your telephone communicator can become a "career" employee, although because of increased call efficiencies the "production-line" system can usually improve productivity and lead to higher profits through control of costs and maximization of call contacts. Many call programs operate very profitably for their companies on a salary-plus-commission compensation base, despite the fact that a commissioned phone sales representative often stays on a single call for 25 to 30 minutes.

That is often necessary in selling Yellow Pages advertising ($1 billion annually), or in selling steel (Valley Industries, $85 million per year). Every sale depends on the sales ability of *that* individual operator. He or she is only human, and results will vary with the weather, the situation at home (do you know where your children are?), and with individual moods and styles.

Just as all sales personnel hit highs and lows, so commissioned sales results must vary, depending on the salesperson's input. Thus constant incentives are necessary; commission is essential for profitability—"If you don't produce, you don't get paid." The absolute necessity to produce adds pressures all along the line: the operator for income, the prospect for a sale, the management for profit. Most commissioned phone operations function under high pressure and communicate that atmosphere over the telephone.

Environment–The Third Consideration

Your staff of communicators has been selected from among the many applicants who have made themselves available for interview and assessment. You have administered a carefully planned and expertly supervised training course, complete as to both theoretical instruction and practical practice sessions.

But your preparatory operations are not yet quite complete. With your trained communicators eventually scheduled to work at the telephone from four to eight hours daily, they will require optimum physical environmental conditions to produce the results you anticipate getting from them. Certainly it would be shortsighted to spend time, money, and effort training the most qualified individuals in the best possible manner, only to provide them with working conditions that could serve to hamper their efforts and dim their enthusiasms.

How to go about providing the proper environment and the elements of the system it must service are the major concerns of the next discussion.

chapter seven/

The Interdependency
Factor

GRANTING THE POINTS of superiority enjoyed by the telephone as a mass-marketing medium, and even projecting the manner in which it will be enhanced and broadened by future technological developments, one thing must be emphasize continually: that to achieve optimum total effect each aspect of a telephone-marketing program must be considered in its relation to all the other facets of the system for achieving maximal returns.

To cite just one typical example, costs must be evaluated in terms of the number of calls that can be resultfully completed within a given time span. Since it is highly probable that, in any marketing effort, only a minority of those approached will respond in a manner hoped for by the marketer, every effort must be made to (*a*) eliminate at the very start all those who cannot be expected to respond at all (a list-selection function) and (*b*) promptly terminate conversations with those who quickly indicate that they are not likely to be converted to completed sales (a facet of script preparation). Taken together, these two factors can be controlled to maximize the call-per-hour figure.

In the same manner, there exists a close relationship between ultimate results and choice of personnel, training, selection of equipment, presentation of offer, and the other factors involved in the total telephone operation. To ignore any single element, or to stress any at the expense of any others, is to create a serious imbalance that will quickly be manifested in the condition of the bottom line.

Regarded in this light, the design of your telephone room or workshop and the conditions provided for your communicator crew represent elements in your planning that cannot safely be undervalued.

Designing Your
Telephone Workshop

So that nobody would know where the calls came from, some earlier-era marketers of dubious integrity had their calls placed from basement boiler rooms. But working in the old-fashioned "boiler room" or "bucket shop," with all that those rightfully disparaging terms imply, is not satisfying to the students and/or homemakers who make up the bulk of today's telephone communicators.

The conditions under which they ultimately will function should be the conditions under which they are trained, so that there will be a minimum of transitional feeling when they shift from training sessions to workdays. Analyze, with thoroughness and in considerable depth, exactly what equipment and furnishings will be required to enable them to do their jobs best and, when you have arrived at your decision, set up those conditions before they begin their training operations.

Your routine, and the equipment required to carry it out, should be fully production-oriented. Think not only of the immediate challenge at hand, but about the potential for expansion as well, and plan your physical space needs with the future in mind. Experience in this field has made it clear that there are certain fundamentals to be regarded as essential for the attainment of maximum efficiency from your communicator staff. Make sure the space you set aside and furnish reflects these basis needs (see Figure 4).

1. *Use a room that has windows.* The nature of the work your people will be doing demands that they have an opportunity to stop for a short period every so often and look out at something beyond the four walls within which they are functioning. To a person sensitive enough to function well as a communicator, the stress and strain of repeating the same call routine as many as perhaps 40 to 80 times in a normal work shift can create problems. An opportunity every so often to look out of a window and to recognize that there's a "real world" still at hand can prove an important factor in the communicator's ability to function at top productive levels.

2. *Provide for control of temperature* and consistent, controlled

airflow. A stuffy, overheated room (or, for that matter, one that's too cold and drafty) can quickly lead to the inefficiency that stems from the need to pay attention to something other than the job at hand.

3. *Set up a logical work flow procedure.* Make it as easy as possible for your communicators to function without constant getting-up-and-going-somewhere movements. See that they have easy access to their supervisors (and vice versa, of course) and that the materials they require for effective telephone productivity are available at all times.

4. *Provide the mechanical bases for efficient operation.* Make sure communicators have at hand whatever report forms you require them to fill out after each call. If each station requires shelving to hold needed forms, build in shelving; if your operation uses small cards for reference materials or as report forms, construct properly sized bins at each station, and so on (see Figure 5).

5. *Provide adequate supervisory attention* for your communicators. At a minimum you should have one supervisor for five or six salespersons. Normally the supervisor can effectively direct 10 communicators. The communicators should know that he or she is there to help, not to hinder or criticize. Give the supervisor a separate booth, glass-enclosed for easy observation of the communicator group, so that the supervisor has an opportunity to notice whenever an individual communicator shows signs

Fig. 4. A typical phone-room installation.

Fig. 5. Shelving and bins are designed and constructed to meet the specific needs of the program.

of not functioning smoothly or easily, and can, if need be, retrain the communicator in privacy.

6. *Arrange for monitoring operations* in such a way that the equipment will not interfere with the monitored communicator or be noticed by the prospect or customer on the other end of the line. It is important that the communicators know that monitoring will go on from time to time, but as a help to them, not as a means of being critical or harmful to their operations. If the communicator agrees to the monitoring of his or her own calls, you must have a written acknowledgment to that effect from that communicator. But at least one state regulatory agency has suggested recently that such monitoring cannot be done under any circumstances. While that does not appear to be the general law, certainly at least written consent is necessary.*

7. *Anticipate the need for supporting clerical activities.* Does your operation call for mail follow-up after each successful telephone contact? If so, make sure that an operational routine is established to ensure smooth and prompt functioning. Keep your telephone communicator area and your fulfillment center close together to avoid loss of time and energy in carrying out the essential contact and communication between them.

8. *Give each communicator ample space in which to work properly.* The size of each individual's booth will depend upon the nature of your own operation and the functional requirements you accordingly set up for

* See App. 7 for legal information.

each person's workday. Provide ample electrical outlets for lighting equipment, tape players, etc. Make sure there is a large enough area—and easy access at hand—for such items as price lists, catalogs, scripts to which reference might be required, index cards, etc., (see Figure 6).

Experience has demonstrated that individual communicator booths, lined with acoustical tile and separated by glass or Plexiglas upper partitions through which visibility of surrounding areas is permitted, provided the optimum conditions under which communicators should be asked to function (Figure 4).

In general, keep in mind the principle that your communicators will work better when operating under physical conditions designed for privacy, but without a feeling of isolation. The difference is as important as it is subtle.

Work-Control Forms

Essential to the production-line operation are the work-control forms that constantly provide you with an ongoing record of how each communicator is performing, what has been the result of each individual call placed, and the overall total picture of what is happening relative to your entire program.

While the actual physical design of each of these three fundamental control forms will vary to some extent with the details of your own pro-

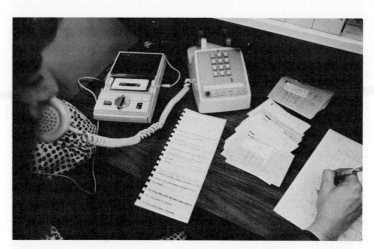

Fig. 6. Communicator tools: tape player, telephone, flip-chart, Production Call Cards, communicator production tally sheet.

gram, the necessary basic elements they should contain will become apparent through a close study of the following examples, taken from actual use and experience.

Production Call Card The individual production call card serves to accomplish a significant range of important functions. Related directly to an individual call to a specific customer or prospect, it is created when the name of the person to be called (normally in label form) is attached to it (Figure 7). When used by the communicator directly following completion of each call, it serves to provide essential information:

- It places value on the name of each prospect.
- It details the actual result of each and every dialing.
- It enables accurate coding to be applied with subsequent program measurement.
- It ensures a controlled work-flow pattern.
- It provides the base for correct follow-up procedures.
- It makes available whatever historical documentation may ultimately be needed.
- It eases and speeds up communicator tasks by permitting standardized use of abbreviations.
- It provides opportunity for qualitative feedback and program interpretation and analysis.

All in all, the individualized production control form furnishes every service its title implies.

Production Tally Sheet This record form provides you with a complete record, at a quick glance, of the experience of each individual communicator over the course of any one hour or day of operation (Figure 8).

As indicated in the illustrated example, it shows what kinds of responses were evoked and the total number of each, as well as the total number of calls both initiated and completed, thus furnishing a continuing daily basis for comparison with the production records attained by other members of the communicator staff.

Program Master Log Sheet Put together by clerical personnel from the individual production call cards turned in each day by each communicator, this important form gives you a consistent, up-to-date, cumulative overview of the progress of your telephone-marketing program, enabling you to spot strong points and shortcomings that require correction on a day-to-day basis. It also makes possible the creation of a daily result curve chart

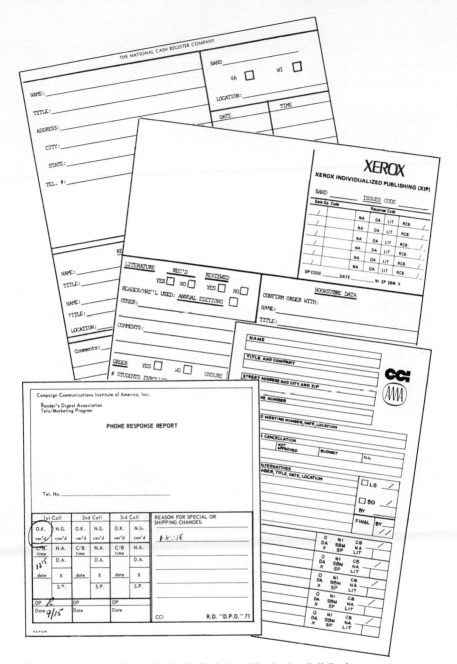

Fig. 7. *A montage of several individually designed Production Call Cards.*

COMMUNICATOR PRODUCTION TALLY SHEET

DATE _1/6/76_   PROGRAM / CODE _X & Y_

COMMUNICATOR _R. Baker_   TOTAL TIME _3 hrs._

	(A) ORDER	ITEMS 1	2	3	4+	LIT. REQ	NOT INT.	SBM	SPEC.	REC. C/B	COMP. CALLS	N/A	D/A BUSY	X	TOT. DIAL.
1 00 15 30 45															
2 00 15 30 45															
3 00 15 30 45															
4 00 15 30 45															
5 00 15 30 45															
6 00 15 30 45															
7 ⓪⓪ 15 30 45	/		/			//	++++	/		/	9	//	++++	//	18
8 00 15 30 45	/	/				///	++++		/	//	12	///	//		17
9 00 15 30 45						////				///	7	///	++++ ++++	/	21
10 00 15 30 45															
11 00 15 30 45															
TOTALS	2 (1)	1	1		3	5 (2)	14 (3)	1 (4)	1 (5)	6 (6)	28 (7)	8 (8)	17 (9)	3 (10)	56 (11)

Fig. 8. A communicator production tally sheet. Key:

(1) 2 orders totaling 3 product units; (2) 5 requests for literature; (3) 14 prospects who were "Not Interested" in any offer; (4) 1 prospect who had already SBM'd (subscribed by mail); (5) 1 Special (the response was that the prospect had previously bought from the company, had returned the merchandise and was being billed; would buy when credit was received for that return); (6) 6 requests for Call Back (the communicator *spoke to the decision maker* who for one reason or another—busy with children, still deciding, etc.—asked to be called back at a later time; (7) 28 completed calls (total of columns 1 through 6); (8) 8 N/A's (the company answered, but the decision maker was "Not Available"); (9) 17 D/A's (no one answered, or the line was busy); (10) 3 X's (phone number disconnected, with no new number, or party had moved); (11) 56 total dialings (total of columns 7 through 10).

CCI

CAMPAIGN COMMUNICATIONS INSTITUTE OF AMERICA, INC.

PROGRAM MASTER LOG SHEET

X & Y PROGRAM

DATE	ORD. #	%CC	Item 1 #	%CC	Item 2 #	%CC	Item 3 #	%CC	Item 4+ #	%CC	LIT. REQ.	NOT INTERESTED #	%CC	SBM #	%CC	SPECIAL #	%CC
C-T-D	211	22.2	155	16.3	23	2.4	33	3.5				581	61.0	59	6.2	46	4.8
1/7	16	16.2	15	93.8			1	6.3				61	61.6	12	12.1	5	5.1
C-T-D	227	21.6	170	26.5	23	2.2	34	3.2				642	61.1	71	6.8	51	4.9
1/8	108	18.2	84	1.4	12	2.0	12	2.0				374	63.2	44	7.4	28	4.7
C-T-D	335	20.4	254	15.5	45	2.7	46	2.8				1016	61.3	115	7.0	79	4.8
1/9	13	15.1	9	(10.5)	3	(3.5)	1	(1.2)				56	65.1	10	11.6	1	1.2
C-T-D	348	20.1	263	(15.2)	48	(2.8)	47	(2.7)				1072	62.0	125	7.2	80	4.2

Fig. 9. *Program master log sheet.*
Key:

C-T-D = Cumulative to date
%CC = Percentage of completed calls
SBM = Subscribed by mail (prior to call)
RCB = Requested callback

N.A. = Not available
D.A. = Did not answer
X = Specials
TD = Total calls dialed
CC = Completed calls

that will enable you to see how well your results are holding up on a consistent basis, and to spot any sharp deviations from the norm (Figure 9).

The Importance of the Interdependency Factor

When it is realized that only three communicators working an average of but six hours daily, 50 weeks out of the year, can contact some 31,000 decision makers,* the importance of accurate, ongoing record keeping and record analysis becomes clear.

But such records can have real meaning only when a telephone-marketing operation is so planned and organized as to concentrate every effort of every component part of the operation to the attainment of bottom-line results. Your decision to embark on such a step, as part of your total marketing operation, must therefore be tempered by your own evaluation of your readiness and ability to:

■ Develop an accountable telephone-marketing plan

---

* 3 × 7 completed calls per hour (average day and night) × 6 hours daily × 5 days per week × 50 weeks = 31,500.

RCB		COMPLETED CALLS		N. A.		D. A.		X		T. D.		TOTAL HOURS	TOTAL CC HR.	TOTAL TD HR.
#	%CC	#	%CC	#	%TD	#	%TD	#	%TD	#	%TD	%	%	%
55	5.8	952	35.2	426	15.8	1277	47.3	47	1.7	2702	100.0	105.75	9.0	25.5
5	5.1	99	20.2	38	7.7	352	71.7	2	.4	491	100.0	10.5	9.4	47.2
60	5.7	1051	32.9	464	14.5	1629	51.0	49	1.5	3193	100.0	118.0	8.9	27.0
38	6.4	592	35.9	278	35.9	742	45.0	37	2.2	1649	100.0	68.0	8.7	24.2
98	6.0	1643	33.9	742	15.3	2371	49.0	86	1.8	4842	100.0	178.5	9.2	27.1
6	7.0	86	23.7	53	14.6	217	59.8	7	1.9	363	100.0	9.0	9.6	39.9
104	6.0	1729	33.2	795	15.3	2588	49.7	93	1.9	5205	100.0	182.0	9.5	28.6

- Structure systems for specific sales programs
- Create the materials needed for call and program support, such as tape messages, scripts, communicator response modules
- Establish a series of controls, including record keeping and cost accountability procedures
- Devise recruiting and training programs for supervisory and telephone communicator personnel
- Analyze and evaluate programs, project cost and response factors
- Pretest before-program implementation to develop scripts, operator norms, response feedback, and cost-per-order data

The experience of one marketer dramatically demonstrates how failure to integrate even one portion of the overall program with all the other elements of the operation can result in costly and highly ineffective involvement on the part of dozens of people.

Working from what was represented as an accurate and up-to-date list, communicators were set to work calling magazine subscribers who had failed to respond to the normal cycle of mailed expiration notices and renewal appeals. Surprisingly, the call reports revealed that over 40 percent of those called resentfully reported that they had in fact long since renewed their subscriptions by mail. Investigation at that point uncovered the facts:

a recently installed computer operation held data showing the authenticity of those claims, but no one had seen fit to provide the updated, accurate records to those making the calls. Instead, an older, hand-compiled, and hardly accurate expiration list had been furnished for testing.

Not only was a costly test undertaken on a basis that never should have

TELEPHONE MARKETING SYSTEM

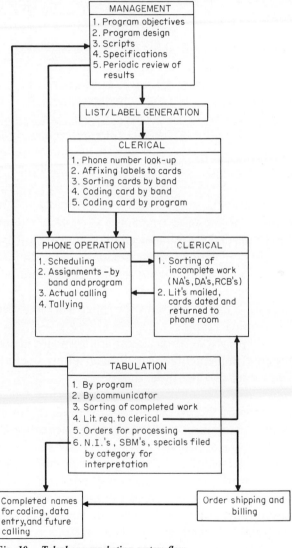

Fig. 10. Telephone marketing system flow.

been permitted, but the general expressions of annoyance that were received from among the publisher's best customers indicated a significant
decline in the level of consumer relations that every business operation
strives to maintain.

If and when you feel you are prepared to attest without reservation to
your readiness—and the ability of your organization to offer personnel
and resources support—to integrate all of the many vital facets of successful telephone operations, then you may very well be fully prepared to
begin thinking about the possibility of launching your own internally
staffed program.

The flow of operations and the relationship of each portion of the total
operation to each of the others is graphically shown in the accompanying
Telephone Marketing System diagram (Figure 10). Each of these factors
depends completely for its successful operation on the professional implementation of each of the others, and a weakness or shortcoming anywhere along the line can result in a breakdown of the entire operation.
Ironically, such a breakdown may be difficult to trace to its cause once the
program is operative, since the very shortcoming itself may well make it
difficult to isolate the weakness in call response that caused the problem.

But no analysis or projection of possibilities is feasible without a mature
and thorough consideration of the total economics of your telephone
marketing program. So let us now proceed to a full discussion and analysis
of the numbers that characterize mass-marketing operations via the telephone.

chapter eight

Telephone Economics

AS IN ANY FORM of promotional or sales activity, the success of your telephone marketing campaign will always be measured in terms of profitability. Your ultimate cost per order can readily be measured because the cost factors related to telephone operations are easily isolated. Since telephone is frequently used in combination with other media, or with the follow-up efforts of a sales force in the field, final cost-per-order calculations must await definitive sales conversion results.

Generally speaking, your cost factors break down into two broad categories: *telephone-activity costs* and *supportive costs*. Your ability to budget-estimate your telephone program investment thus becomes a facet of your basic planning strategy.

Telephone-activity Costs

Charges in this area refer directly to those items which go into the actual making of a call to a customer or prospect, and include all setup charges for operations essential to the launching of your program. Again, as in other areas of promotional activity, the basic costs of preparation are fixed and can be amortized over the series of total calls made; in this respect "background" activities can be considered much in the same light as are copy preparation, typesetting, layout, and production costs in the areas of print-media advertising and direct-mail operations.

Here is a list of the fundamental charges to be taken into account in relation to direct telephone-activity costs:

1. Creative design and development
2. Acquisition of lists
3. Phone number look-ups
4. Labor: salaries, fees and/or incentive payments and bonuses for supervisors, communicators, and clerical staff.
5. Telephone-workshop costs: space rental, phone booth construction, establishment and maintenance of file and control systems, monitoring equipment purchase or rental
6. Actual telephone equipment and call charges
7. Preparation of material for control forms
8. Time involved in analysis and interpretation of results
9. Prorated general and administrative costs

In each of these areas, individual organizational conditions will affect specific cost-allocation figures.

Creative Costs   Creative design and development costs, for example, will vary to the extent that your creative personnel devotes full time to the preparation of scripts and tapes or whether the individuals you assign to those functions devote only part of their payroll time to them. Included in this area also are the costs of tape preparation, fees paid to name personalities for their participation, and the manufacture of additional duplicate tapes for simulations and continuing use by several communicators.

List Costs   As already noted, lists will generally average about $25 to $30 per 1,000 names, but this figure must be tempered by the number of nonusable names (unlisted, moved, unavailable, etc.) in each batch of 1,000 rented and paid for by you. Your "drop-off" ratio can vary widely, depending upon the nature, recentness, and demographics of the list you are using; in some rural areas, where only delivery route numbers serve as addresses, you might experience as high as a 60 percent loss, while a recently compiled business list might prove locatable by phone for over 90 percent of available names. Look-up charges, as we have seen, will add anywhere from 8 to 25 cents per name when such supplementary activity is required.

Call Charges From the standpoint of economics, this represents a complex area of operations, since a wide variety of individual factors must be taken into account before you can safely predict, with any realistic amount of accuracy, how much it will cost to make a call.

The nature of your offer is of primary concern here, since it controls the amount of time required per call to make your message clear to the prospect. Whether you use direct dialing or WATS lines (or incoming "800" calls, which are reverse WATS calls), your offer will determine the number of calls per hour you will successfully conclude. In either case, the hourly payment to your communicators is thus reflected on a per-call basis; with WATS usage, the per-call allocation becomes a factor of the number of hours each day your WATS lines are used.

Taking into account such important details as time of day, geographical distance from caller to prospect, proportion of call-backs required to reach a prospect, and similar factors, anywhere from $3 to $10 an hour will probably be the final figure for phone costs alone. Knowing in advance, as you will, what your WATS time-lease rates are makes it possible for you to budget on a cost-per-minute basis, against which the variables noted above will have to be calculated.

WATS can prove a complicated "nut to crack," particularly since telephone company tariffs are changing with frequency because of their own cost crunches. Your local phone company will supply the information you should have available before you make a decision as to what arrangements will prove best for your specific kind of operation. The kind of equipment you should rent is also a matter requiring some expert knowledge and evaluation, so you may wish to consult with local phone company representatives or seek out the services of recognized and authoritative phone consultants before making any decisions in this vital area of basic costs.*

The Communicator Hour

Taking all of these factors into consideration, an average and "normal" measurement for costs (for a centralized workshop) can nevertheless be developed, based on the experiences of a number of successful telephone marketing programs undertaken by a variety of firms and individuals over a period of time. The best standard unit of such calculations available is the "communicator hour," a figure against which you can measure the

---

* See App. 9 for listing.

efficiency of your own operations. It can average about $20 per hour, based on these projections:

Communicator wages	$5.00
WATS (average monthly line cost)	
$1,600—200 hours of actual use	$8.00
Supervisory costs (@ $6.00 per hour	
—10 communicators)	.60
Clerical operations	.25
List costs (including look-ups, forms,	
preparation @ 6 per hour @ 15 cents each)	.90
	$14.75
General administrative and overhead	5.25
TOTAL HOURLY COSTS	$20.00

These calculations are based on current rate structures and ongoing averages in effect in 1975, and will be subject to changes during this era of unpredictable inflation. Nevertheless, they do provide a basis for use as a yardstick against your own experiences.

Miscellaneous Minor Costs Preparation of materials for record-keeping purposes and for tabulations of results, payroll costs allocated for time spent on analysis and interpretation of call results, departmental charges for proportions of rent and other overhead considerations such as furniture and equipment, while relatively minor, are factors that should be included in your cost records and properly charged against total actual and projected investment in your telephone marketing program.

While not comparable to the direct cost of communicators' remuneration, training programs, lists, and actual call charges, they can nevertheless—particularly in a project of major proportions—mount up to a point at which they can mark the thin line of difference between outstanding success and merely acceptable results.

Supportive Costs

Over and above the direct-cost factors noted above, there are additional considerations you should take into account in calculating and/or projecting the price of any telephone-marketing program.

The length of each individual call, already touched upon in terms of its cost relationship to hourly charges, will be directly affected by the nature of your objectives. Aiming for direct sales at "cold calls" (about which the prospect has no prior awareness) will require calls involving one "time" duration (usually longer), whereas other call goals (renewals of magazine subscriptions, for example) will make possible a different (usually shorter) call rate per hour.

Among the objectives you may have in mind, each of which will affect the time involved in making a productive call, are contained such variants as lead generating or prospecting, verifying previous orders to eliminate costly unaccepted deliveries, setting up appointments for salespersons, renewing orders for merchandise or services with which the prospect or customer is already intimately familiar, credit jogging, or information-producing survey operations, among others. Each such objective will result in a different time-per-call factor, and thus will leave its imprint on your overall hourly cost figure.

Concentration of your prospects geographically will affect both look-up time and WATS call figures, while the combination of your telephone program with a direct-mail operation will add another call cost factor as well. The costs of the latter must be taken into account, as should also any fulfillment costs arising in connection with telephone contact procedures.

The payroll costs of your communicator staff will also be materially affected by such considerations as the need to concentrate staff operations at a specific time of day, seasonal responsive patterns, and any other factors that might tend to deviate from the normal course of an ongoing, continuous full-day operation.

How Much Do "Costs" Really Cost?

The experienced marketing executive knows that the cost of any sales effort is not an absolute entity. Promotional and sales costs are always relative to the nature of the individual effort.

To reach approximately three-quarters of a million people through a full-page ad in the Sunday edition of a major city newspaper can cost an advertiser about $10,000; with that same investment, an advertiser can use direct mail to bring a message to about 35,000 prospects. Yet the experienced marketing executive does not therefore automatically reject direct mail in favor of newspaper advertising, knowing that there are other criteria that must be applied in determining the choice of media for each individual sales challenge.

A marketer knows, for example, that if a specific offer is aimed at a pinpointed audience, advertising it in a publication of general circulation entails great wastage. It is of course possible to include in a seemingly more expensive direct-mail package more complete, more detailed, more color-ful, and more stimulating direct-response mechanisms than might be crammed into a single-page newspaper advertisement. In short, the as-sessment of cost factors is based on professional understanding of the nature of the offer, the type of audience one is trying to reach, and the requirements of the creative approach.

Telephone marketing must be considered in a similar context, with cost factors subject to the same analysis. The investment of $20-per-hour opera-tional costs and added basic creative and preparatory costs still proves profitable if just two of a projected six calls completed in an average hour result in eliminating nonprospects, with possible savings of $120 to $200 that would otherwise have been fruitlessly spent on travel to nonproductive personal sales calls.

Telephone costs vary considerably from product to product, from objec-tive to objective, from audience to audience. At current rates, telephoning to consumers in their homes during evening hours might cost roughly from $1 to $2.50 per call, while attempts to reach business executives in their offices during normal commercial hours can amass charges of anywhere from $3.50 to $6 for the average call. However, the business call usually involves a product or service of significantly higher dollar value than the normal consumer call, in which case, based on cost-as-percentage-of-sales factors, the business daytime call might well prove the better investment.

The key element in any consideration of financial operations in any direct-response program is *cost-effectiveness*—and, faster than any other direct-marketing medium, telephone is completely and accurately measurable.

Considered from that highly pragmatic viewpoint, telephone can actu-ally be a more economical medium than any other you might employ, when properly used in combination with other media, and when results are correctly assessed.

A Practical Example   Exemplifying this approach is the experience of the telephone-marketing program run on behalf of the Public Broadcasting System, which showed results indicating that while telephone is neither the most effective nor the least expensive fund-raising medium, it will raise more money and generate more contributors than will any other existing medium—providing it is directed toward highly selective prospect lists.

The Station Independence Project—funded by the Ford Foundation on behalf of PBS in 1973—was based on the concept that the multimedia, mass-marketing approach habitually employed in the commercial world could be successfully applied to the raising of public moneys in support of a nonprofit organization.

The technique. Using tape messages prepared by leading PBS television personalities, the telephone call represented the first step in the fund-raising efforts. A pledge of a specific contribution was sought—and achieved, in various cities, from 22.7 to 36.1 percent of the time—and followed up immediately with the mailing of a contribution form. Analysis of returns thus made it possible to know, on a day-by-day basis, which pledgees had not actually fulfilled their commitments.

If within 10 days a pledgee had not fulfilled his or her promise, a follow-up letter went out. A third letter and, if required, a fourth prompting letter were also available for mailing. With the four-letter cycle, the conversion rate ran at a high of 86 percent. But equally gratifying is the fact that the average contribution actually received was encouragingly higher than the amount originally pledged via telephone!

Here is a summary of the operations in six tested communities:

	Total Calls	Pledges Rec'd	Average Pledge	Average Actual Contribution
New York	7,575	31.5%	$14.42	$14.85
Philadelphia	5,075	25.8%	$12.48	$13.07
Portland, Me.	2,579	36.1%	$11.02	$11.63
Cincinnati	1,828	25.5%	$11.62	$13.16
Dallas	3,232	22.7%	$16.83	$18.14
San Francisco	2,783	28.6%	$15.96	$16.47

Results of this nature were achieved largely because of the nature of the lists selected for telephone use. An average return of 34 percent was attained from lists of individuals who had been annual supporting members of their local PBS television station, but who had permitted such membership to lapse. Over 30 percent average response came from viewers whose names were available because they had previously indicated in one manner or another that they were fans of a particular program (it was in connection with this type of list that the earlier-discussed individually taped messages of TV program hosts or hostesses, like Alistair Cooke and Julia Child, were most productive).

Among more broadly based prospecting lists, those categorized as "local"—including educators, doctors, lawyers, supporters of symphonies and museums, etc.—averaged over 27 percent pledges, while various national lists responded with an average return of slightly over 30 percent. Here is a summary of results, by lists:

Type of List	Total Calls	Pledges Rec'd	Average Pledge
Viewer	3,577	30.13%	$12.62
Lapsed Members	4,810	34.01%	$15.85
Local Lists (arts, professionals, educators, etc.)	7,008	27.42%	$14.22
National Lists (McGovern, *Sat. Review*, college faculty, cultural donors, etc.)	2,602	25.98%	$12.24

Some relative cost numbers. Original tests were immediately projectable in developing the cost-effectiveness ratio between direct-mail and telephone approaches.

On a broad scale, it was determined that for $50,000 direct mail could deliver the message to a universe of 333,333 individuals. The cost per letter would thus be 15 cents. Projections based on a direct-mail test indicated an anticipated 2 percent response, or 6,666 contributors, with an average donation of $15. In total, this meant that the $50,000 direct-mail investment would produce $100,000 in funds raised.

Projecting other segments of the same lists via telephone, higher per capita costs per each contact meant that for the identical $50,000 budget, only 44,445 people could be reached, calculated at the rate of $1 per call, plus 50 cents follow-up charge per actual pledge obtained. But an average of 25 percent return was projectable, with 75 percent of these convertible to actual cash donations. The total projection: 11,110 pledgees, with 8,333 actual new contributions resulting. The identical average donation of $15 meant that, in the case of telephone usage, a total of $125,000 would be raised for the same $50,000 investment that produced $100,000 by mail.

Here again is the summary:

	Mail	Telephone
Budget	$50,000	$50,000
Appeals Delivered	333,333	44,445
Response	2%	25%
New Contributors	6,666	8,333 (after 75% conversion of pledges)
Average Contribution	$15	$15
Total Raised	$100,000	$125,000
Cost per $ raised	50%	40%

An additional test was implemented in Philadelphia in which mail and telephone appeals were addressed to the same prospects. Call response indicated that *triple* the dollar result was obtained over the mail-only panel when prospects received both the mail and the telephone appeal! A further bonus inherent in this dual-contact technique is represented by the fact that 80 percent—compared to 75 percent by phone only—were converted to actual cash donations, while another 10 percent over the normal mail-only response came from those subjected to both types of contact, thus bringing to 90 percent the total conversion rate from use of the telephone.

Another Typical Experience An additional case in point is the telephone marketing experience of Academic Media, publishers of reference books:

A former division of Cordura Corporation, Academic Media, used a combination of mail and telephone to achieve its sales results at lowest possible cost. While, in absolute figures, it cost 50 percent more when telephone was used in concert with mail, the absolute increase in cost was more than offset by the fact that each sale was just about double what it was when direct mail was employed alone.

The publisher's cost, for example, ran about 20 percent when only direct mail was used. Using telephone to close the sale, as a follow-up to earlier mail efforts, the cost of getting that customer moved up to 30 percent—*but*, the normal direct-mail response of two books per order became a significantly larger 3.7 books per order when telephone was used to support the mailing program. Thus what seemed to be an increase in cost factors actually resulted in an equally favorable cost-effectiveness when telephone was judiciously and scientifically employed.

Telephone can be highly cost-effective, too, when applied to a specific portion of a market where sales might otherwise be achieved at relatively high cost. This experience, as reported in the magazine *Sales Management*, provides indication of the effectiveness of such an approach:

> Inside salesmen aren't the hottest new idea in selling, but lingering effects of the energy crisis and, especially, inflation's added burden on selling costs are prompting more companies to try selling via telephone. One of the latest converts is U.S. Gypsum, which now has 23 inside salesmen.
> "We have the same incentive program for them as we do for our outside salesmen," marketing vice president Bob Day says. "And we measure their performance in the same way—on the sales dollars they bring in." The big difference, Day says, is the kind of account they handle. Gypsum sales executives believe that *telephone selling works best with those customers who have fairly regular buying patterns or who don't need much personal follow-up.* [Italics mine, M.R.]

How cost-effectiveness factors vary with the product, the prospect, and the offer is exemplified by the contrasting telephone-marketing experiences of *Saturday Review* magazine and Xerox's University Microfilm, both of which were regarded by their sponsors as highly successful projects. To achieve $25 in sales results, the magazine invested $10 in total telephone costs, while the publisher of the $800 set of books invested no more than $2.50 for each $25 of sales achievement.

The difference, of course, lies in the nature of the offer. For all intents and purposes, University Microfilm's income from its telephone program was a final and complete dollar return on its investment, whereas *Saturday Review* was interested in obtaining continuing circulation which would then be translated into additional corporate income through the sale of advertising space in the pages of the magazine. In addition, periodical publishers traditionally spend more on attaining initial subscription goals, since renewals are then normally obtained in future years on a less costly basis. The two experiences provide just another example of how costs must be assessed in the light of individual operations, offers, audience, and ticket level.

Some Costs Are Down

The cost of long-distance telephone operations has been significantly reduced in some instances.

Cost Per Station-to-Station Call 8 A.M. to 5 P.M.

N.Y. to	1950	1976
Philadelphia	.45	.99
Chicago	1.55	1.18
Denver	2.50	1.24
San Francisco	2.50	1.30

And if you wait until after 5 P.M., which is 2 P.M. San Francisco time, the cost drops down to 53 cents for three minutes.

With WATS lines, of course, even those low rates are materially reduced for the telephone marketer.

When you study projected telephone-marketing cost data, remember that cost-effectiveness can be achieved in a wide variety of ways. Over and above straight sales, consider the following dollar-related factors and give thought to how they might be applied to your own situation:

1. A sales force always needs screened, qualified leads, frequently specific sales appointments.

2. Where high-cost sales calls exist, marginal accounts must receive continual coverage as an area of future growth.

3. "Trial" prospects and "annual" customers must continue to be converted and renewed at the highest rate.

4. New product launches require maximum media usage to generate awareness, market position and share of market, and to achieve payout objectives.

5. Customer service and credit are closely interrelated but in either case telephone can produce excellent results.

An Eye to the Ticket Level

While you can in fact reach virtually everyone today who is a prospect for your goods and services by using telephone-marketing techniques, caution should be observed where low-ticket items are involved.

Such offers as book club memberships, magazine subscription renewals and even industrial or business-related products that sell at relatively low prices must be carefully controlled and supervised to ensure cost-effective results. Where nationally distributed prospects are concerned, required analysis of potential volume in any given local area must warrant the costs of establishing a local telephone operation. In such cases, you may also discover that the cost of calling to sell low-ticket items, from a centralized operation, will result in prohibitive WATS rental-per-call assessments.

One way to handle the low-ticket item is to make it part of a "piggyback" or multiprogram operation, in which some of your WATS time is used to offer a higher ticket product or service to a different audience, thus proportionately lowering the shared WATS line cost that has to be allocated to the lower-priced offer.

In any case, with careful cost-conscious projections and calculations, you will find—as other marketers can testify—that the telephone provides an effective, economical, flexible sales tool that meets requirements which other media cannot match.

chapter nine

The "800" Route
to Sales

THE TELEPHONE OCCUPIES a key position in the multimedia mix in those operations in which prospects are urged, through advertising in other media, to initiate their own calls to the marketer.

Basic to the implementation of this approach is the advertised "800" telephone number. In essence, this is an incoming WATS telephone system set up on a nationwide or regional basis that encourages potential customers to respond to national media advertising by long-distance telephone to a publicized number. The service is provided by the marketer, without the customer incurring any long-distance charges.

These "800" operations can be and are employed to attain a broad variety of marketing objectives, but their logistical details are often extremely complex. Cost factors have to be anticipated—and later projected from test experience—on the basis of average volume of incoming calls expected. Taken into account also should be such varied factors as time and frequency of the distribution of the print-media advertising that is aimed at stimulating incoming calls, setting up operations and forming adequate crews to handle evening activity in response to televised stimulation of calls, seasonal variations in patterns of demand for your own specific offer, etc.

What "800" Can Do for You

That the "800" approach works—and works well—is indicated by the experiences of successful users of the system:

■ When broadcast commercials offer both write-in and phone-in operations in the same announcement, "800" calls outpull incoming mail responses threefold.

■ Tested in print-media advertising and in direct mail, the "800" option consistently adds incremental sales of 25 to 30 percent.

■ Call-in suggestions included in merchandise catalogs have resulted in sales increases up to triple normal volume.

With a telephone company survey demonstrating that almost 9 out of every 10 Americans have either used "800" numbers or are at least familiar with their existence, the alert marketer will recognize many varied ways in which this approach can be of profitable use. The prospect who takes the trouble to pick up his own phone and initiate a call in response to a printed or broadcast request to do so is a live prospect, who has virtually screened himself. His readiness to contact you can be viewed as a positive factor that can lead to maximizing your sales potential, since it represents an indication of basic interest in your offer.

Incoming calls, therefore, can be used to:

1. Take orders directly
2. Fulfill requests for product information
3. Identify the caller's nearest dealer
4. Obtain demographic and psychographic data
5. Screen credit
6. Upgrade sales by suggesting additional products or services
7. Quote prices
8. Accept memberships and/or reservations
9. Improve customer service and increase customer satisfaction by minimizing delay between response and fulfillment
10. Offer alternative payment methods and terms
11. Stimulate faster cash flow by obtaining immediate credit card data
12. Offer alternative styles, colors, price ranges, sizes, etc.
13. Convert information calls to sales calls
14. Build repeat sales

The "800" technique, popular with both customers and marketers, owes its growth largely to its capacity to meet the needs of today's "new breed" of consumers for direct verbal contact with another live human being who can talk to them and answer their questions.

Solving A Basic
Marketing Problem

Bringing the prospective customer and the retailer together is a major problem that faces many manufacturing organizations. How the use of "800" has helped solve that question is reflected in the experience of the Lane Company of Alta Vista, Virginia, one of the nation's largest furniture makers.

Despite its $120 million annual sales volume, Lane is but one of some 5,000 furniture manufacturers operating in the United States. It produces a broad line of bedroom and dining room furniture, chairs, tables, cedar chests, and so forth. Within each such category, Lane makes a substantial number of products of different designs and price ranges. But with some 40,000 retail furniture outlets throughout the country, Assistant Advertising Manager William R. Martin, Jr., notes that "A manufacturer's well-accepted group of merchandise may not have more than 2,000 retail furniture outlets."

Thus the prospective customer, exposed to a Lane product advertisement in a national publication, enjoys but a 1-in-20 chance of finding the advertised item at any given furniture store. How does Lane use the "800" approach to solve this problem?

The Technique The Lane Company carries a prominently displayed "800" number in each of its national advertisements, inviting the customer to call in order to get the name and the location of the dealer nearest his or her home. Using the facilities of a fully computerized service organization, Lane is able to furnish this information to the prospect literally within seconds.

With different retail outlets handling one, some, or many of Lane's varied product groups, the service agency is furnished with up to 43 separate dealers' lists. The communicator asks the caller to identify the product group in which she is interested, and while punching up the list of dealers handling that specific merchandise for its appearance on an electronic screen, asks the prospect for her zip code. In a relatively few seconds, then, it becomes possible for the communicator to match the prospect's zip code with that of the nearest listed dealer and to inform the customer as to the store name and address.

Experience demonstrates that, immediately following the newsstand date of a nationally distributed publication carrying a Lane advertisement, several hundred calls per day will come in consistently over a

10-day period. For this reason, the company has found it inadvisable to attempt to set up its own telephone answering service, using the existing facilities of Listfax, instead. Lane's headquarters location, in a small community with a limited labor supply, would make it difficult for the company to staff up properly for the required concentrated service effort. In addition, Mr. Martin notes that the service agency's charges, based on the circulation bracket of the publication in which any ad appears, are more reasonable than would be the cost of any attempt by Lane to set up its own in-WATS operation.

Subordinate Benefits   In addition to its valuable dealer locator role, "800" performs other important functions for Lane as well.

The direct contact with an interested consumer makes it possible for the manufacturer, through open questioning of the caller, to test the relative pulling power of split-run ads in contrasting formats, and to test the appeal of one publication versus another. Headlines and copy approaches are also tested in this manner.

A special promotion, in which miniature Lane cedar chests are made available to graduating high school senior girls through local dealers, is promoted in national advertising, with the reader asked to call the "800" number to learn where the nearest participating dealer is located. The "800" approach augments a direct-mail program used to announce the dealers' offer, as schools grow increasingly reluctant to release their student lists for commercial purposes. Lane receives some 20,000 calls during the month of the promotion and notes that a call from but one member of a graduating class leads to word-of-mouth promotion that results in over 400,000 graduates getting Lane miniature chests.

The use of a separate "800" number on each page of a multipage magazine insert is a device employed by the furniture manufacturer to encourage dealers to stock up on various categories of Lane products. Callers are referred to dealers on the basis of the kind of merchandise stocked, so that to increase traffic maximally, a dealer is prone to consider having himself fully represented by stocking at least some of the items from each separate page.

"She Likes What She Sees"   Pointing out that where ads solicit either a mail or a telephone response, test results from each method completely support one another, Mr. Martin says:

> The '800' number seems to be a reasonable solution to one of our main marketing problems, and that is, to take the work out of the consumer finding

the product we are advertising. In that respect, it has been a successful effort for us . . . we are all in all very pleased with our use of the '800' number.

And commenting upon the level of response achieved from mail as against telephone, he adds:

We find that the telephone inquiry means that the consumer likes what she sees and is interested in buying. The written inquiry simply means that she's possibly interested in buying furniture and she wants to see what you make in addition to what's advertised. That can be a sale 30 days, 60 days or a year later. But the telephone inquiry means that she's a very live prospect, and so we are most anxious to get her into the store stocking the advertised merchandise as quickly as possible.

Overcoming Restrictive Regulations

The use of the "800" technique can prove most valuable in soliciting inquiries in fields which pose marketing problems by reason of governmental or industry-wide restrictions on the nature and content of permitted advertising appeals.

Dreyfus Liquid Assets (DLA), like all other money market funds, is regulated by the Securities and Exchange Commission and the National Association of Security Dealers. Under federal securities laws, mutual funds advertisements may say somewhat more than normal security advertising is permitted to say, but are still subject to very stringent rules. "Tombstone" advertising is the rule; little is permitted to be said, and NASD must clear the wording of all headlines and body copy.

Further, details of funds cannot be discussed with any prospective investor who has not previously received a printed prospectus—a regulation that seriously inhibits selling procedures because the cost of printing bulk prospectuses and mailing them to major lists can prove prohibitive.

Working within the framework of these limitations, Dreyfus neverthe-less succeeded—through a combination of print-media advertising, mail response, and incoming telephone calls—in enrolling over 60,000 investors and in building a total fund of more than $900 million within one year of the operation's inception.

Procedures Using *The Wall Street Journal, The New York Times,* daily newspapers in other major cities, and specialized financial publications, Dreyfus employs the combination response appeal of a mail coupon and an "800" phone number.

The mailing piece sent to the inquiring prospect includes a prospectus and an application form, a letter from the organization's chairman, a question-and-answer booklet, a schedule of the fund's current investments, and a reply envelope. This original packet is supported with a letter containing additional sales materials, sent every fourth week over a 16-week period. The conversion rate has consistently hovered around 20 percent.

Success via Telephone   From March 1974 through January 1975, Dreyfus received in response to its print-media appeals more than 55,000 incoming calls for Dreyfus Liquid Assets prospectuses, and an additional 110,000 for further information. The current average for incoming calls has levelled off at about 17,000 each month since that time.

Analysis indicates that about 40 percent of those responding to print-media advertising for DLA do so via telephone, calling the listed phone number. Those who answer these incoming calls must be registered with NASD to permit them to answer technical questions. A full-time communicator staff of 26 people, plus 4 part-timers, handles the workload.

Two telephone numbers are included in the effort: an "800" WATS number for respondents living outside New York State, and a local New York City number for the remaining prospects. Since these lines are available to Dreyfus continuously on a rental basis, costs are kept to a workable level by using them for dual purposes; existing investors can make toll-free calls to these numbers to obtain up-to-the-minute information about the status of their accounts. Readily available computer terminals are at hand for the use of incoming-call communicators, who can instantly retrieve the desired data from a local bank and pass it on immediately to the inquiring investor.

"800" and the Business Prospect

Use of the promoted call-in technique is not limited to the area of consumer marketing. Numerous firms doing business with the business community have learned to employ it in pursuit of their varied marketing objectives.

One example of how a service can be provided through "800" operations, resulting in actions leading directly to greater profitability, is provided by the experience of the Sweet's Division of McGraw-Hill Information Systems Company, publishers and distributors of construction product information files, whose telephone survey program has been noted in Chapter 3.

Thousands of firms buy participation each year, listing their companies' products and services in the Sweet's catalogs that have been distributed—without charge—to nearly 75,000 architects, engineers, government agencies, and commercial firms, who then use these files as major sources of information about available products and services required in performing their jobs.

After referring to the Sweet's Catalog Files, these users frequently want to contact a local dealer or representative for details about prices, delivery, and similar special information. The purpose of the "800" operation is to provide a centralized calling point where the local user's most conveniently located representative can be identified for him.

The program was originally launched in two test areas: New York City and Dallas–Fort Worth. Users of the file in those two centers received a specially prepared folder announcing the new service, and pointing out that ". . . a new Sweet's telephone service—free to architectural and interior design users—now enables you to make immediate contact with manufacturers' representatives whenever you need their help but don't know who they are or where to reach them."

Implementing the Test Program   Campaign Communications Institute of America, Inc. (CCI), was commissioned to carry out the test operation over an eight-month period in the New York market area.

Projecting the amount of incoming phone traffic this program would generate, CCI interviewed, hired, and trained a group of communicators, each of whom was subsequently furnished with a detailed, eight-page typed summary document. Its contents included a script setting forth the questions to be asked of the caller, an outline of the files operation, and the purpose of the phone program and a description of the "operator tools" with which each communicator was provided. The latter included a Rolodex file carrying, in alphabetical order, the names of the manufacturers participating in the Sweet's Catalog Files and the individual products listed for each such manufacturer. Each such card, of course, listed the name, address, and telephone number of each of the representatives in the New York area who carried that particular item.

As a supplement to the communicator operation, index books were also provided, which enabled the communicator to locate—by parent company, product name, or trade name—any name inquired about which could not be found in the manufacturer Rolodex file. Under such special references, the manufacturer could easily be located, following which the communicator could then return to the Rolodex and provide the caller with the information he sought about the local area representative.

Carefully analyzed test results convinced Sweet's Division executives of the value of the program. Today it continues on a national basis, with a nationwide "800" number serving all callers in place of the two local test call-in numbers. The Rolodex has been replaced by a totally computerized file, with data electronically retrievable and placed instantly on CRT screens directly in front of the individual communicator responding to the incoming call.

The geographical distances between all zip codes are programmed into the system, making it possible to locate the closest representative quickly and accurately in each case. The operation, which is maintained by the Information Management Workshop of Mission, Kansas, also furnishes Sweet's with a list and tally of calls related to nonparticipating manufacturers, thus providing Sweet's with a highly effective sales weapon. The entire system can be revised and updated every day.

Sponsor Benefits   The economics of the Sweet's File operation relate closely to those of the traditional controlled-circulation magazine, in that a published product is circulated without charge to the user and the entire operation made financially viable (without charge to the user, except for a small distribution charge instituted in 1975) through the support of advertisers interested in reaching a targeted, specific market segment.

In the case of Sweet's Files, the publication is a series of voluminous catalogs, organized, indexed, and distributed annually; the advertisers pay Sweet's for the opportunity of including their own catalogs (often hundreds of pages in length) as component parts of the overall file.

Thus it follows that whatever special services the publisher can offer to demonstrate not only that the files are extensively used by their recipients but also that sales-related activity is stimulated by them, contributes to the sales and promotional arguments that go into selling the concept of participation.

Sweet's Division's extensive financial support of the nationwide "800" operation consistently results in proving to existing and potential participants that the publisher offers a product in which their participation means traceable increased product sales.

In this manner, the ostensibly costly "800" service operation actually aids the publisher in maintaining a profitable enterprise and in continually expanding the range of participatory activity.

Some "800" Caveats

The use of the incoming-call technique has proved profitable and practicable for marketers of goods and services in many areas of enterprise. But success, as in other areas of telephone operations, is not automatic. There are pitfalls to be avoided, details to be considered, decisions to be made if the marketer is to make the most of the opportunities offered by this type of operation:

1. Keeping in mind that one of the attributes inherent in an incoming-call operation is its ability to serve as leverage for upgrading a sales ticket or promoting related products or services, the alert marketer will recognize that *communicators* assigned to "800" work may require skills somewhat different from those possessed by operators initiating calls.

While any well-organized "800" program will provide communicators with all factual details required for a successfully completed call, it is nonetheless true that some different quality of "sales ability" is needed to achieve this end. Materials must be furnished that will serve to familiarize the communicator with the detailed advantages of ordering additional or better-quality merchandise, but the individual communicator must possess the sensitivity to know if and when to introduce the subject.

The "800" number is geared and costed on incoming-call volume. Its lowest cost is based on taking down simple information, only a name and address, for example. The more information required—color, size, additional product information, etc.—the greater the cost per call.

Cost-per-order factors are no less critical for incoming than they are for outgoing calls. Switching directions for the communicator who is merely taking down a name and address in less than a minute into a selling or upgrading mode requires new skills, new training, new adaptability— and a special cost structure.

While it might appear superficially true that costs can be minimized by making use of outgoing operator "downtime" by having idle communicators handle incoming calls, don't assume this to be the fact. The airlines have tried to use their downtime reservation personnel to handle incoming calls, some banks have experimented with the use of their deposit clerks for this purpose, but experience indicates the need for separate call staffs to attain optimum cost-efficiencies. Analyze the essential differences between the goals of your incoming and your outgoing calls and then decide whether or not different personnel is required to maximize results.

2. Since you will be paying for your incoming WATS line on a rental basis, you must make every effort to stimulate *continuous use* of it, so you

will require advertising support that fully emphasizes your "800" number and the benefits to be derived by the consumer in using it.

Stress that number everywhere—on the outside envelope of your mailing pieces, on catalog covers, on your order forms, in print-media advertising headlines, and in your television commercials, where it should be superimposed over a considerable length of your air time, not just tagged on at the very end. Make sure your copy approach stresses the fact that this convenient service is an important consumer benefit.

3. On the other hand, when you stimulate incoming calls to the fullest extent possible, make sure you are *completely set up* for this capacity required—both in available WATS lines and in personnel—to handle the anticipated influx of calls. There are few experiences that will cause a prospect to forget the whole thing as quickly as will repeatedly making calls and getting a busy signal.

How a failure to anticipate with reasonable accuracy the volume of calls your announcement will generate is illustrated by the sad experience of one of the nations's leading automobile manufacturers who decided to generate call-ins from dissatisfied owners. Fortunately, the program was tested in only one section of the country.

The influx of calls was so great that the agency that had contracted to handle them was unable to fulfill its responsibilities under the terms of the agreement. Additionally, such a huge burden was placed on lines and cables that the telephone company threatened to discontinue service to the announced number. Legal complications followed, and the net result was that the organization which had anticipated handling a lucrative operation ended up with a staggering financial loss.

An additional example of improper gearing—but in the opposite direction—is provided by the history of an organization established for the announced purpose of making any published book available to the consumer in response to a call to an advertised "800" number.

In this case, two factors contributed to the failure of the endeavor: first, too few calls were received to support the cost of the incoming WATS line charges; additionally, those orders that were received involved a high percentage of requests for hard-to-find, out-of-print single book copies, resulting in excessive fulfillment costs that ultimately caused the demise of the entire operation.

4. *Gear your service* to the needs of your offer and your audience. "Call now" is a powerful stimulus to consumer action, but remember, if those words are part of a commercial appearing on California stations at

10 P.M., you must be fully staffed to handle the expected calls at 1 A.M., if your communicators are East Coast-based.

The Optimum Response Mechanism

The use of the "800" technique is consistently growing, because marketers recognize that it provides a means whereby the customer can immediately respond to advertising—conveniently and without cost to himself—at the very moment of greatest advertising impact.

But the specialized requirements of many programs make it cost-ineffective for a number of firms to set up and implement their own operations for the handling of incoming calls. Seasonal peaks and valleys of ordering activity, headquarters locations in small communities with in-adequate labor pools, the problems inherent in hiring and training a significantly sized staff for specialized work that might last but a few days or weeks at a time, problems related to availability of space for limited-time operations (many companies close at 5 P.M.)—these and related conditions make the implementation of an "800" program difficult for many business organizations.

The complications of logistics that can accompany a decision to use the "800" approach are exemplified by the experience of a national advertiser owning and operating a vacation facility.

A two-hour holiday eve network-special television program was projected which would have invited viewers to call a specified "800" number immediately for the purpose of obtaining a free brochure about travel and the advertiser's vocation resort. Estimates of anticipated responses were elicited from no fewer than six different specialist firms, whose average opinion indicated that the sponsor might expect from 50,000 to 75,000 responses in approximately three hours. Further professional opinions projected that any one single communicator would be able to handle about 40 calls per hour. This made it clear, when taken into consideration with the estimate of total intake, that no one facility in the United States could be depended upon to handle the volume satisfactorily.

It was further recognized that the location of the advertised facility would result in a greater number of calls from areas east of the Mississippi than from other parts of the country; on this basis, optimum locations were charted on a projected call basis for the handling of the expected volume of incoming calls.

The total volume thus anticipated was then broken down into a series of estimates for each of some 205 metropolitan market areas in the U.S., and incoming facilities were contacted in accordance with these individual estimates. As a result of this detailed planning, production, and cost analysis, the program was never implemented. It was judged to be too costly and too risky in terms of the projected results.

Service Organizations Can Help You   The specialized organizations that were consulted in this instance are representative of a number of such firms that can provide the required services on a straight fee basis for marketers. They are set up to receive calls over their WATS lines (whose cost you thus share with their other clients) to the "800" number they supply you, and are fully staffed with trained and experienced personnel. They are computerized to allow their communicators to punch up your specifications on electronic screens for the purpose of presenting your sales appeals; responses can be fed back to you on printouts or on magnetic tape, or fed directly into your own EDP system. They are organized to follow through on credit card checkups, to produce shipping labels, to file daily activity reports with you, and to carry out a broad variety of services connected with your program.

Used the right way and in the appropriate situation, the "800" technique has already amply proved its worth in many marketing programs. So whether you are in position to handle it internally or whether you may benefit from the extensive services of a professional outside operation, it will pay you to investigate the possibilities it holds for you.

chapter ten/

Some Guidelines for the Independent Salesperson

VIRTUALLY EVERYTHING SAID THUS FAR has emphasized the employment of specialized approaches to telephone marketing problems, mainly applicable to business firms or quasi-public organizations of some size. Yet many of the principles involved can well merit the consideration of the one-man or one-woman operative—the real estate or insurance agent, for example—who uses or contemplates using the telephone for any of a dozen marketing purposes.

As has already been stated, telephone marketing in today's highly competitive world has developed into a complex, sophisticated, and highly projectable operation requiring specialized expertise every step of the way. So while the individual salesperson might find extensive services to be far beyond what his or her needs or means require, employment of some professional consultation aimed at positioning the operation on a contemporary basis should be given serious consideration. A few hours spent on the phone each day by your spouse, or by an experienced communicator, can maximize your own selling time by helping you identify qualified leads for you to visit; a few well-planned, well-directed phone calls each day can save you lots of valuable time on your personal sales-call schedule.

Taking into account the various steps and procedures already outlined in earlier pages, it can be seen that the application of experience and trained knowledge might well prove helpful to the smaller entrepreneur—the local retailer or the travel agent, for example—in a number of areas:

1. *List selection and testing.* If you have been doing some telephone marketing, or contemplate undertaking such an operation, based solely on cold calls to persons whose names you take at random from a local telephone directory, you should be reminded that cost-per-order can be greatly reduced and generally results can be significantly increased by relating the demographics* of your list more directly to the nature of your offer.

In every community of any significant size, there exists at least one professional list broker organization that specializes in keeping its fingers on the pulse of the list-renting business. Locate one or more in your town and consult with their experts about the kind of people you are trying to reach and influence. Not only can such a professional suggest the best possible list or lists for you to test, but he or she can be equally helpful in recommending scientifically projected test percentages against which to measure your results and can help you set up forms that will make it easier for you to spot those lists that are paying off best.

2. *Script preparation.* Although you know exactly how effective a salesperson you are, it should be stressed here once again that the techniques required for telephone salesmanship differ materially from those you may have very successfully employed during face-to-face selling activities.

Among the differences is the need to be able to respond immediately and unhesitatingly in a variety of ways to a whole series of questions, or indeed even comments or objections, posed by individuals whom you call. Such responses must be made far more promptly than in face-to-face selling procedures, and totally without the defense of the casual, personal kind of banter you can carry on in someone's presence while working out a logical and acceptable reply.

The answer to this problem is the script, already described and discussed in Chapter 5. Together with a local advertising writer of your choice, work out a series of anticipated queries that might be expected to follow the announcement of the offer you are planning to make via telephone. Give careful consideration to the responses you will give, and

---

* See App. 3 for explanation of demographic indicators.

then have the local writer prepare this data in the form of professional, concise, convincing, and natural wording for you.

Transfer each such question or comment, and its written answer, to a flip-chart, and keep it close at hand whenever you make a call. In this way, you can be sure that your responses will always be correct; but, above all, they will always be *consistent*, and will not vary with your mood or the nature of the individual conversation.

In the preparation of your opening message, it is conceivable that there may be certain types of offers and operations which could profitably use a taped message of subtle endorsement from some locally prominent person or from your boss. Here, too, you will require the services of professionals to prepare the message to be taped, to make the recording, and to select and install the equipment that will make it possible for you to play it in connection with each telephone approach to a prospect.

3. *Training*. While you may not be required to provide formal training for a staff of assistants, even your own individual approach to the specifics of telephone marketing will, as has already been noted, dictate that you expose yourself to the specialized techniques of this unique medium.

4. *Operations*. Once your telephone-marketing program gets under way. it is important that immediate and accurate results of each and every call be set down for your records. Subsequent analysis and study will provide the major means that will enable you to judge the degree of success that is meeting your efforts. And only with such data at hand can you make realistic decisions regarding lists, testing procedures, and possible changes in your approach or even in your offer.

The ease and accuracy with which you analyze and interpret such records depends in considerable measure upon the physical format of the record sheets themselves. In this area, too, you might find it helpful to call upon the services of some local person whose regular occupation is related to statistics, record keeping, and the like, and let him or her help you draw up the forms best suited to supply you with the information you will constantly need.

This is of considerable importance, because the flexibility provided by an understanding of what is actually happening—on an hour-to-hour or day-to-day basis—can prove an important factor in your cost-per-order calculations and to your overall percentage of sales or conversions.

The Dial with the Smile

Since the first salesman sold the original apple to his first prospect, the *principles* of salesmanship have not changed.

But successful developments in the art and science of getting someone to buy something have led to changes in the *application* of those principles. Competent sales letter writers, for example, know that choice and juxtaposition of words must be employed as tools to substitute for voice tones and facial expressions when mail is used instead of person-to-person sales approaches. The television announcer is aware that he must add an acceptable *visual* appearance of credibility to achieve the acceptance that sincerity of *verbal* approach alone accomplishes for the radio announcer.

And, as a telephone marketing operative, you must recognize that, for maximum effectiveness, it is necessary to take into account some unique facets of this instrument that the eyeball-to-eyeball salesperson rarely has to be concerned about.

The New Approach *Brevity* is the key to the successful telephone approach to a sales challenge.

Because the person you have called cannot see you, it is not feasible to try to open your contact call with the same personalized techniques that many salespeople have learned to use with such great success in their personal calls. No comments about the weather . . . no jokes about golf . . . few personal asides will ever serve to smooth the path to a sale when you use the telephone as your marketing medium.

Instead, the very nature of the electronic contact makes it essential that you get directly into your main subject, and that you do so promptly. The reason for your call must quickly be made clear to your customer or prospect; and the nature of your offer must be presented in such a direct and unequivocal manner as to be immediately and unquestionably understandable.

You must speak at a pace that is somewhat slower than you would employ in person-to-person conversation—a rate of about 150 words per minute will be most readily received. And whereas a warm voice and an ingratiating personality are important to the personal visiting salesperson—his or her appearance, facial expressions, and voice inflections might well serve to establish friendly contact—those qualities are absolutely critical in your telephone contacts—because, in effect, they are the only means you have of convincing the person you're talking to that you are a reliable, authentic, and dependable source of information.

Remember, when you telephone, you do not have the backing of flipcharts, films, promotional leave-behind pieces, or any other kind of visual aids. Your sales success depends to a large extent upon how you use your voice box to convey your personality and your message.

While your prepared script (as discussed in an earlier chapter) might well guide you in *what* you should say, only your own understanding of your personality and delivery can give you the answer as to *how* you should say it.

Getting Maximum Verbal Effect One of the first things you might do, before going into a program of attempted telephone sales, is to get some idea of just what you sound like to the people you're planning to call.

Arrange to hold a reasonably lengthy and complete telephone conversation—about almost anything at all—with a colleague or a friend, and tape-record it with his or her permission. Then play it back to yourself, listen carefully—and prepare to be astonished! The likelihood is that you will not sound anything like the way you think you sound.

There will be, in all probability, syllables that will sound as if you've swallowed them. There will be phrases you intended lightly that will sound like solemn declarations. There will be jokes that might well be interpreted to be insults! Find out where the unknown shortcomings lie in your own delivery, and make sure you've done everything in your power both to be constantly aware of them and to overcome them, before you make your first attempt at a telephoned sales call.

For the power of the *voice alone* can be a significant factor in your attempts to influence the recipient of your call to take the action you want him or her to take. How often have you been carried away emotionally by the efforts of a great vocalist singing an operatic aria in a language of which you cannot understand one single word?

Although it will be helpful, as suggested above, to study your own voice and its individualities, try to correct whatever shortcomings you may find without losing your own *naturalness*, for that is one of your key sales attributes. Since each call you make will be a short one, it must quickly establish the level of contact that is required—you must be warm, you must be natural. There are those who tend to tighten up when making a tele-phone sales call, reflecting some sort of standardized printed page rather than the individualized approach that is the essence of the demand made by today's consumer. And, when working with a predetermined script, allow yourself the necessary luxury of adapting it, as you go along, to your own way of saying things. Your naturalness—or its absence—will quickly be apparent over the telephone to whomever you may be talking to.

That in itself is a good reason for you to train yourself always to "smile when you dial." Corny as it may sound, experience amply demonstrates that it works. If you've had a bad session with an unreceptive prospect, if you're upset about a spat you've had with your spouse, if there's anything bothering you that has affected your outlook about the world in general—then postpone the next call until you get over that bad mood. For it most certainly will be immediately reflected in your tone of voice and, more seriously, in the diminishing sales returns you will achieve.

Impatience, irritability, grouchiness, all will be readily transmitted to your contacts over the wires. Keep in mind at all times that, in addition to trying to make a sale you're always trying to build a long-term customer, too. When you talk to anyone by telephone, *you* are your company's representative, and it is only your *voice* that can lead your prospect to evaluate what kind of organization you represent.

The Other Side of Talking

There is another side to talking that is of extreme importance to the successful telephone communicator—and that is *listening*.

For just as your own tone of voice and your own mood are instruments that key your contact to whether or not he wants to do business with you, so are the remarks of the person you're talking to a dependable indicator of *his* or *her* mood and attitude. The highly successful telephone salesperson quickly learns to develop what amounts to a veritable sixth sense in his or her contacts with customers and prospects.

Every person-to-person salesperson knows this; sensitivity to the moods of the potential buyer he or she may be visiting results in immediate reconsideration and adjustment of the approach that is being used during such a sales visit. In exactly the same manner, you must learn how to listen for the sometimes extremely subtle indications of how your contact is reacting to your telephone message. And even when working with a set script, you must quickly adjust your own thrust to meet the prospect's position. Remember that you must retain at all times control of the conversation that you have initiated. You must direct the flow of the dialogue to serve your own objectives, and so you should always include pertinent questions in your script that will serve to evoke responses from the prospect.

If you, and you alone, do all the talking, you will end up not with a conversation but with a monologue—and an experienced, professional radio announcer can do a better job of that than you can! Your communicator script should include keywords or phrases specifically designed to get responses from the prospect, and to lead those replies in a direction that will permit you to come back with one or more of your major sales points.

For example, here is an excerpt from a script for a call made to individuals who have failed to renew their credit card privileges:

> Mr(s) _____, we are concerned about serving you properly, and I'd be grateful if you would tell me if the Heritage Book Club has failed you in any way.

Related to this question is a whole series of communicator script cards setting forth specific benefits of the club's service to which the communicator can quickly refer as soon as the customer responds with a particular complaint.

Or again, this is the approach used to stimulate increased sales of office copying machine supplies among active customers whose volume of orders has declined during any given period; following the playing of a tape message from the supplier's sales manager, the communicator returns to the phone with this:

> Now, as Mr. Burns said, we've noticed that you've been ordering a smaller amount of paper supplies than previously. Is that the result of anything that we might have done? . . . any way in which we have failed to satisfy you?

Approaches of this nature not only demonstrate your interest in the customer's satisfaction and welfare, but they also serve to provide the basis for a generalized survey, pinpointing those areas in which your product or service might stand some improvement. But, equally importantly from the standpoint of the objective of the individual telephone call, they lead the prospect or customer into a frank and open discussion that smooths the way to a presentation of sales points that might otherwise be subject to awkward introduction.

Your adjustment to what your prospect tells you requires a sensitivity solely to what you hear, for there is nothing to see. Voice tone, inflection, choice of words are your only clues to how your prospective customer feels, not only about what you're trying to tell him, but about life and the world in general at that particular moment.

By listening carefully, you should be able to discover in fewer than 100 calls your own ability to evaluate the nature of each individual prospect you talk to, and pretty soon you will be able to tell, within the first 200 words of any conversation, just what kind of person he or she is, and how to adjust your own approach to that awareness.

How to Speak via Telephone

Because the telephone is extremely sensitive to the sounds that are directed at it—as your experiment with your own tape-recorded voice will have already demonstrated—it reproduces those sounds exactly as it receives them. That's why such fundamentals as breathing, diction, emphasis, and voice quality are important factors you must constantly take into account.

Few things are as basic to successful telephonic communications as are a proper transmittal and understanding of numbers. This is especially true in a sales effort, where prices, sizes, lot numbers, and delivery dates have such a vital bearing on the completion of the transaction. Numbers, therefore, must be pronounced with a very special quality of distinctness. The telephone company long ago learned this, and has always insisted that its own operators pronounce numbers in a very special way, which you should train yourself to use:

One	"Wun"	Six	"Siks"
Two	"Too"	Seven	"Sev-ven"
Three	"Th-r-ee"	Eight	"Ate"
Four	"Fo-wer"	Nine	"Ni-yen"
Five	"Fi-iv"	Zero	"Oh"

Learning to pronounce your numbers in this strange and initially awkward way will serve you in good stead, since no customer or prospect will ever be able to claim that he or she was told a product you're selling costs $5.94 when you've told him that the price was $9.94. Misunderstandings that can lead to the loss of sales—or even of a customer—will thus be completely avoided.

The Importance of Correct Inflection   That highly successful telephone salesman Jack Schwartz is perhaps the best authority on the key topic of the importance of proper inflection. Here is what he says about that vital subject in his widely read "How to Get More Business by Telephone":

> Inflections reveal motive, hidden meaning, sarcasm, contempt, anger, indifference, interest, concern, love, respect, etc. Anticipation is denoted in an upward inflection. The voice naturally rises in inflection when one is interested, inquiring, seeking, anticipating. Voices fall at a "period," on arrival at a decision, completion. Therefore a too frequent use of the downward inflection gives the impression of self-importance, of "know-it-allness," of finality, or firm, dogmatic decision; if overdone it is particularly dangerous in telephone use, as it runs the risk of being considered "bossy," argumentative and dictatorial. A mild use of it, however, is liked, as it registers decision and competence. A too generous use of inflection, up or down, gives a rather dizzy sense to the hearer; and a tone with little or no inflection is on the other hand monotonous and colorless.
>
> A trained voice ascends and descends the scale with a nice fitness and ease. A voice that stays at one key "gets on the nerves" of the hearer, quite as does one note struck constantly on a piano. A voice that runs up and down the scale at the right periods and without showing too giddy a temperament is best.

Tempo and Volume as Sales Factors Everyone has his or her own natural tempo of speech, but in your telephone sales efforts it is important that you try to adjust your rate of speech to the indicated needs of whoever is on the other end of the line.

Keeping in mind that about 150 words per minute is a good "average" rate, remember nevertheless that even that basic pace should be adapted to the personality of your contact. If the initial response you get from the person you call is delayed, and then finally comes through with pauses, and with hemming and hawing, cut back on your own tempo when you reply. Most people don't like "fast talkers," and they particularly arouse not only discomfort but suspicion—a bad trait to stimulate when you're trying to sell something!—in the listener, who thinks that maybe you're trying to put something over on him.

On the other hand, the person whose reply to you is couched in language delivered in machine-gun fashion may very well become provoked and impatient if you dawdle and hesitate with your own part of the conversation. Your real job here is to catch the pace of your opposite number, and to talk to your prospect so that he or she feels entirely comfortable with and confident in you.

You might also find it distinctly advantageous to vary the rate of speech between things you say in general conversation and items of specific importance related directly to sales points of your offer, slowing down and speaking with particular clarity and at a slower tempo when mentioning price, special sales points, etc.

The volume at which you deliver your message can also have an important influence on your degree of success as a telephone salesperson. No matter how far your voice is going to be carried over telephone lines, don't forget that it's moving with the aid of electronic and electric devices; you don't have to shout to carry out a conversation between Boston and San Diego!

In fact, it is best always to modulate your voice so that you consistently speak at normal conversational voice level. If you train yourself to keep your lips at just about a half-inch from the transmitting mouthpiece, and talk directly into it, your message will come over much more clearly at an ordinary decibel volume than it will if you get trapped into shouting. Too much volume can result in annoying sounds coming out the other end that will serve only to turn your prospect off completely.

How Good Diction Helps You Sell Diction, combined with properly used emphasis, represents an asset to the telephone salesperson because its employment helps create respect and admiration for the caller in the mind of the hearer.

Contrary to popular belief, diction does not refer solely to the act of sharp and clear pronunciation; in fact, Webster's first definition of the word reads, "Choice of words to express ideas; mode of expression in language." Thus, diction and emphasis, taken in combination, enable the caller to make points subtly and, in many cases, through an appeal to the prospect's subconscious.

There is a difference in effect, if none in thought, between "We will ship your order today," and "We will ship your order *this very afternoon*." The customer might take umbrage at "I'll get around to handling your complaint as soon as I can," but he or she is likely to be well satisfied with, "I'll handle your complaint *just as promptly* as I *possibly* can."

By giving weight to certain significant words or phrases, you can create an image of intent or action far in excess of what the words might barely mean. Diction and emphasis are not the property of the highly educated specialist alone, for their use is not purely a matter of knowing special words. They are there at the beck and call of anyone who speaks the language.

Courtesy Can Make the Difference   Along with diction in importance to your efforts as a telephonic salesperson, courtesy over the telephone takes its place of equality. Telephone courtesy is a subject all by itself, because people will tend to do things via this electronic instrument that they wouldn't dream of doing in person. Have you ever, for example, been in the process of ordering drugs or sundries in person at a store, only to have your order filling interrupted by a telephoned order from another customer who hasn't bothered leaving her home? Had she entered the store, no doubt she would have waited patiently until you had been waited on; in fact, had she made an effort to break in ahead of you, it's likely that the clerk would have ignored her. But somehow, when the telephone rings, you answer it!

As a result, some people even today resent the telephone as an instrumentality of discourtesy. Your own careful efforts can help overcome that concept.

A Vastly Different Level of Challenge

Virtually every experience to date in the rapidly developing area of telephone marketing has served to make one primary point exceptionally clear:

an entirely different degree of personal competence is required to sell successfully by telephone than through the traditional person-to-person confrontation.

To achieve a sale within a very few brief minutes, without the benefits inherent in sitting down face-to-face with a prospect in his own office, without showing him any kind of visual sales aids, without "softening him up" through personal and informal conversation about his family or his activities—to achieve that sale just by talking to the prospect over the telephone is a harder job.

But, as compensation, it can be a very rewarding job. It can be accomplished with far less physical strain, since no travel, no waiting time, no wasted hours are involved. It can be accomplished at far lower cost per sales call, and many more calls can be made in the course of a normal business day. So from every standpoint it is obviously well worth your effort to develop for yourself the new and superior techniques and approaches that are required.

Although today it has developed and continues to develop into a solid marketing science, replete with research, planning, testing, training, demographic and psychographic analyses, scripts and tapes and computers, telephone marketing still remains basically a person-to-person sales operation.

It cannot succeed properly for you without application of all its contemporary facets, but even with them, it will not prove successful without the application of the fundamental human touch right at the point of basic contact: the telephone sales call. The communicator is the heart of the system, his or her personality the fundamental factor that makes everything else work properly.

When you're at that telephone, when you're making that call, when you're talking to your prospect, sensitivity and flexibility are the keys to your success. Listen as hard as you talk and, in the final analysis, when the prospect tells you she wants "nyther" the blue model nor the beige one, don't tell her in response that you will send "neether" of those colors to her.

chapter eleven

The Eleven Commandments

IN THE BROADEST SENSE, an added dimension is vital if telephone marketing is to continue to be employed as a successful medium at the service of American business.

Beyond knowing how to choose and test lists, over and above selecting and training communicators, supplementing the professional preparation of tapes and scripts, and transcending an awareness of how to keep and analyze accurate and meaningful records, the advertiser must—under pain of the threat of losing control over this unique medium—add one more fundamental facet to phone operations: *business integrity*.

Door-to-door salesmanship, as experience demonstrates, has suffered immeasurably over the years, the direct result of alienated prospects who felt put upon—even openly cheated—and whose strident, justifiable complaints have led to a series of local restrictive regulations. Direct mail, as well, having been exploited by irresponsible practitioners—including some pornographers—seeking the quick buck any way they could get it, has seen its reputation tarnished with the term "junk mail."

The telephone, coming as it does directly into the home on so intimate and direct a personal basis, is vulnerable to national, state, and local legislative action that may seriously restrict the operations of marketers, if not eliminate them entirely. The only protection against such an eventuality is the maintenance of the highest standards of integrity on the part of the nation's telephone marketers.

Consumer Reactions

The man who has been angered or deceived by a telephone contact or sales effort will quickly react by reporting the experience to any of a dozen public or private agencies at his disposal, or by relating his unpleasant experience to his business colleagues. The homemaker who has been called away from her dinner preparation chores and treated rudely when she asks to be called at another hour will see to it that her bridge circle immediately shares the experience with her—and a dozen potential customers will be forever lost to all telephone marketers.

For prospects have, at all times, an immediate, definitive, and final answer to any telephone approach: they can just hang up! And more and more of them will do just that, if irresponsible marketers use the medium to provide the type of disillusioning contact that leads to a spreading of the negative word.

Already reactions have set in, on a fairly broad geographic basis, in this country. Many states and dozens of localities have either considered or actually introduced legislation seriously restrictive of telephone-marketing operations. Newspapers and magazines have alertly seized on examples of misuse of the telephone to publish articles about marketers who use this entry into offices and homes often for less than honorable purposes. The files of the Better Business Bureaus and the Federal Trade Commission are full of the shoddy, shady, and sleazy attempts—sometimes highly profitable—of telephone hoodwinking programs:

Phony stocks, marginal land, pyramiding costs for dance lessons, false and misleading "home siding" and "chemical" sales, high-pressure electric light bulb sales efforts by handicapped persons on specially rigged "charity" phones, contests for newspaper subscriptions and uneconomical five-year magazine subscription programs with "small type" contract clauses, all have taken their toll on the believability quotient of a no longer gullible public.

That this undertow of publicity has not been without effect is amply attested to by the fact that today more than 4 million Americans have agreed to pay an extra monthly fee to keep their names out of their local telephone directories. The percentage of such unlisted numbers in some of our major cities is beginning to run at a substantial rate: about 18 to 20 percent in Los Angeles, 14 percent in Chicago, 11 percent in Seattle, close to 10 percent in New York.

In California, legislation has been considered that would direct the telephone company to asterisk the listing of any subscriber requesting such action, with a legal reaction in store for anyone who called such a number for commercial purposes. Dozens of states and hundreds of local communities have placed—or at least seriously discussed placing—rigid limitations on the practice of calling anyone for purposes of advertising or selling. And Tampa, Florida, has completely outlawed telephone soliciting except where the individual called has invited such contact as part of a "current business or commercial relationship."

In response to public reaction to the activities of shysters, hucksters, and "bucket shop" operations, three states—Arizona, Colorado, and Delaware—have enacted legislation prohibiting "harassment" by telephone. California, Colorado, Oklahoma, Oregon, and Wisconsin have laws on their books requiring caller identification within a specified time of the opening of each commercially inspired conversation. Nevada requires immediate disclosure of the fact that a call has been made with an intent to sell something. Hawaii requires either a permit or a payment for a license, and also prohibits the offer of certain types of inducements to encourage sales or appointments. On the local level, Cincinnati prohibits the enforcement of any telephone sales agreement unless the buyer has been notified, during the call, of his or her right to cancel the purchase after receipt and inspection of the goods.

Responsible Marketing Required

Numerous other such legal enactments exist throughout the country. What is significant about them is that none would ever have had to be considered or legislated into law unless the actions of certain irresponsible telephone marketers had given rise to a broad series of consumer complaints. The corollary is that responsible marketers, operating properly and decorously, giving due recognition to the dignity and the rights of privacy of each person called, can act to reverse any negative consumer reaction currently existing and thus bring to a halt any need to spread further the blanket of legal restrictions on their operations.

The telephone is today's most responsive communications tool. Responsibility of operation, careful executive control, and high standards of professionalism are the attributes that must be projected by telephone marketers to avoid offenses—both deliberate and unintentional—that lead to consumer complaint.

The Common Offenses

While much of the restrictive legislation that has been enacted results from complaints based on deliberate unethical conduct on the part of some irresponsible telephone marketers, a considerable amount of consumer dissatisfaction springs from unintentional shortcomings, nurtured by such factors as pressure to obtain results, lack of qualified and trained personnel, insufficiently applied supervision, crash deadlines, and absence of adequate verification systems.

Responsible firms do not indulge in bait-and-switch advertising, nor do reliable organizations fail to deliver the quality or amount of merchandise that has been ordered by a customer in good faith, but managerial shortcomings in handling a telephone marketing operation can easily result in negative consumer reaction. Such well-meaning inadvertences lead to a falloff of credibility—and low credibility levels not only reduce results; they affect negatively every public contact a company makes or plans to make.

Too often guidelines adopted for telephone marketing are different from those used in other media, because some marketers reason that the person-to-person relationship offered by the telephone limits to a single individual the amount of negative result that can be provoked. This is fallacious reasoning. Precisely because it is so personal and so intimately effective, the telephone must be used with great care and consideration.

A Responsive Medium

The telephone is properly used as a marketing medium when the caller elects to contact only those believed to have a reasonable interest in the offer, when calls are made at a time that is not inconvenient to prospects, when the purpose of the call is clearly explained, and when the prospect is given the choice of listening or not listening. Used according to these standards, the telephone can prove the most responsive, sensitive, and achieving marketing medium available today.

What are the most common offenses encountered in the use of the telephone as a marketing medium? . . . offenses often committed unknowingly.

1. *Telephoning a person who has already been telephoned.* This, of course, is also a problem with direct mail, where it is certainly not as offensive since, upon receipt of a duplicate-mailing package, all the recipient has to do is throw it away.

Careful list apportionment—by alphabet or by geography—is essential if repeating is to be minimized. Each communicator should, in addition, be instructed to screen his or her own list prior to calling, to make sure the same name does not appear more than once in the list of assigned calls to be made.

Future developments will make possible the economic feasibility of computerized optical scanning of select lists for duplication, but even then there may be some inadvertent repeating. So what is perhaps more important than elimination of duplication is the matter of how the accidentally repeated call is handled. Make sure your communicators don't simply hang up without a word. See to it that they don't try to wriggle out of the embarrassment of the situation with, "Well, you know how it is . . . we've got all these names to call. . . ." Present a message that honestly and sincerely apologizes for your error.

2. *Wasting people's time.* Total controls must be exercised to make sure that all communicators are saying the same thing, and that the message has originally been created to make all necessary points in the shortest possible time.

When communicators take it upon themselves to waste time at the opening of a conversation ("Hi, my name is _____. I'm sure glad that you're home, because I want to . . . etc., etc."), you're likely to get a hang-up followed by a complaint to some agency.

Besides arousing antagonisms, such an approach is just plain bad sales strategy—the prospect spends so much time trying to get through to the reason for this unexpected call from a total stranger that he or she doesn't really hear your offer. By the time your communicator gets the main message under way, the prospect is completely turned off and about ready to hang up, which he or she frequently does.

3. *Varying the phone message from the follow-up.* Don't expect to get away with saying one thing on the telephone and following it up with a written agreement that says something else. Make sure your original verbal message is the truth, the whole truth, and nothing but the truth. Offending one individual more than offsets the positive effects of a dozen successful calls, because the individual whose antagonism you've aroused becomes an influential door-to-door *unsalesman*, telling countless other people how your company attempted to dissemble.

4. *Calling at the wrong time.* Remember your audience; you do just that when you prepare your script, which is always phrased in terms of prospect interest and benefits, so do it when you schedule your contact hours.

This requires some subjective judgment on your part since, for example, what you consider not to be a late evening hour may be just that for an elderly couple living on a farm. You don't make 9 P.M. calls to people who have to be up and about milking cows at 5:30 the next morning.

Keep the country's four time zones in mind, too. If you're telephoning from the West Coast, don't forget that 9:30 P.M. for you is already well past midnight for residents of Pittsburgh.

And keep the concept of daylight saving time in mind, as well, when projecting the hour in whatever city you're planning to have called.

Obviously you will not call businesspeople in their offices over the weekend, but be careful about making residence calls then, too. Many people deeply resent having their precious leisure time interfered with by someone trying to sell them something. There are certain areas of the country where you *just don't call* on Sunday; everything is shut up tight, and Sunday is a day of rest. You wouldn't think of having a door-to-door salesman go around calling on prospects in their homes under such circumstances, so don't attempt to impose yourself via telephone either. For the very same reason, if you're calling for a special cause and using a membership list of Jewish-oriented organizations, don't make Saturday calls.

Some Basic Principles

The person you are calling is more than a name on a list. He or she is a human being—much as you are—with individual interests, emotions, hopes, fears, and a point of view.

You must gear your program activity, therefore, to your own sensitivities in order to maximize the type of sympathetic response you anticipate getting from your telephone-marketing efforts. The key to your success is to get the person who answers the telephone to *listen* to the message you have prepared. One who feels antagonized or put upon will respond in a negative manner. How *both you and your prospect* respond to the person-to-person medium is the difference between the sale and the hang-up. So, follow these special telephone-marketing commandments:

ELEVEN COMMANDMENTS FOR TELEPHONE MARKETERS
"CODE OF ETHICS"

1. Thou shalt not lie or deceive or make false promises in fast words or small print.
2. Thou shalt not dishonor privacy or disturb the peace by calling at ungodly hours.

3. Thou shalt not set "hooks or snares" for your neighbors with false bait.
4. Thou shalt not make calls on the sabbath—the seventh day.
5. Honor the father and mother by not taking advantage of the child, the weak, the aged, or underprivileged in a household.
6. Thou shalt not kill the sale or the goose that lays the golden egg by overselling the product.
7. Thou shalt not commit the crime of adulterating the offer with false claims.
8. Thou shalt not abuse the privilege of privacy by questioning in the guise of research and survey—then acting the merchant who sells the names for profit.
9. Thou shalt not bear false witness, and will keep a proper and accurate account for thy client's sake.
10. Thou shalt not hide behind false identity and will always state thy true number.
    —and—
11. Thou shalt not bring down the wrath of the federal gods by breaking *their* commandments!

The Industry's Response

Lest any marketer think that concern about consumer reaction to some aspects of telephone marketing is being overdramatized, it should be noted that the telephone company—certainly a major beneficiary of all telephone marketing activity—has felt sufficiently worried about developments to devote some portion of its advertising budget to reassuring its customers that there are defenses against unpleasant and misleading calls.

A typical advertisement of New York Telephone, for example, running some 1,200 lines of space in newspapers throughout New York State, shows a guarded, suspicion-radiating housewife, listening to her kitchen wall telephone instrument. "Can't something be done about nuisance telephone calls from salesmen?" reads the large headline, which then proceeds to answer its own question: "Yes. There are things *you* can do and things *we* are doing." And here is what the text of the advertisement says:

> Most salespeople who use the phone are anxious to please you. But an aggressive telephone solicitor with a "pushy" sales pitch can be a real nuisance. We're concerned about the inconvenience and irritation such calls may cause you, and we're trying hard to eliminate them. But if you should receive such a call *Here's what you can do:*
>
> The best way to handle a nuisance sales call is politely, but firmly, to refuse the offer and hang up.
>
> In a persistent case, ask for the salesman's name and company and report him to his firm. Reputable companies know it's bad business to annoy or mislead potential customers.
>
> If you feel a call is unethical or offensive, call your telephone business

office. Or report the incident to your local Better Business Bureau or Chamber of Commerce.

Here's what we are doing:

When we're told about firms that have unethical or offensive sales practices, we call or visit them and review the complaint.

We meet with industry associations and discuss the proper use of the telephone. This includes keeping telephone selling free from deception and pressure, calling at the prospect's convenience, using only specially trained people, emphasizing good telephone manners and calling only bona fide prospects.

We are conducting a public-information program to eliminate undesirable practices.

We are required by law to provide telephone service for any legal purpose. Selling by telephone is legal, and, when properly conducted, is a mutually beneficial way to conduct business with customers. But, like many other things, it is subject to misuse. You should be protected against misuse, and we are doing our best to see that you are.

As the telephone company ad says, "Selling by telephone is legal. . . ." You can help see to it that it is kept that way.

chapter twelve

The Future State
of the Art

ANNUALLY, THE AUTHORITATIVE PUBLICATION *Advertising Age* summarizes by various media the amount invested by business in advertising during that current year. Its latest figures showed a total of some $26.5 billion.

Yet it is a mark of the newness of the use of the telephone as a marketing medium that the publication fails to include in its summary of some eight different categories of media any mention of that growing tool of the contemporary marketer.

In spite of the great volume of activity recorded for mass-marketing telephone usage, the total sum invested in the past on this person-to-person approach represents but a fraction of the potential it projects for both the immediate and long-range futures. Growing recognition of the benefits to be derived from the correct use of this newest marketing tool, plus the clear indications of technological developments already over the horizon, make it obvious that the reign of the telephone as the dominant monarch of the marketing world is just beginning.

A Glance at the Future

The scope of telephone marketing as well as its techniques are constantly evolving as the technology of telephony continues to make significant progress. Right now we have the basic technology to produce Dick Tracy's two-way wrist watch picture telephone. Ten years from now we will be able to use the phone as an automatic message-taker and for ordering theater tickets without uttering a word. The technology of the next decade might well herald a significant turning point in the scope and approach of telephone marketing. Individual switchboard operations will be eliminated during the 80s. The caller will thus be able to reach the desired party without any intermediaries—saving precious phone time and giving the telephone communicator a far better chance of effectively reaching the sales prospect.

Tools that are already becoming part of business life will also revolutionize telephone marketing in the coming decade. But even today, if you are one of the 100,000 Toronto trading area residents whose home is equipped with a 12-key Touch-Tone phone, you can order out of the Simpson-Sears catalog simply by pressing a combination of keys on your instrument. By 1980, Ma Bell anticipates the existence of one million Picturephones, which are expected to bring the telephone sales call almost to the level of an individual sales visit. Imagine the boost to telephone selling when you can both talk about and demonstrate the use of your product over the phone!

Automatic transfer is also slated to become a fact of life by the 80s, and the telephone communicator will by then be able to initiate a three-way conversation or transfer a prospect to another line for further information. These are but a few of the changes in store for telephone marketers in the near future, an age during which new satellite applications for telephony will enable telephone marketing to retain its relative cost-effectiveness.

In addition to these and other technological advances, the rapid emergence of telephone as an increasingly accepted tool in everyday life throughout the world should radically broaden the horizon of telephone marketing. There are now more than a quarter of a billion telephones installed throughout the world. While the United States and Canada far outpace other countries in telephone use, the rest of the world is rapidly catching up. In 1960 there were 134.6 million telephones; by 1970 the world total had very nearly doubled.

Increasing use of telephone the world over combined with broader-range automatic dialing capabilities should directly affect your marketing in the coming years. Automatic dialing has already enabled telephone-marketing programs to reach beyond national borders, especially between the United States and Canada, where it has been in effect since 1952. By the 60s European countries were direct-dialing each other, and automatic transatlantic dialing has since become a reality. In recognition of the increasing importance of telephone communication, the International Telecommunications Union (ITU), the United Nations agency responsible for overseeing communications arrangements between nations, has already prepared a worldwide telephone numbering plan that will accommodate all the world's phones until the year 2000.

Considering the technological and marketing advances in store for telephone, the day seems not too far off when a telephone communicator calling from Chicago will be able to sell a United States-made tractor to a farm cooperative in the Soviet Union over the phone!

Applying the Principles Profitably

Working with present reality or projecting the potentials of the future, the alert marketer will recognize that optimum employment of the telephone as a direct-response mass-marketing medium can be developed only with planned and controlled application of the fundamental principles that have been evolved through the efforts of those who have successfully used the phone during recent years.

Basic to the implementation of these standards is a full appreciation of the Levitt concept: the application of production-line manufacturing techniques to this person-to-person service process. While there are numerous examples of successful sales programs conducted via phone by career salespersons, they fall mainly into the category of highly specialized situations. Where mass-marketing problems are involved, the application of the "production-line approach to service" has distinctly proved its fundamental validity.

It is time, therefore, to review briefly what has been detailed in the preceding pages, remembering always that the various integral segments of any overall telephone marketing effort are completely interdependent, that equal importance must be attached to each, and always under responsible management control.

1. *Recognition of consumer attitudes.* Today's consumer regards the telephone as a way of life, using it for every communications purpose imaginable. While taking advantage of this highly positive development, the contemporary marketer must always remain aware that the modern consumer demands a dignified yet personalized approach. The person-to-person medium that is the telephone must be handled in such a manner as to cater to every human-related aspect of its highly intimate characteristics.

2. *Defining and identifying the market.* The theoretically optimum market segment must be clearly recognized and profiled well in advance of any movement to pick up the instrument and begin dialing. Such factors as previous purchasing history, educational background, cultural and social habits and standards, ethnic interests, business needs, and similar identifying characteristics should be projected and built into a list of the factors marking the "ideal" prospect. Lists can then be selected and, only then, be rented or exchanged.

3. *Selecting lists.* As in any direct-marketing effort, telephone results will prove only as good as the validity of the lists that are employed.

Once the type of prospect has been identified and categorized, the marketer can turn to a series of varied sources to obtain the names of those seemingly best suited to be approached. Such sources include your own business files, the specialized business and consumer press, other noncompetitive business organizations maintaining their own lists, and professional list brokers who, in particular, can prove most helpful if their services are correctly and efficiently employed.

Readily available census tracts and zip-code data, combined with common sense, can serve to expand a known market to include names of those similarly situated. Americans have a tendency to group themselves, both residentially and by activity, and the alert marketer is aware of the sales possibilities inherent in this national characteristic. If, for example, country-club members living in New York's affluent Westchester County have proved a valuable source of earlier profits for your product, it is well worth a test or two to probe the high degree of probability that others of similar affiliation will also respond to your offer, whether the county of their residence is named Dade, Contra Costa, Lake, Orange, or Harris.

4. *Script preparation.* Success on the telephone is highly dependent on the employment of a standardized, carefully structured message that allows but a minimum of individual communicator deviation. Experience has indicated the desirability of having it follow a carefully constructed format, combining the proved strengths of advertising copy employed in other forms of direct-marketing efforts, while simultaneously taking full advantage of telephone's unique ability to allow the marketer to react instantly to each individual prospect's personally stimulated questions or objections.

A script professionally created to maximize the opportunity to sell the interested prospect while at the same time allowing the communicator to terminate at an early stage a conversation with an obviously unqualified lead can prove a potent factor in cost control and thus exert a significant influence on your cost-per-sale figures.

Tests have repeatedly demonstrated that the inclusion of a taped message from a prominent public or quasi-public figure related to the interests of your audience can materially upgrade final total results.

5. *Presenting your message*. While the *basic principles* of salesmanship. apply without regard to the form of medium used, telephone demands a new and different application to achieve its anticipated results. Long, detailed copy may well be the key to attainment in many direct-mail efforts . . . handsome design and packaging of the message frequently enhance the appeal of print-media offers . . . exploitation of a personal relationship often smooths the way for the salesperson visiting his or her prospect in person . . . but telephone demands brevity and the immediate identification of the caller and the offer.

The communicator's personality—a prime factor in either befriending or alienating the prospect—can be projected only through his or her voice; there are no flip-charts or diagrams or illustrations to pave the road. Thus proper use of the voice is an essential that must be combined with a sensitivity to the need to *listen*, as well. Here once again the interdependence of the various facets of telephonic marketing becomes vital, since just accepting a question or objection is of no value unless it is combined with an opportunity to respond—an opportunity that can be provided only by a properly prepared script that furnishes the answers to anticipated prospect reactions.

6. *Selection and training of personnel*. The process of telephone marketing begins with the recruiting of adequate personnel—people who by personality and temperament are suited to fulfill the unique requirements of the medium and, in addition, possess the interest and the ability to lend themselves to proper training. Experienced and competent instructors are vital ingredients of preparation for your communicator crew. The employment of role-playing techniques is an important segment of proper training and instruction, along with constant monitoring of simulated phone-sales efforts and accompanying taped playbacks plus critiques.

For the individual planning his own telephone marketing operations, or for the smaller business organization employing only a limited staff, exposure to the local telephone company's "Phone-Power" materials and organized classes is highly recommended.

7. *Creating and installing optimum work conditions*. The organization of your telephone-room working area represents a significantly important area of your total operation. Physical arrangements must be designed with both comfort and efficiency clearly in mind. Work-flow procedures must be planned to ensure an absolute minimum of wasted time and effort.

Temperature, airflow, visibility, supervisory control station site, equipment, and furnishings must all be given full consideration and should be adequately built into your entire operation. Fundamental to the maintenance of high standards is the requirement for supervision, with spot monitoring and taping, so that the individual communicator can from time to time have his or her efforts become the subject of constructive discussion with a supervisor.

The final conditions under which you expect your telephone-room staff to work can have a marked effect upon the results you can expect to achieve. A fair compensation base must be assured, but results can frequently be improved through the institution of such morale-boosting factors as incentive awards, special bonuses, etc.

Basic to the creation of good working conditions for your communicators is the precept that they always be provided with *privacy*, but never be subjected to *isolation*.

8. Handling production forms and controls. Ongoing clerical and analytical operations are as essential to the successful conduct of a telephone-marketing program as are any of the other numerous factors. Full advantage of the medium's unique adaptability to virtually instant testing can be taken only if current results are carefully recorded and promptly evaluated.

To expedite the work of the communicators, and to provide a basis for efficient operations on the part of those who retrieve, record, and evaluate results, it is necessary that a specific form be designed to match the requirements of each individual telephone campaign.

9. Maintaining ethical standards. The constantly burgeoning telephone-solicitation effort to which the nation's consumer and business public alike is exposed brings in its wake a serious set of problems. Constantly alert to their traditional rights guaranteeing protection against "invasion of privacy," some Americans have registered objections to being called at their homes, or even in their business offices, by those whom they see only as strangers intent on selling them something.

Those who conduct telephone marketing operations must do so on a level of integrity, courtesy, and common decency that will assure the continued availability to them of the telephone as a marketing tool.

With a number of states and municipalities having already instituted controlling legislation or regulations of one sort or another, the telephone marketer should be familiar with these laws and ordinances to ensure that none are violated by personal efforts. In the past, business practices that have been carried out in excess of acceptable levels have often resulted in restrictive legislation and in public reaction that has led to public rejection.

The telephone represents a legitimate and effective means of communicating with the nation's customers and prospects, and responsibility lies with those who use it to make sure that it is not abused.

10. *Projecting and analyzing your costs.* Profitability, of course, is the name of the game, so, as in every form of advertising and sales effort, cost factors in telephone marketing operations must ultimately be assessed in terms of bottom-line results, not gross investment figures.

Telephone cost figures take on an entirely new perspective when analyzed, as they should be, in relation to the goal attained through their expenditure. For example, a $3 (WATS) phone call that serves to screen out what would have proved to be an unproductive $90 to $100 personal sales visit is obviously a prudent and inexpensive investment. A 60 cents to $1 local phone call that offers and screens credit privileges for a retail store can be a very profitable investment if the response levels are 2 out of 10 completed calls. The total cost of testing two lists, with 200 calls made to sample names on each, represents a substantial saving if it serves to demonstrate that mailings to one such list will prove significantly more productive than to the other.

As in any form of direct-marketing operation, the key element to be considered and evaluated is *cost-effectiveness*. Accurate record keeping, plus prompt analysis of test results, provides you with immediate ability to check out this fundamental.

Telephone-marketing costs should not be analyzed or judged on the basis of total outlay, but rather on the basis of cost-per-sale or cost-per-inquiry statistics.

An Opportunity at Hand

The telephone is a reality, its current validity as a marketing medium already proved, its possibilities for the future subject only to the limitations of the imagination of mankind.

With an instrument at hand on the desk of every single American business executive and in the homes of about 95 percent of the nation's meaningful consumers, you have the opportunity to establish person-to-person sales contact with virtually everyone in the country you may choose to approach. Pioneers have already indicated, through painfully learned trial-and-error techniques, what can be done and what must be done to obtain profitable marketing objectives. The lessons they have learned are at your disposal; the telephone is ready for you, if you demonstrate that you are ready to use it.

It will be the marketing marvel of the twenty-first century, but it is ready, here in the final quarter of the twentieth, to serve those who know how to make maximum use of this mechanized, electronic, magical communications tool. Your voice is somewhere out there on microwaves or with the stars, bouncing off a speedy satellite and shooting back down to earth to just one human being you'd like to talk to personally and naturally.

It still boggles my mind. I hope you feel the same way.

Total Expenditures
for Media in U.S.—1975

		% Change From 1974
Television	$5.33 Billion	+10
Newspapers	8.45 Billion	+6
Magazines	1.48 Billion	−2
Radio	2.02 Billion	+10
Display	3.40 Billion	−1
Direct mail	4.13 Billion	+4
Telephone	*8.5 Billion+	+5

* The figure for telephone expenditures is not directly comparable to those given for other media, in that it combines selling expense with advertising expense. It is simply not possible to apply a rule of thumb that would accurately reflect the correct proportion of advertising and selling expenses in the $8.5 billion total. The figure stands, nevertheless, as a valid indicator of the vast annual investment in telephone sales and marketing activities.

Substantiation for Estimated $8 Billion Telephone Sales/Marketing Medium 1975 Expenditures

Definition and Expenditure Inclusions The telephone is a two-way medium primarily dependent on human communicators for message delivery and receipt. Technological developments now permit broader use of automatic message delivery and receipt, but this still represents a relatively small part of the total medium expenditures.

The medium-cost expenditures include all outgoing and incoming calls of a lead generation, sales appointment, sales closing, message delivery, and market research nature, to and from consumers, businesses, institutions, and governments. The two major cost items are monies paid for:

   A. Equipment (plus message units/tolls) and
   B. Labor (paid by businesses) for phone staffing and time spent on the phone.

Network Overview Updating figures from AT&T's, "The World's Telephones as of January 1, 1974," in 1975—in the United States—there were nearly 210 billion phone conversations (over 900 per capita population) conducted on approximately 152,000,000 phones. Billings were made by the 1,705 United States phone companies. Breakdown:

1975 Estimates	Total Phone	Main Nos.	Percent Total
U.S. Totals	152,000,000	81,400,000	100.0
Residence	110,976,000	68,783,000	84.5
Business	41,024,000	12,617,000	15.5

Overall Revenues for Equipment and Tolls Only   Updating AT&T figures published in *The New York Times* and *The Bergen Record* re U.S. Justice Department suit against AT&T, the 1,705 phone companies (including AT&T with 86 percent share of the market) had an estimated $32 billion in revenues for 1975, about 15 cents per phone conversation held. Estimated breakdown:

Residences. Based on an estimated $240 per year ($20 per month) per residence main number, total phone company revenues for this sector are approximately $16.5 billion.

Business. Total of $32 billion less $16.5 billion residence, or $15.5 billion paid by companies for their numbers as well as use of other phones (hotel, motel, pay phones, etc.).

Telephone Sales/Marketing Medium Expenditures

Residences. At least 2 percent (CCI estimates $330 million) of $16.5 billion involve consumer-activated purchasing/inquiry calls to retail merchants, catalogue/mail-order houses, airlines, etc.

Businesses (Equipment/Tolls). At least 25 percent (CCI estimates $4.1 billion) of $16.5 billion involve sales (purchasing)/marketing type calls to and from consumers, businesses, institutions, and governments.

Examples

■ In 1974 businesses spent $975 million, according to AT&T figures published in *The New York Times* and *The Bergen Record* re U.S. Justice Department suit against AT&T, on WATS alone, (estimated at over $1 billion in 1975). WATS is the Wide Area Telephone Service: flat monthly rates for fixed number of hours with rates governed by geographic coverage. This includes the much-advertised "800" toll-free call-in numbers as well as high-volume sales and market research calls to consumers as well as businesses, institutions, and governments.

■ One major airline stated in 1972 that its phone-related reservation systems cost was over $40 million.

■ United States businesses spend $1 billion a year just for Yellow Pages advertising (another medium and not included in the $8 billion) of their phone numbers.

Business equipment total: $4.1 billion

Business (Labor). For every dollar spent on telephone equipment and tolls in sales and marketing, at least that much again is spent on telephone labor.

Long Distance—Equipment and Tolls—costs higher than labor

WATS (Average)—Labor about same as equipment and tolls

Local—Labor costs higher than equipment and tolls

Examples

■ A major United States retailer estimates that 23 percent of its business emanates from its catalogue operations, and 75 percent ($2.25 billion) of that amount is written over the telephone by consumers calling in. Although the company incurs little equipment cost (rental but not tolls), its labor cost is at least $25 million for order taking.

■ There are hundreds of thousands of people in the United States making toll-free soliciting calls from their homes (local area) but who are paid for their labor: piece work, commissions, etc., but at least minimum wage.

■ There are hundreds of local answering services who specialize in handling inquiry and order calls from consumers and businesses motivated to call through print and broadcast ads.

Business Labor Total: $4.1 billion

Estimated Grand Totals: $8.53 billion

appendix two/ *Identifying the Audience-Criteria*

***Standard Industrial
Classifications (SIC)***

All of America's commercial enterprises have been divided into 13 major groupings, each of which has been assigned a two-digit classification number.

Within these broad categories, several hundred narrower classifications have been established and, from that level, each specific type of enterprise has been given an additional number. Thus every business or service organization within the United States falls into some specific four-digit numerical group, enabling the marketer to specify, by SIC number, all of the firms he or she may want to reach.

The first two digits, providing the key to a major industry group, have been designated as follows:

01 to 09	Agriculture, Forestry, and Fisheries
10 to 14	Mining
15 to 17	Contract Construction
19 to 39	Manufacturers
40 to 48	Transportation and Communications
49	Utilities
50	Wholesale
52 to 59	Retail
60 to 62	Finance
63 to 64	Insurance
65	Real Estate
67	Holding and Investment Companies
70 to 89	Services

Assume that it is decided that an optimum marketing target area lies within the field of those companies manufacturing *footwear* of various kinds. Within the *manufacturing* category, the marketer will find classification 30 (Rubber and Miscellaneous Plastics Products) and classification 31 (Leather and Leather Products). Referring to SIC tables, available from government sources and published by marketing service organizations, he or she would find three sub-areas related to the manufacture of various kinds of footwear:

3021	Rubber footwear
3141	Footwear, except house slippers and rubber footwear
3142	House slippers

135

Somewhere within these three subdivisions, every manufacturing organization in the country producing footwear of one kind or another will be included. Thus, the marketer need only specify to the list source that he or she wants the names of all the organizations within those three categories to insure complete coverage of his or her indicated market.

To refine his or her needs further, of course, the marketer might specify that he or she wants only those organizations in one, two, or all three of those sections "located within the six New England states," or all SIC 3141 companies "employing more than 250 people," or perhaps all SIC 3021 companies "with an annual sales volume of more than $500,000."

The use of SIC designations enables the marketer to obtain all of the names and addresses within exactly the category of prospect he or she is interested in reaching.

A four-digit directory, called *The Standard Industrial Classification Manual 1972*, is revised every five years. It costs $6.75. The seven-digit *Numerical Listing of Manufactured Products In 1972 SIC Basis* breaks down manufacturers by product. It costs $4. Both directories are available from the Superintendent of Documents, Government Printing Office, Washington, D.C. 20402.

appendix three / ## Demographics, Psychographics, and Census Tracts: Using Zip-code Data to Zero in on a Market Segment

INCREASING COSTS AND THE CONSEQUENT NEED to concentrate direct-marketing programs on carefully selected targets of maximum opportunity have led marketers to seek means whereby they can readily define and isolate such cost-effective prospect segments. This requirement is at least equally applicable to telephone activity as it is to other forms of direct-marketing operations.

The development of computer technology, combined with data available from both governmental and private sources, makes it currently possible for marketers to design programs responsive to this need and to test-market segments chosen with respect to the indicated life-styles of residents of narrowly defined geographic areas.

Demographics and Psychographics   While some gray areas of overlap do exist, sometimes obliterating sharp differences between *demographic* and *psychographic* considerations, in general it can be stated that the former relate to clearly measurable statistical data about people (e.g., age, income bracket, size of family, level of completed education, means of making a living, etc.), whereas psychographic considerations are based on cultural measurements (e.g., membership in a country club, nature of magazines subscribed to, attendance at symphony concerts, etc.).

Since people tend to flock together in neighborhoods in which they feel comfortable, the tendency develops for specific geographic residential areas to be inhabited by persons of like characteristics, as related both to economic standards and cultural life-styles. Reference sources exist, and are available, to help the marketer pinpoint the kinds of prospects sought in terms of the areas in which they reside. (See Figure A-1.)

Census Tracts versus Zip Codes   The universal application of the zip-code addendum to every known address in the United States sharply narrows

137

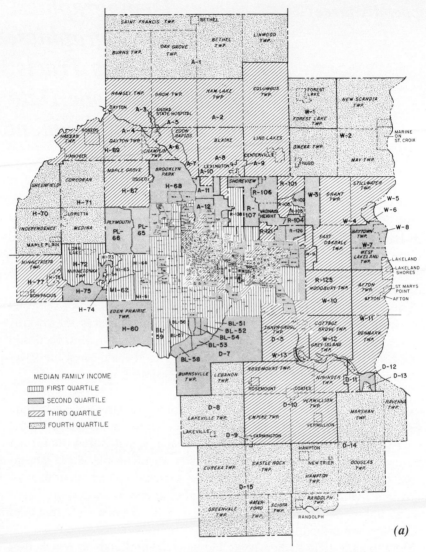

MEDIAN FAMILY INCOME
- FIRST QUARTILE
- SECOND QUARTILE
- THIRD QUARTILE
- FOURTH QUARTILE

(a)

Fig. A-1. (a) The Reuben H. Donnelley Network Map of St. Paul showing census tracts; (b) various demographic cross sections (National Demographic Research Corporation).

identification of every prospect to a point not attained by earlier use of census tract data. See Figure A-2.

Census tract data are developed from a series of questions asked individuals during each national census carried out by the United States government at 10-year intervals. Thus they provide generalized summary information about the "average" of a population segment within a given

(b)

geographic area. Thus, a marketer can discover that some 30 percent of the residents of New York State were under the age of 18 in 1970.

Census tract data can be purchased from the U.S. Government Printing Office, and are also available for examination at major public libraries, university libraries, or at local Census Bureau offices (see Fig. A-2).

SECTION II – DETAILED CHARACTERISTICS
TABLE D, ITEMS 57-79

REZIDE™ The National ZIP Code Encyclopedia

ZIP CODE	Family Life Cycle Code	Families % With Children Under 18	% With Female Head	Males Per 100 Females	% Pop 14 Years & Over Married	AGE OF DISTRIBUTION OF THE TOTAL POPULATION % Under 6 Years	% 6-13 Years	% 14-17 Years	% 19-24 Years	% 25-34 Years	% 35-44 Years	% 45-54 Years	% 55-64 Years	% 65 Years & Over	Median Age In Years	RACE White % Tot. Pop.	Negro % Tot. Pop.	DOMINANT ETHNIC GROUP Abbrev. Name	% Tot. Pop.	Spanish Americans % Tot. Pop.	RESIDENCE IN 1965 % Diff. House Same State	% Diff. State or Abroad	% Non-Pop. Movers
ITEM	57	58	59	60	61	62	63	64	65	66	67	68	69	70	71	72	73	74	75	76	77	78	79
30184	F2-6	51.9	12.4	102.3	64.5	11.6	14.7	6.9	11.1	12.0	11.4	13.9	7.9	10.5	29.7	N/A	N/A	--	N/A	N/A	15.3	.4	70.3
30185	F2-5	52.9	15.7	95.5	65.7	10.5	16.5	7.5	12.6	10.4	10.1	10.8	11.7	9.9	27.6	89.1	10.9	UK	1.5	N/A	45.6	5.7	43.0
30186	F5-3	53.6	9.7	102.8	61.4	10.2	15.8	9.6	9.6	10.3	11.4	9.7	12.0	12.0	29.5	N/A	N/A	--	N/A	N/A	34.0	2.4	57.7
30187	F4-6	60.7	6.9	98.3	68.5	12.0	20.0	8.8	9.2	12.6	12.1	9.7	6.6	9.5	25.0	N/A	N/A	OT	.2	N/A	30.4	2.8	61.6
30188	F2-9	62.2	7.7	97.3	74.5	13.9	17.1	7.3	11.6	17.0	10.8	9.6	6.2	6.5	25.1	4.5	N/A	GE	.5	N/A	48.8	12.6	32.4
301	F2-7	56.4	9.6	94.4	66.8	11.4	16.2	7.6	11.6	13.2	11.5	10.6	9.2	8.7	27.4	89.2	10.7	OT	.2	.2	35.8	6.2	53.8
30201	F3-9	57.5	6.0	97.8	71.2	11.3	17.1	8.2	9.3	14.8	12.2	9.6	9.1	8.4	27.7	93.6	2.2	GE	.4	.2	42.8	7.2	45.3
30202	F5-7	53.0	16.8	87.3	51.1	11.6	19.5	11.6	11.8	6.9	6.9	8.5	10.4	13.3	21.4	87.3	N/A	CA	.7	N/A	34.7	2.7	57.6
30203	F2-9	59.6	10.8	101.6	68.1	12.1	15.2	7.4	12.3	13.6	10.8	10.9	8.0	9.7	27.1	N/A	N/A	--	N/A	N/A	40.5	3.5	52.2
30204	F5-4	52.6	8.3	91.4	53.9	10.7	16.9	9.8	11.4	11.9	11.0	9.8	10.7	9.9	26.3	54.1	45.9	OT	.6	N/A	32.2	3.0	60.2
30205	F5-8	53.5	8.7	93.4	69.1	9.5	17.2	9.3	8.3	7.9	13.4	11.7	10.7	9.8	30.9	N/A	N/A	OT	.8	N/A	40.1	1.2	54.0
30206	F5-3	53.6	11.5	96.4	57.0	12.1	18.3	10.0	11.1	7.9	9.5	10.0	11.7	9.8	23.7	47.5	52.5	CA	.7	N/A	34.3	2.7	54.9
30207	F2-7	60.7	9.7	98.4	67.7	13.1	16.0	7.4	10.4	15.3	11.0	10.0	7.8	7.0	25.4	76.4	23.4	OT	.7	N/A	43.3	9.2	44.3
30209	F5-7	57.4	13.5	93.0	62.4	12.5	17.3	8.4	11.2	13.2	11.0	9.6	9.6	7.4	25.4	56.7	43.3	OT	.5	N/A	36.1	5.7	51.5
30211	F2-8	53.7	9.6	99.0	66.3	11.5	16.0	8.2	11.1	13.1	13.1	11.0	9.1	10.1	27.4	92.6	7.4	OT	.2	N/A	35.2	2.1	60.9
30212	F6-1	45.0	7.4	83.5	68.4	12.8	13.0	5.7	10.8	10.8	11.5	12.7	17.0	10.3	36.4	34.3	N/A	--	N/A	N/A	34.3	2.8	59.2
30213	F4-6	59.7	10.0	95.9	64.6	11.1	18.4	9.0	7.9	12.3	12.9	10.1	9.2	9.2	27.9	79.2	20.8	OT	.4	.1	39.3	3.8	49.6
30214	F3-7	59.2	9.0	95.0	68.6	11.7	19.0	7.5	9.4	15.6	10.6	10.1	8.5	7.6	26.5	88.3	11.7	GE	.4	N/A	38.7	7.7	48.9
30215	F3-9	56.5	9.1	100.0	64.2	11.1	17.1	9.5	10.7	11.4	9.0	11.4	8.0	8.0	23.1	65.1	34.9	OT	.8	N/A	34.8	3.0	57.7
30216	F2-7	46.7	16.7	101.6	64.0	11.1	15.8	8.2	9.4	12.3	11.8	11.8	11.9	11.9	30.8	71.8	28.2	CA	1.1	N/A	35.5	2.1	56.9
30217	F5-5	51.5	12.2	94.2	60.9	10.0	18.0	9.7	11.4	10.5	9.1	12.2	12.7	12.7	29.1	66.3	33.7	CA	.6	N/A	31.8	3.8	63.6
30218	F5-5	52.1	16.4	85.9	51.8	10.6	20.3	10.9	6.8	6.8	6.3	8.8	10.1	13.8	21.5	N/A	N/A	CA	.6	N/A	34.7	2.8	57.9
30219	F5-1	51.0	18.2	92.1	55.6	10.7	18.2	10.7	5.9	8.8	7.0	11.9	13.3	13.2	25.3	70.4	29.6	CA	1.8	N/A	19.5	1.5	78.9
30220	F5-1	48.9	11.1	91.0	63.9	11.7	19.1	9.3	10.0	15.3	11.0	12.9	11.4	9.9	30.0	75.8	24.2	IT	.3	N/A	26.6	3.2	66.3
30221	F2-1	52.8	11.6	85.9	68.2	8.2	19.1	9.4	11.5	11.8	14.7	8.1	9.7	8.5	26.7	99.3	.7	OT	1.6	.0	47.6	5.7	39.6
30222	F2-1	48.7	16.9	92.7	56.2	12.5	16.8	9.6	8.2	9.8	9.0	11.3	9.9	12.9	27.8	45.4	54.6	OT	.6	N/A	21.4	2.6	72.7
30223	F2-6	53.9	15.2	91.3	62.5	11.0	17.1	7.5	10.0	12.8	11.5	11.9	9.1	9.1	28.5	77.1	22.9	OT	.2	N/A	37.1	4.4	55.3
30228	F2-5	67.8	10.8	101.4	66.4	13.8	19.9	9.8	9.8	11.9	11.1	10.6	5.8	9.1	22.0	88.7	11.3	CA	2.0	N/A	43.7	20.1	32.0
30229	F5-7	56.5	9.6	97.4	63.4	12.1	19.0	9.7	11.9	8.3	7.7	8.9	8.9	11.1	26.3	63.7	36.3	CA	1.0	N/A	30.6	2.8	58.5
30230	F5-5	45.3	14.7	90.2	63.0	12.1	15.0	8.1	10.0	11.9	8.0	7.7	14.6	11.4	33.1	59.4	40.6	OT	N/A	N/A	31.4	4.1	53.1
30231	F2-4	47.3	17.0	101.7	63.0	10.6	17.7	8.5	10.0	9.1	12.3	11.8	11.8	11.8	30.1	86.7	28.5	UK	.8	N/A	35.0	2.3	56.7
30232	F3-1	57.6	10.1	93.6	66.3	10.6	17.7	9.5	10.9	13.0	10.3	10.7	9.4	10.8	26.4	86.2	13.8	--	.3	N/A	39.5	5.4	50.8
30233	F2-2	54.1	15.4	91.9	63.2	10.7	18.2	9.5	11.9	11.9	9.7	9.3	9.4	10.5	28.5	63.2	36.8	CU	.8	N/A	39.5	5.4	50.8
30234	G3-4	47.9	15.5	74.3	55.8	11.2	13.3	6.2	8.9	10.6	10.6	10.5	6.7	24.7	34.9	65.9	34.1	CU	2.8	N/A	52.7	6.2	39.1
30235	F2-7	61.6	5.9	97.7	68.2	10.8	18.1	9.6	9.6	8.9	10.6	10.6	8.7	7.3	25.7	89.0	11.0	OT	N/A	N/A	44.7	1.7	51.3
30236	F2-8	67.4	6.1	98.0	72.5	15.2	18.7	6.9	12.3	18.4	12.4	7.8	4.7	3.6	23.5	92.1	7.8	OT	.9	.6	42.8	15.8	32.5

Zip	Code																					
30240	F2-4	51.3 16.0	88.1 60.7	10.6 15.6	8.4	11.8	10.5	11.9	11.3	12.2	10.3	10.1 29.1	72.7 27.3	OT .4	N/A	31.9 6.5 58.4					
30245	F2-7	60.6 7.5	97.3 69.2	12.7 16.9	8.5	10.7	12.4	15.2	11.8	7.8	5.8	4.9 25.4	95.1 4.9	OT .4	.0	41.9 7.3 43.6					
30247	F2-7	64.3 5.8	96.7 75.4	13.2 18.4	7.0	10.7	11.6	12.4	9.6	7.8	9.2	9.2 25.4	99.5 4.5	OT .5	.3	40.1 13.0 39.5					
30249	F2-9	51.2 13.7	98.6 65.9	11.4 17.2	7.5	10.0	10.9	12.5	9.6	7.8	8.0	9.2 28.6	91.1 32.8	GE .3	.0	36.2 6.1 37.1					
30250	F5-3	60.8 4.0	104.1 73.3	10.8 17.2	8.8	10.9	12.4	12.7	9.8	8.0	6.2	10.6 25.5	90.4 8.9	CA 11.3	.0	33.3 13.3 45.7					
30251	F2-7	55.1 25.1	130.5 56.7	12.9 21.0	8.8	10.0	11.4	9.4	12.7	6.2	7.0	25.5	90.4 9.6	-- N/A	.0	31.3 1.3 66.7					
30252	F2-7	57.8 14.6	96.3 59.8	14.3 17.2	8.8	10.0	11.4	9.4	8.4	8.4	10.6	24.8	46.6 53.4	-- 1.8	N/A	26.4 .9 68.7					
30253	F3-9	61.1 4.3	102.4 72.9	11.8 16.5	8.2	12.8	10.6	11.6	5.8	4.7	4.7 25.3	100% .0	UK 1.7	N/A	38.0 21.1 36.6						
30254	F2-9	62.9 6.6	103.1 72.7	15.3 18.1	7.3	13.6	13.9	11.6	9.0	8.8	8.8 22.9	74.3 25.7	OT 1.0	N/A	53.2 4.9 40.4						
30255	F3-6	52.3 11.0	96.1 63.4	13.0 18.3	6.5	11.3	10.5	11.1	9.0	10.4	10.4 25.9	65.3 34.7	-- N/A	N/A	37.2 9.6 52.5						
30256	F4-3	49.0 7.1	109.9 60.3	11.0 18.3	8.1	8.5	10.2	9.5	9.7	13.0	13.0 29.1	81.3 18.7	OT .4	N/A	29.6 5.6 61.8						
30257	F4-9	46.4 9.1	94.4 61.8	9.0 20.2	9.8	9.4	12.1	9.5	8.9	11.2	11.2 26.4	72.5 27.5	N/A	N/A	39.7 2.7 57.2						
30258	F2-4	53.9 11.6	95.9 57.1	12.1 18.4	9.8	11.2	7.9	9.5	9.5	10.7	10.9 23.8	47.5 52.5	IT .1	N/A	34.3 2.7 54.9						
30259	F3-8	55.1 12.2	87.7 56.9	16.0 16.0	7.6	10.6	11.1	12.4	9.0	12.6	12.6 31.0	77.7 22.3	IT 1.2	.6	35.7 2.0 60.3						
30260	F3-8	73.1 5.6	96.8 73.7	14.1 20.9	7.6	8.8	19.8	8.2	11.0	3.3	3.3 23.9	92.6 7.3	GE 1.2	.6	39.4 14.5 37.2						
30261	F5-5	54.8 7.2	97.6 63.5	17.5 17.5	10.5	11.6	8.6	11.0	11.8	7.3	7.3 24.6	77.4 22.6	UK 1.7	.6	29.4 4.5 63.5						
30262	F3-6	52.3 11.4	97.2 63.3	13.2 18.2	6.6	7.9	9.8	11.0	10.3	10.3	10.3 25.4	64.7 35.3	N/A	N/A	37.2 9.7 52.4						
30263	F3-9	55.5 12.7	91.4 63.4	13.1 17.0	7.9	10.1	12.8	11.6	9.6	3.6	3.6 28.0	61.9 38.1	UK .4	.5	35.7 5.7 56.1						
30266	F5-4	50.2 11.7	94.8 62.3	10.1 18.6	10.3	10.7	10.3	9.5	9.0	9.8	9.8 25.4	79.1 20.9	GE .6	N/A	36.5 3.5 58.7						
30267	F2-9	50.6 10.5	98.8 64.0	12.0 15.9	7.9	14.3	11.7	10.8	9.0	7.5	7.5 24.9	85.3 14.7	OT 1.2	N/A	33.8 9.6 50.5						
30268	F5-8	54.7 11.5	96.1 65.2	12.2 20.1	7.8	10.4	12.5	11.4	10.3	8.7	8.7 24.7	70.5 29.5	CA .0	.0	32.9 6.0 53.5						
30269				SEE ZIP 30214																		
30270	F2-9	56.8 8.0	95.0 68.1	17.0 17.6	9.7	14.2	10.3	9.8	11.7	6.2	6.2 26.5	85.9 14.1	GE .4	N/A	30.8 5.2 50.8						
30271	F3-1	60.2 9.0	90.2 71.2	13.9 20.5	11.7	13.8	11.4	10.5	7.2	7.2 25.5	90.5 9.5	IT .5	N/A	32.4 2.7 61.6							
30272	F3-9	58.7 10.2	95.4 69.2	14.0 20.1	9.1	7.5	12.0	12.3	7.5	4.5	4.5 25.6	93.6 16.3	CA 2.1	1.0	33.7 13.7 43.6						
30273	F3-8	58.7 9.2	95.5 65.9	10.1 19.5	10.7	7.5	12.0	12.3	7.5	6.0	6.0 23.8	91.1 8.9	OT .5	N/A	37.0 8.5 43.9						
30274	F2-8	72.0 5.0	99.0 75.6	15.1 19.5	6.4	11.4	12.1	10.9	9.4	3.4	3.4 23.8	82.6 17.4	GE .7	.6	46.4 15.6 29.2						
30275	F3-8	58.0 5.9	103.8 66.3	11.0 18.2	8.5	7.7	13.5	11.6	10.8	6.6	6.6 26.6	82.0 17.4	CA .4	.2	40.8 9.2 60.2						
30276	F2-6	58.6 14.1	96.3 61.1	12.3 21.7	8.5	9.1	11.5	10.1	9.2	8.6	8.6 23.8	69.2 30.8	OT 1.4	N/A	26.5 1.9 60.5						
30277	F3-9	58.5 14.3	96.3 61.0	12.2 21.7	8.6	9.1	11.4	9.2	9.1	8.6	8.6 23.7	69.1 30.9	OT 1.8	N/A	26.5 2.0 60.5						
30278	F2-8	61.8 4.0	101.6 75.2	12.2 18.0	8.7	8.7	16.1	11.3	7.4	5.6	5.6 24.7	96.9 3.1	UK .8	N/A	47.0 7.7 41.3						
30279	F2-3	52.4 15.3	89.4 61.6	11.8 15.5	9.9	9.9	11.0	10.6	9.4	10.7	10.7 22.6	69.5 30.4	GE .5	N/A	37.1 3.5 55.6						
30280	F2-3	55.4 13.6	98.3 65.6	13.1 15.6	8.8	14.8	8.8	9.5	10.5	8.7	8.7 22.6	69.6 30.4	SW .9	N/A	34.9 12.8 48.6						
30281	F3-9	57.7 7.8	99.7 66.4	12.0 17.1	9.0	9.9	12.1	10.4	7.6	7.0	7.0 24.9	78.8 21.2	OT .7	1.2	31.2 5.0 55.3						
30282	F2-1	61.1 6.4	91.6 67.4	12.6 17.1	8.4	11.4	14.4	10.4	7.6	7.2	7.2 25.0	93.5 5.7	GE 1.2	N/A	41.8 3.8 50.6						
30283	F2-1	50.2 11.7	99.0 59.1	11.9 17.7	8.9	11.3	14.5	9.5	10.8	16.5	16.5 29.5	69.1 30.9	UK .4	N/A	24.3 8.6 63.2						
30284	F2-6	55.8 10.5	100.0 68.1	13.1 17.7	7.7	11.2	14.5	10.8	8.0	8.0	8.0 25.2	82.7 17.3	CA .6	N/A	42.2 7.9 45.1						
30285	F2-6	52.3 6.6	94.9 67.5	13.1 16.1	7.3	12.8	13.6	12.1	6.5	6.5	6.5 29.2	69.3 30.7	GE .6	N/A	36.3 7.3 56.7						
30286	F3-5	51.1 11.4	91.8 64.6	10.2 15.5	8.2	9.4	11.3	11.8	9.2	8.9	8.9 30.9	73.7 26.3	GE .1	N/A	34.7 2.6 58.8						
30289	F3-8	58.9 14.5	97.7 60.1	12.4 21.0	9.1	10.2	11.0	9.7	9.0	8.8	8.8 23.2	68.9 31.1	OT 1.9	N/A	26.5 2.4 59.9						
30290	F2-7	60.2 9.3	97.1 69.4	13.3 17.8	7.6	10.2	12.4	11.9	10.0	6.5	6.5 24.5	N/A N/A	CA 1.0	.0	37.4 10.7 49.6						
30291		62.0 9.7	93.0 66.9	13.1 18.8	7.5	10.9	13.7	11.0	8.5	7.9	7.9 24.8	76.9 23.1	GE .3	.6	38.5 4.0 54.2						
30292	F3-9	53.6 6.7	107.1 66.3	11.5 24.1	9.0	9.5	10.8	8.4	7.9	8.2	8.2 22.2	58.5 41.5	CA .5	N/A	39.5 .3 59.1						

c. 1973

CLARITAS CORPORATION
3600 M Street N.W.
Washington, D.C. 20007

Fig. A-2. Part of a page of REZIDE, Section II, the 5-digit zip-code data book.

Application of *zip-code data* can narrow this vital information down to a factual conclusion as to whether this identical proportion holds true within an area comprising only a few square blocks within the city of Syracuse. One major source of zip-code data is the REZIDE directories furnished to subscribers by Claritas Corporation. (See Figure A-2.)

These sources provide the answers to well over 100 questions regarding the characteristics of households within each of the nearly 38,000 zip-code areas in the United States. It is easily possible, for example, to look up the household income distribution, by bracket percentage, of the residents of a specific section in Sioux City, Iowa, or the median number of housing rooms per resident—for both owners and renters—in any given zip-code area in Chicago, or the percentage of professionals as against the proportion of service workers living in a given part of Phoenix, Arizona.

With this type of data available, the marketer can pinpoint exactly those small geographic areas throughout the country which the marketer's judgment and experience lead him or her to conclude represent the most viable market segments for the product or service he or she wishes to offer to prospects.

Zeroing in on the Optimum Segment With this type of operation made feasible through technology and the availability of basic data about people, the alert marketer can readily test a small sampling of those zip-code areas whose residents he or she believes reflect the characteristics of his or her best market. Telephone techniques make it possible to test such areas quickly and economically and to evaluate the results promptly. Where such tests prove out positively and profitably, the marketer can then readily extend the operation to a wider segment of those zip-code areas reflecting essentially the identical characteristics of those which have proved out during test operations.

appendix four/ *List Brokers and Compilers*

List Brokers

Accredited Mailing Lists, Inc.
15 East 40th Street
New York, NY 10016
(212) 889-1180

Americalist (Division of Haines & Co., Inc.)
8050 Freedom Avenue, NW
North Canton, OH 44720
(216) 494-9111

American Mailing Lists Corporation
777 Leesburg Pike
Falls Church, VA 22043
(703) 893-2340

George Bryant & Staff
71 Grand Avenue
Englewood, NJ 07631
(201) 567-3200

Concepts for Children, Inc.
58 Anderson Avenue
Englewood Cliffs, NJ 07632
(201) 947-8888

The Coolidge Company, Inc.
11 West 42nd Street
New York, NY 10036
(212) 695-2010

Creative Mailing Consultants
8800 Edgeworth Drive
Capitol Heights, MD 20027
(301) 350-5600

Dependable Lists, Inc.
257 Park Avenue South
New York, NY 10010
(212) 677-6760

Dillon, Agnew & Marton, Inc.
654 Madison Avenue
New York, NY
(212) 832-2233

Direct Marketing, Inc.
90 South Ridge Street
Portchester, NY 10573
(914) 937-2003

Alan Drey Company, Inc.
600 Third Avenue
New York, NY 10016
(212) 697-2160

Alan Feldmar List Information Company
4215 West Grand Avenue
Chicago, IL 60651
(312) 235-4922

Saul Gale Associates, Inc.
57–03 Kissena Boulevard
Flushing, NY 11355
(212) 353-5757

George-Mann Associates, Inc.
Six Old Cranbury Road
Cranbury, NJ 08512
(609) 443-1330

Guild Company
160 Engle Street
Englewood, NJ 07631
(201) 569-5151

Helix, Inc.
1015 18th Street, NW
Washington, DC 20036
(202) 223-8016

Leonard G. Holland Associates, Inc.
549 Allen Road
Woodmere, L.I., NY 11598
(516) 374-1624

KMS-List Brokers
1000 West 25th Street
Kansas City, MO 64108
(816) 842-7267

Walter Karl, Inc.
20 Maple Avenue
Armonk, NY 10504
(914) 273-3353
(212) 324-3336

The Kleid Company
605 Third Avenue
New York, NY 10016
(212) 867-1340

E. J. Krane, Inc.
89 Washington Road
Princeton, NJ 08540
(609) 452-8000

Listservice/GRI
623 South Wabash Avenue
Chicago, IL 60605
(312) 922-6075

Otto F. Meyer & Associates, Inc.
92 Young Road
Mercerville, NJ 08619
(609) 586-7237

Mosely Mail Order List Service, Inc.
38 Newbury Street
Boston, MA 02116
(617) 266-3380

Names in the Mail
8035 Thornton Freeway East
Dallas, TX 75228
(214) 324-0577

Names in the News, Inc.
31 East 28th Street
New York, NY 10016
(212) 889-1850

Names Unlimited, Inc.
183 Madison Avenue
New York, NY 10016
(212) 481-1555

Omega List Company
301 Maple Avenue, West—Suite 2B
Vienna, VA 22180
(703) 281-2522

Preferred List, Inc.
203 North Main Street
Culpeper, VA 22713
(703) 825-5213

Prescott List, Inc.
17 East 26th Street
New York, NY 10010
(212) 684-7000

Regency Group, Division of Russ
   Reid, Inc.
80 South Lake, Suite 524
Pasadena, CA 91101
(213) 684-1920

Religious Lists
43 Maple Avenue
New City, NY 10956
(914) 634-8724

Reynard Press
P. O. Box 1383
Evanston, IL 60204
(312) 465-4309

Russell Rose Associates, Inc.
27 Locust Avenue
White Plains, NY 10605
(914) 946-3270

Russ Reid, Inc.
80 South Lake, Suite 500
Pasadena, CA 91101
(213) 684-1920

William Stroh, Inc.
568–570 54th Street
West New York, NJ 07093

Target Mailing Lists, Inc.
1140 Avenue of the Americas
New York, NY 10036
(212) 575-1020

A. R. Venezian, Inc.
211 East 43rd Street
New York, NY 10017
(212) 661-9242

Woodruff-Stevens and Associates
235 Great Neck Rd.
Great Neck, NY 11201

List Compilers and Managers

Ed Burnett, Consultants, Inc.
176 Madison Avenue
New York, NY 10016
(212) 679-0630

Compilers, Inc.
Suite 1814
225 West 34th Street
New York, NY 10001
(212) 736-2288

Dunhill International List, Inc.
444 Park Avenue South
New York, NY 10016
(212) 686-3700

The Educational Directory
1 Park Avenue
New York, NY 10016
(212) 889-8455

New Resi-Data Marketing, Inc.
77 Brookside Place
Hillsdale, NJ 07642
(201) 666-2212

Zeller and Letica, Inc.
15 E. 26th Street
New York, NY 10010
(212) 685-7512

appendix five /

A Graphic Tool
to Help "Zero In"
on the Market

MARKETERS WHO ARE UNFAMILIAR with the various telephone companies outside of their immediate geographic districts will find the map in Figure A-3 useful when planning their campaigns.

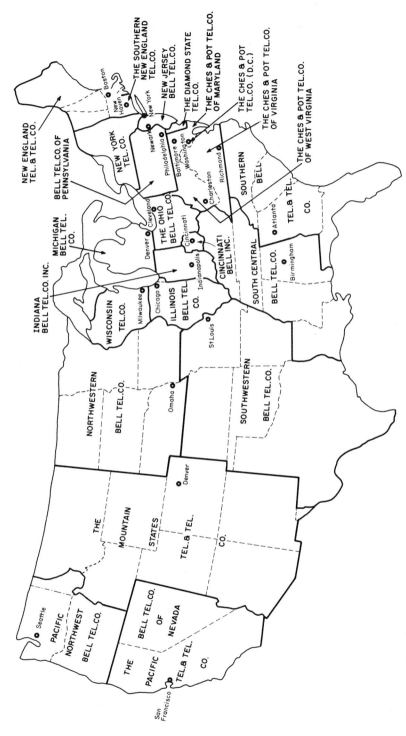

Fig. A-3.   The Bell Telephone System operating companies and jurisdictions.

appendix six/ *Voices on Tape: The Influential Persuaders*

FOLLOWING IS A PARTIAL LIST of business leads and important individuals whose messages have been recorded on tape by CCI, and used in telephone-marketing programs. NOTE: Titles of individuals are those that were correct at the time the tape readings were made.

Reaching Business Executives

American Management Associations: James L. Hayes, President and Chief Executive Officer
    John P.R. Budlong, Senior Vice President, Operations
    Dr. Franklyn Barry, Director, Center for Planning and Implementation
    Roblee Martin, President, President's Association
    Blaine Cooke, Senior Vice President, Trans World Airlines
    Donald H. Lyons, Vice President, Purchasing and Engineering Services, Johns Manville Corporation
    Bayard Rowan, Vice President, Marketing Services, The Singer Company
    Edward Smith, Vice President, Pfizer Inc.
American Metal Market: Robert J. Mastro, Publisher
Amsterdam News: Clarence Jones, Publisher
Barron's: Robert Bleiberg, Editor
    Alan Abelson, Managing Editor
Bell & Howell: David Jones, Group Vice President, Business Equipment Group
    John Marken, Micro Photo Division
Chemical Engineering: John Mitchell, Director of Sales, McGraw-Hill
Commercial Credit Equipment Corp.: Jack McDonnell, President
Communispond (J. Walter Thompson): Kevin Daly, President
Curtis 1000: Robert Brown, Advertising Manager
Dartnell Corporation: Joseph Batten, Sales Consultant; Arnold Palmer
A.B. Dick: Richard Whalen, Branch Manager, Boston
    Harold Doss, Branch Manager, Atlanta
Direct Mail/Marketing Association: Robert DeLay, President
F.W. Dodge Division, McGraw-Hill: William Dowling, Manager, Advertising/ Promotion
Encyclopaedia Britannica Educational Corp.: Prof. Howard Taiffa, Harvard Business School; Marion Sloane, Education Consultant
Equitable Life Assurance Company: Richard Hageman, Executive Vice President; Harry Walker, Executive Vice President
Goldman Sachs and Company: Gustave L. Levy, General Partner
Information Handling Services: H.C. Judd, Jr., Vice President, Marketing

IBM Corporation: Jerry Reilly, Customer Service Manager
Money Manager: Albert Kraus, Editor
Monsanto: Dr. Jerry Caulder, Technical Herbicide Manager
Nashua Corporation: Lawrence Burns, National Accounts Manager
National Cash Register: Gil Williamson, Vice President, Marketing
New York Affairs: Richard Netzer, Dean, Graduate School of Public Administration, New York University, Editor
Parade Magazine: Arthur ("Red") H. Motley, Chairman of the Board
Pepsico: Millard Styles, President, Chandler Leasing Co.
Pfizer Inc.: Dr. Paul H. Blatchley, University of Oregon
  Dr. Manuel M. Pearson, University of Pennsylvania
  Dr. Robert E. Litman, University of Southern California
Research Institute of America: James Cheeks, Senior Editor
  Charles Elting, Managing Editor
Sweet's Architectural File, McGraw-Hill: Robert Nichols, Chairman, Professional Engineers in Private Practice
Standard and Poor's: John Oppenheimer, Publisher, *Outlook*
Hearst Publications: William Campbell, Vice President, *Popular Mechanics*, *Better Homes and Gardens*
Hanover Shoe Company: Gordon King, President
International Correspondence Schools: Dr. John E. Walsh, President
Margrace Corporation: Mickey Mantle
Montgomery Ward Auto Club: Richard Cremer, President; Zsa Zsa Gabor
National Organization for Women: Betty Furness
National Women's Political Caucus: Betty Friedan
  Gloria Steinem
Old American Insurance Company: Joseph McGee, President
Psychology Today, John Suhler, Publisher; *Art in America*, Brian O'Dougherty, Publisher
Public Broadcasting System and Ford Foundation: Alistair Cooke, Julia Child, David Susskind, William Buckley, Margaret Chase Smith, Erica Wilson
Saturday Review/World: Norman Cousins
  James Michener
Studio Girl Cosmetics: Doris Day
Time-Life Records: Edmund Schooler, Director
United Planned Parenthood: Bess Myerson, Hugh Downs, George Plimpton, Dr. Gunnar Myrdal
Warner Communications: Charlton Heston

Reaching Educators and Institutions

Academic Media Cordura Corp.: Robert Bleiweiss, Publisher, Smithsonian Institution's Science Research in Progress Series
Behavioral Research Laboratories: Dr. William Sullivan, Founder
  Ms. Cynthia Buchanan, President
U.S. Department of Commerce National Technical Information Service: William T. Knox, Director

United States Steel: John Kennedy, Superintendent, Fairfield Mill
Wrightline Corp.: E.W. Housh, President

Reaching Consumers

American Express: John Anderson, Vice President, Marketing
   Phillip Kraczkowski, Sculptor
American Red Cross: Fred D. Thompson, Vice President, *The New York Times:*
   Chairman, New York Campaign
Architectural Digest: Cleon Knapp, Publisher
Canadian Olympic Coin Program: Austin Page, Director
Center for the Study of Democratic Institutions: Robert Hutchins, J.K. Gal-
   braith, Dr. Erich Fromm, Dr. Kenneth Clark, Vice Admiral Hyman
   Rickover, Dr. I.I. Rabi, Arthur Schlesinger, Jr., Dr. B.F. Skinner, Justice
   Warren E. Burger, Walter Lippmann, Ramsey Clark, W. Averell Harriman,
   Senator E.W. Brooke, Senator J.W. Fulbright, Justice W.O. Douglas,
   Rexford G. Tugwell, Thurgood Marshall, Senator Hubert H. Humphrey,
   Cesar Chavez, Senator Eugene J. McCarthy, Edwin O. Reischauer, Arthur
   Goldberg, U Thant, Lord Caradon, Aldous Huxley, Abba Eban, George F.
   Kennan, Rev. Martin Luther King, Jr., Steve Allen, Newton N. Minow,
   Sander Vanocour, Sen. Sam Ervin, Frank Mankiewiecz, Hon. Henry
   Kissinger, Daniel P. Moynihan
Chase World Information Corp.: Putney Westerfield, President
Colonial Penn Group: Robert Pollack, President
Dreyfus Corp.: Jerome Hardy, President
Encyclopaedia Britannica: Senator William Benton, Chairman of the Board
   Peter Norton, President
Encyclopaedia Judaica: Ambassador Chaim Herzog, Golda Meir, Premier
First National City Bank: Carl Gambello, Assistant Vice President
   Dennis Burns, Assistant Vice President
Guarantee Reserve Life Insurance: Richard Seidel, President
CBS "Face the Nation": Jeffrey Norton, Publisher, Holt Information Systems
Educators' Purchasing Guide: Frank Nemeyer, Publisher
Prentice-Hall: Dr. James Popham, University of California Los Angeles, author
   "Teacher Competency Development System"
   Dave Amerman, Director of College Marketing
   David Guralnik, Editor in Chief, Webster's New World Dictionary
Scott Education and Associated Press: Don Perkes, Special Projects Director
   Shirley Chisholm, Congresswoman
   Shirley MacLaine, Actress
   Joseph Montoya, Senator
   Lawrence O'Brien, Chairman, National Democratic Committee
   Robert Dole, Senator
   William Rogers, Secretary of State
Van Nostrand Reinhold Co. Litton Corp.: Benjamin F. Plummer, professor,
   author, Trinity College
   Harold Titus, professor, author
   Frank Greenagle, Vice President

Xerox Individualized Publishing: John Maroszan, Product Manager
Xerox University Microfilms: Robert Asleson, President
 Sir Frank Francis, Past Director, British Museum re: Ovid's *Metamorphoses*,
 Englished by Caxton

Political

Senator George McGovern; Rep. John Ashbrook; Rep. Herman Badillo; Rep.
 James Scheuer; Gov. John Gilligan; Ms. Elaine Siris, Chairperson Women's
 Division, and Morris Levenson, Past Chairperson, United Jewish Appeal;
 Sen. Edward F. Kennedy; Sen. Edmund Muskie; Sen. Jacob Javits; (for-
 mer) Gov. Nelson Rockefeller; (former) Vice President Hubert Humphrey.

appendix seven / The Legal Aspects of Telephone Marketing

TELEPHONE COMPANIES OPERATE IN ACCORDANCE with tariffs promulgated by state regulatory bodies. Legal problems of all kinds arise which relate to the use of the telephone by marketers. Daniel Markewich, Esq., of the firm Markewich, Rosenhaus, Markewich & Friedman, P.C. of New York City, has specialized in such problems. We have asked him to provide us with some general guidelines, and to highlight specific areas that should be of interest to those who use the telephone in marketing:

Companies in the telephone marketing field have an evergrowing number and variety of state and federal regulations to be aware of, if not afraid of. This summary can, at best, touch on only a few of the liveliest areas. Generally, the best advice is: when in doubt, check with your attorney, *in advance*.

For example, many states prohibit harassment by telephone, and some regulate methods of debt collection, whether by telephone or otherwise. A few require that the caller immediately identify himself as a solicitor, or that he immediately disclose his intent to sell. In some places, certain kinds of sales inducements are banned, while elsewhere permissible hours for solicitation are regulated. There may even be a permit, or a license fee, or registration required for certain kinds of solicitation. And in some states, consumers are afforded the right to cancel sales contracts made over the telephone within a limited number of days after delivery of goods. The movement of the future may be towards requiring initial contact by the consumer, or his written permission, in advance of telephone solicitation; alternatively, some states may give the consumer the right to insist on having, next to his name in a telephone directory, a symbol prohibiting solicitation. In short, the telephone solicitor must keep continuously up-to-date with the applicable laws of 50 states and the federal government.

Often, these laws apply to far more than the telephone. Thus, for example, a company performing marketing programs for the federal government will have to comply with Department of Commerce Regulations requiring non-discrimination, equal opportunity, employment of the handicapped and the listing of job opportunities with the state unemployment office. And, in the entire broad area of solicitation and market research, whether by telephone or in person, the effect of the federal tax laws will be a growing consideration.

It is of key importance to all companies whether telephone and in-person solicitors and market research survey interviewers are independent contractors or employees. If the former, the Self-Employment Contributions Act applies to the independent contractor, and the company is free of tax liability; but if the latter, the Federal Insurance Contributions Act, Federal Unemployment Tax Act, and Collection of Income Tax at Source of Wages Act apply to the employer. The clear trend, as exemplified in two current rulings of the Internal Revenue Service, is to fit as many such persons as possible under the umbrella of "employees."

Revenue Rulings 75-242 and 75-243 use the following guide for determining whether the employer-employee relationship exists:

> when the person for whom the services are performed has the right to control and direct the individual who performs the services not only as to the result to be accomplished by the work but also as to the details and means by which that result is accomplished. That is, an employee is subject to the will and control of the employer not only as to what shall be done but as to how it shall be done. In this connection, it is not necessary that the employer actually direct and control the manner in which the services are performed; it is sufficient if he has the right to do so.

Thus, when telephone solicitors are paid on an hourly basis, provided with company training and required sales talks, furnished a list of prospective interviewers to call, and must perform the services on days and at times prescribed by the company, they are employees although they perform the services in their own homes on their own telephones. But when such solicitors, operating from their own homes on a part-time basis without supervision, pay their own expenses, submit no report other than sales orders, are not required to devote any certain amount of time to the work or perform any services on the company's premises or produce any minimum amount of sales, are assigned only certain pages of the telephone directory from which to make the calls, and are paid straight commissions with no advance or draw, they are independent contractors.

Further, when the market research survey interviewer, whether on the telephone or in person, is obliged personally to perform the services, specific instructions are issued with respect to conducting the interview, the type of people to be interviewed and the questions to be asked, he is required to make daily progress reports to the company, the company retains the right to designate the areas where interviews will be conducted when it deems such action appropriate, and the company has the right to control and direct the interviewer to the extent necessary for the satisfactory conduct of its business, the interviewer is an employee. But when such interviewer is engaged on a short-term basis and furnished with a brief training period after which all other contact with the company is usually by mail or telephone, the interviewer is not required to perform the work personally and is free to accept or decline an assignment, and any accepted assignment is to be done according to the company's specifications but without its supervision, the interviewer is an independent contractor.

The above guidelines are so imprecise as to furnish almost no guidance at all, other than the obvious warning that the Internal Revenue Service will treat solicitors and market research survey interviewers as employees whenever possible. The real danger, of course, is that this strict rule may be applied retroactively, thereby submitting innocent companies to large additional tax bites for prior years. Presently, the Market Research Association is engaged in an attempt to persuade the government to apply the new revenue rulings only prospectively. But even if this effort is successful, most companies can expect to have their solicitors treated as ordinary employees for tax purposes in future years and should plan accordingly.

There may arise situations where, under special state laws, both the employer and the employee will have to register as solicitors. For example, the area of charitable solicitation is replete with regulation. Thus, in New York all companies that solicit for charities must register as professional fund-faisers, pay a fee, obtain a bond, submit a registration statement, and file contracts and reports; each of their employees who does such solicitation must also pay a fee for registration as a professional solicitor. There are civil and criminal penalties for non-compliance.

Other areas where the telephone marketer may easily go wrong include travel group charters, where there is the Civil Aeronautics Board to contend with; insurance sales, where there is likely to be a vigilant superintendent of insurance; and land sales, where both the State of Florida and the local attorney general may display a regulatory interest. Thus, a company whose callers solicit for insurance over WATS lines from a state where the insurer is not licensed to a state where the insurer is licensed stands a reasonable chance of avoiding the unlicensed salesman prohibitions of the local insurance laws of the state from which the calls are made only if: its solicitors are paid salaries instead of commissions, all responses to the solicitation are made directly to the insurer, *and* during the program the solicitors are paid by and treated as employees of the insurance company itself. And, in the real estate field, it is presently a matter of contention whether a telephone solicitor needs a salesman's license simply to solicit personal interviews by other, duly licensed salesmen.

The field of civil rights, too, demands the attention of the telephone marketer. In many jurisdictions, there may be laws protecting the right to privacy, so that a person's name, or even perhaps his identifiable voice, may not be used for trade or advertising purposes without his written consent to such use. Generally, it is against the law to monitor an employee's telephone calls without his consent; and substantial damages as well as criminal liability may result. Even where such consent is given in writing, it may be regarded as coerced and therefore a nullity where the giving of that consent is made a condition of employment, particularly where the scope of the required consent is broader than that necessitated by the nature of the employment. Thus, it would almost never be proper to monitor the employee's *personal* telephone conversations; but, it is submitted, a telephone marketing company might reasonably require its employee's consent to monitoring of his *business* telephone conversations *solely* for purposes of training and quality control.

Such consent may be useful in states where any *one* of the parties to a telephone conversation may consent to its being overheard, as under New York or federal law; but in jurisdictions where the consent of *both* parties to the conversation is required, surreptitious monitoring may amount to illegal electronic surveillance and be punished as a crime, not to mention the serious lawsuit that might result. As a general proposition, when it is not criminal to monitor a conversation, it is not criminal to record it; and vice versa. But criminal liability and civil suit are not the only dangers, for it is against both Federal Communications Commission and New York State Public Service Commission provisions to record a telephone conversation without the use of a "beep tone." The New York rule was unsuccessfully challenged before the state commission in 1975 by both the New York State Association of Chiefs of Police and Campaign Communications Institute of America, Inc. Thus, it is illegal, although not criminal, under New York and federal law to record a telephone conversation without the use of a "beep tone," even with the consent of *one* of the parties; it may even be the position of the regulatory commissions that the "beep tone" rule applies even where *both* recorded parties consent. The ultimate available penalty for non-compliance is removal of the offender's telephones.

This, after all, is the age of the consumer; new rules, laws, commissions and agencies have seemingly sprung up on all sides to protect the solicited at the expense of the solicitor. But unless telephone marketers recognize that it is largely the long history of abuse of consumers that has stimulated legislatures now to leap to their defense, still broader statutory proscriptions will result. It is only the telephone solicitor's strict adherence to the law that can and will protect him/her against still more onerous regulation to come; he/she therefore must seek, and follow, the advice of his/her attorney.

Dated: February 2, 1976

Direct-Marketing Agencies

Ahrend Associates, Inc.
64 University Place
New York, NY 10003
(212) 533-1640

Altman, Vos and Reichberg, Inc.
485 Madison Avenue
New York, NY 10022
(212) 371-5100

N. W. Ayer
Ayer/Direct
West Washington Square
Philadelphia, PA 19106
(215) 829-4000

Ronald A. Bernstein and Associates,
Inc.
John Hancock Center, Suite 1414
Chicago, IL 60611
(312) 664-4244

The DR Group, Inc.
342 Madison Avenue
New York, NY 10017
(212) 682-1015
(sales promotion)

EGR Marketing Group, Inc.
275 Madison Avenue
New York, NY 10016
(212) 725-1600

The Fidler Group, Inc.
801 Second Avenue
New York, NY 10017
(212) 725-9238

Garfield-Linns Company
875 N. Michigan Avenue
Chicago, IL 60611

Garmise Advertising Inc.
522 Fifth Avenue
New York, NY 10036
(212) 869-3535

Kameny Associates
110 E. 59th Street
New York, NY 10022
(212) 421-5522

March Advertising, Inc.
15 W. 44th Street
New York, NY 10036
(212) 867-6683

Marcoa Direct Advertising Inc.
10 S. Riverside Plaza
Chicago, IL 60606

The Mills Agency
527 Madison Avenue
New York, NY 10022
(212) 751-4266

Philip Office Associates, Inc.
720 Harries Building
Dayton, OH 45402
(513) 222-5529

Ogilvy and Mather, Inc.
2 E. 48th Street
New York, NY 10017
(212) 688-6100

J.W. Prendergast and Associates
342 Madison Avenue
New York, NY 10017
(212) 697-2720

Rapp, Collins, Stone and Adler, Inc.
475 Park Avenue
New York, NY 10016
(212) 725-8100

Rapp, Collins, Stone and Adler, Inc.
222 South Riverside Plaza
Chicago, IL 60606
  (312) 648-1199

Sawyer Direct—Division of BBDO
  International
383 Madison Avenue
New York, NY 10017
  (212) 355-5800

Sacli, McCabe, Sloves, Inc.
800 Third Avenue
New York, NY 10022
  (212) 421-2050

Schwab/Beatty
Division of Marsteller, Inc.
866 Third Avenue
New York, NY 10022
  (212) 826-9222

Robert E. Shaller Advertising, Inc.
641 Lexington Avenue, 17th Floor
New York, NY 10022
  (212) 421-9445

Signature Marketing
1115 North Oak Park Avenue
PO Box 227
Oak Park, IL 60302

Maxwell Sroge Company, Inc.
Time and Life Building
303 East Ohio Street
Chicago, IL 60611
  (312) 266-4900

William Steiner Associates, Inc.
527 Madison Avenue
New York, NY 10022
  (212) 688-7030

TLK Direct Marketing
Division of Tatham, Laird and
  Kudner, Inc.
605 Third Avenue
New York, NY 10016
  (212) 972-9000

Throckmorton/Satin Associates, Inc.
880 Third Avenue
New York, NY 10022
  (212) 758-4870

Richard A. Viguerie Company, Inc.
7777 Leesburg Pike
Falls Church, VA 22043
  (703) 356-0440
  (primarily fund raising)

Walter Weintz and Co.
1100 High Ridge Rd.
Stamford, CT 06905
  (212) 586-6730

Wunderman, Ricotta & Kline, Inc.
575 Madison Avenue
New York, NY 10022
  (212) 752-9800

Yeck Brothers Company
2222 Arbor Boulevard
Dayton, OH 45439
  (513) 294-4000

Guy I. Yolton Advertising, Inc.
1509 22nd Street, N.W.
Washington, DC 20037
  (202) 659-2060

Direct-Marketing Consultants

Direct Mail/Mail Order Consultants

Morton Adler
1424 Tallyho Road
Meadowbrook, PA 19046

Axel Anderson
Berner Heenweg 216a
Hamburg 72, Germany

Richard Benson
Amelia Island Plantation
Amelia Island, FL 32034

Henry Burnett Jr.
1422 E. Valley Road
Santa Barbara, CA 93108

Lawrence G. Chait
32 Lynwood Drive
Valley Stream, NY 11580

Henry Cowen
Cowen Group
215 E. Main St.
Huntington, L.I., NY 11743

Gordon W. Grossman
606 Douglas Road
Chappaqua, NY 10514

William Jayme
Jayme-Ratalahti
2306 Leavenworth Street
San Francisco, CA 94133

Ed McLean
Ghent, NY

Eugene Sollo
540 Frontage Road
Suite 259
Northfield, IL 60093

Christopher Stagg
670 Hot Spring Road
Santa Barbara, CA 93108

Cowen Group
215 E. Main St.
Huntington, L.I., NY 11743

Fund-Raising Consultants

American Fund-Raising Services, Inc.
600 Winter St.
Waltham, MA 02154

Blum Associates
annual giving
292 Red Hill
San Anselmo, CA 94960

Richard J. Crohn
105 Wagner Ave.
Mamaroneck, NY 10543

Harold L. Oram
95 Madison Avenue
New York, NY 10016

How to Calculate Telephone Marketing Costs

Cost-per-Order Breakdown

DEPENDING ON THE METHOD OF PAYMENT you choose to make for your telephone services, the calculations necessary to arrive at your telephone cost per order will vary.

Methods of Payment

A. Straight Commission This is the simplest and easiest method since it's based on a flat percent or dollar figure per sale, lead, etc. However, care should be taken in terms of such specifics as whether the percent or dollar is based on gross sales versus net (paid), gross leads versus converted (to sales), etc.

Example:

	Gross	Net
Orders shipped:		
10 @ $50 each	$500	
Orders paid:		
8 @ $50 each		$400
Commission @ 25%	$125	$100

A more subjective but still important aspect of telephone commission sales, particularly when conducted by an outside agency, should be your concern for all those who don't order now, but who may still be good future prospects. Since it is not usual for a commission sales organization to "report" on anything but orders (they are not being paid for anything else), you should be concerned as to whether or not your other prospects (future buyers) have been left feeling that they would appreciate another, later call, or have they been "burned" by high-pressure tactics— based on the maximum effort to generate commissions?

B. Cost per Call The key question here is the definition of a "call." It should mean a contact with a decision maker as opposed to a dialing which includes "Not Availables," "No Answers," "Busy Signals," or

"Nixies"—deceased, wrong number, number not in service. Also, in addition to labor and phone costs, does the cost per call include such items as phone number look-ups, and so forth?

Examples

Allowable CPO	Cost per Call					
	$1.00	$2.00	$3.00	$4.00	$5.00	$6.00
	% Response necessary to achieve CPO					
$ 5.00	20.0	40.0	60.0	80.0	100.0	—
10.00	10.0	20.0	30.0	40.0	50.0	60.0
15.00	6.7	13.3	20.0	26.7	33.3	40.0
20.00	5.0	10.0	15.0	20.0	25.0	30.0
25.00	4.0	8.0	12.0	16.0	20.0	24.0
30.00	3.3	6.7	10.0	13.3	16.7	20.0
40.00	2.5	5.0	7.5	10.0	12.5	15.0
50.00	2.0	4.0	6.0	8.0	10.0	12.0
100.00	1.0	2.0	3.0	4.0	5.0	6.0

C. *Cost per Hour* The key question to be asked here is, how many contacts with decision makers will be achieved per hour? Also, what does the hourly rate include beyond labor and phone costs, if anything?

Examples

(1) Allowable CPO	Cost per Hour (5 completed Calls per Hour)				
	$10.00	$15.00	$20.00	$25.00	$30.00
	% Response necessary to achieve CPO				
$ 5.00	40.0	60.0	80.0	100.0	—
10.00	20.0	30.0	40.0	50.0	60.0
15.00	13.3	20.0	26.7	33.3	40.0
20.00	10.0	15.0	20.0	25.0	30.0
25.00	8.0	12.0	16.0	20.0	24.0
30.00	6.7	10.0	13.3	16.7	20.0
40.00	5.0	7.5	10.0	12.5	15.0
50.00	4.0	6.0	8.0	10.0	12.0
100.00	2.0	3.0	4.0	5.0	6.0

(2) Allowable CPO	Cost per Hour (10 Completed Calls per Hour)				
	$10.00	$15.00	$20.00	$25.00	$30.00
$ 5.00	20.0	30.0	40.0	50.0	60.0
10.00	10.0	15.0	20.0	25.0	30.0
15.00	6.7	10.0	13.3	16.7	20.0
20.00	5.0	7.5	10.0	12.5	15.0
25.00	4.0	6.0	8.0	10.0	12.0
30.00	3.3	5.0	6.7	8.3	10.0
40.00	2.5	3.8	5.0	6.3	7.5
50.00	2.0	3.0	4.0	5.0	6.0
100.00	1.0	1.5	2.0	2.5	3.0

No matter what method you prefer, the primary thing is to get out the "ole" pencil and envelope and do a quick check list and some calculations to be sure you've touched all bases and answered all the major questions.

appendix eleven/ *Selected Bibliography on Telephone Marketing*

Books, Pamphlets, Articles

"ABC's of Telephone Sales: Fourteen Rules for Success," *Direct Marketing*, September 1973.

"An Approach to WATS Feasibility Analysis," *Modern Data*, September 1970.

"Area Code 800 Gives Whirlpool a Solid Consumer Connection," *Sales Management*, Apr. 1, 1970.

Buchanan, L.G.: "The Yellow Page Brigade: Comfort and Privacy: Key to Extra Telephone Sales," *Marketing Times*, November–December 1972.

Burstiner, L.: "Improving the Productivity of a Telephone Sales Force," *Management Review*, November 1974.

Campbell, John L.: "Are You Suffering from Telephobia?" *The Agent and Representative*, June 1970.

"Ducommun's Hot Line II Users Usher in New Era in Telephone Selling," *Industrial Distribution*, June 1975.

Edlund, Sidney, *There IS a Better Way to Sell*, chap. 11, "Selling Tools," New York: American Management Associations, 1973.

"Foundation Funding for PBS Test Reveals Success," *Fund Raising Management*, November/December 1973.*

Greisinger, Frank K.: *How To Cut Costs and Improve Service of Your Telephone, Telex, TWX and Other Telecommunication*, New York: McGraw-Hill, 1974.

"Keep Those Calls Ringing," *Sales Management*, May 1, 1971.

Kuehn, Richard A.: "Controlling Telephone Costs: An AMA Briefing," New York: American Management Associations, 1972.

Kuehn, Richard A.: "Traffic Case Study," RAK Associates, July 1973.

Ling, Mona: *How to Increase Sales and Put Yourself Across by Telephone*, Englewood Cliffs: Prentice-Hall, Inc., 1974.

"Marketing by Telephone: Most Misused Selling Tool," *Industrial Distribution*, February 1975.

"A Marketing Revolution—The Telephone Reinvented," *Sales Executive*, Apr. 3, 1973.*

Peterson, Ken T.: *How to Sell Successfully by Phone*, Chicago: Dartnell, 1975.

"Phone and Ye Shall Receive," *Advertising and Sales Promotion*, April 1970.

"Ringing New Sales for an Old Selling Tool," *Sales Management*, May 29, 1972.

"Sales Action," *Research Institute of American Sales Alert*, March 1974.

Roman, Murray: "How to Market Efficiently and Successfully by Telephone," Address to 7th International Direct Marketing and Mail Order Symposium, Geneva, Switzerland, reprinted by Dartnell, Chicaco, 1975.*

Schwartz, Jack, *How to Get More Business by Telephone*.

"Selling Books by Telephone, the Campaign Communications Way," *Publishers Weekly*, Jan. 21, 1974.*

"Selling by Phone is Ringing the Bell," *Business Week*, Nov. 11, 1972.*

"Selling by Telephone: More Sales, Less Cost," *Industry Week*, Sept. 10, 1973.

* Available from CCI, Inc., 641 Lexington Avenue, New York, NY 10022

Slater, Paul, Senior Vice President, Marketing, American Management Associations, "Marketing by Telephone to Business Executives," Speech at Direct Mail/Marketing Association Convention, October 1973.*

Stone, Robert: *Successful Direct Marketing Methods*, chap. 7, Crane Books, 1974.

Telephone Marketing Is the Only Person-to-Person Mass Marketing Medium That Exists Today, pamphlet excerpting speeches at AMA Seminar, April 1972.*

Telephone Sales Programs (study of effective methods/programs), U.S. Institute of Marketing.

Telephone Selling Skills (training manual), Chicago: Reuben H. Donnelley Corp.

"Today's Most Effective Marketing Medium Is Almost 100 Years Old," *The Wall Street Journal*, advertisement, Oct. 29, 1973.

Using the Telephone for Political Fund Raising, (pamphlet), 1972.*

"Will the WATS Line Replace the Order Form?" *The Reporter of Direct Mail Advertising*, May 1968.

"The World's Telephones (as of January 1, 1976)," American Telephone and Telegraph Company.

Tapes

American Association of Publishers, speech, 1973.*

"The Coming of Age of Telephone Marketing," Boston *Direct Marketing Day*, April 1974.†

"Packaging Your Message for Tomorrow's Market," Direct Mail Marketing Association's 54th Annual Seminar, September 1971.†

"Political Fund Raising," NYU Conference, 1972.*

"Telephone Marketing: Current State of the Art," interview with Pete Hoke, Publisher, *Direct Marketing Magazine*, 1972.†

"Tying the Telephone to Print and TV," Chicago *Direct Marketing Day*, May 1974.†

* Available from CCI, Inc., 641 Lexington Avenue, New York, NY 10022

† Available from Hoke Communications, Inc., 224 Seventh Street, Garden City, L.I., NY 11530.

appendix twelve / *Locating and Identifying Directories*

AN EXCELLENT SINGLE SOURCE for locating and identifying available local directories is the *City Directory Catalog*, published by the Association of North American Directory Publishers, 270 Orange Street, New Haven, Connecticut, 06509, annually at $1 per copy.

It includes a listing of every city directory published anywhere on the North American continent, including those of the national and regional directory publishers such as R.R. Donnelley & Sons Company, The Reuben H. Donnelley Corporation, Cole Publishing, R.L. Polk, Bresser's and others, as well as the substantial number of smaller local directory publishers.

In its pages will be found census data, county lists, automobile owner lists, farmers, householders, property owners, telephone subscribers, rural route resident lists, for example.

New City Directories, published by the Price & Lee Company, also at 270 Orange Street, New Haven, Connecticut, 06509, covers more than 300 United States cities and towns. These are the actual directories, whose individual prices can be obtained by contacting the publisher.

Guide to American Directories, published by Bernard Klein, 11 Third Street, Rye, New York, (914) 967-4340, provides a listing, with concise description, of directories that are available directly from their own publishers—whose identity and address are furnished in each case—for a wide variety of industrial, commercial, and occupational fields.

appendix thirteen/   *Selected Data on*
Telephone Usage
in the United States

NOTE: Charts in this section were furnished through the courtesy of American Telephone and Telegraph. The American Telephone and Telegraph Company offers no warrants with regard to accuracy. However, to the best of the company's knowledge, the information contained therein is accurate and true.

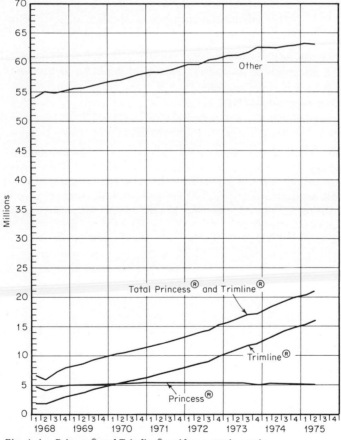

Fig. A-4. *Princess® and Trimline® residence sets in service.*

WATS INTERSTATE RATE GUIDE—As of February 8, 1976

Wide Area Telecommunications Service (WATS) is for customers, with voice or data requirements, who make or receive many long-distance calls to and from many points. The subscriber to WATS by means of a WATS access line establishes long distance calls within specified service areas that he selects. Each line is arranged, at the option of the customer, for either outward or inward service.

WATS is a telephone service available by geographical sections called WATS service areas. The largest service area covers the entire United States, except Alaska, Hawaii, and the customer's home state. WATS is also available on a state-wide basis in most states.

WATS is available at low monthly rates:
Measured Time—10 hours a month, with additional use charged by the Hour.
Full Business Day—240 hours a month, with additional use charged by the Hour.

- Fractional parts of an hour beyond the initial hours are measured in tenths of an hour or a major fraction thereof. The charge per tenth of an hour is one-tenth of the additional hour charge.
- The FIRST inward WATS access line to each WATS Service Area, either Measured Time or Full Business Day, will consist of two transmission paths. When two transmission paths are provided, usage on both paths will be charged as one access line.
- Where the monthly total of completed calls exceeds the number of minutes used, the overtime will be computed by using one minute for each completed call.

FULL BUSINESS DAY

STATE	INITIAL PERIOD FIRST 240 HOURS SERVICE AREAS					EACH ADDITIONAL 1/10 HOUR SERVICE AREAS				
	1	2	3	4	5	1	2	3	4	5
ALABAMA	$1,315	$1,570	$1,630	$1,645	$1,670	$.365	$.436	$.452	$.456	$.463
ARIZONA	1,500	1,630	1,645	1,665	1,675	.416	.452	.456	.462	.465
ARKANSAS	1,315	1,570	1,630	1,645	1,660	.365	.436	.452	.456	.461
CALIFORNIA-NO.	1,570	1,640	1,660	1,670	1,675	.436	.455	.461	.463	.465
CALIFORNIA-SO.	1,610	1,645	1,660	1,670	1,675	.447	.456	.461	.463	.465
COLORADO	1,570	1,610	1,630	1,645	1,670	.436	.447	.452	.456	.463
CONNECTICUT	900	1,315	1,640	1,660	1,675	.25	.365	.455	.461	.465
DELAWARE	900	1,315	1,610	1,650	1,675	.25	.365	.447	.458	.465
DIST. OF COLUMBIA	900	1,315	1,570	1,645	1,675	.25	.365	.436	.456	.465
FLORIDA	1,570	1,640	1,645	1,655	1,675	.436	.455	.456	.459	.465
GEORGIA	1,315	1,570	1,630	1,645	1,670	.365	.436	.452	.456	.463
IDAHO	1,400	1,610	1,645	1,665	1,675	.389	.447	.456	.462	.465
ILLINOIS-NO.	1,150	1,400	1,610	1,640	1,660	.319	.389	.447	.455	.461
ILLINOIS-SO.	1,150	1,500	1,610	1,640	1,660	.319	.416	.447	.455	.461
INDIANA	1,150	1,400	1,570	1,630	1,670	.319	.389	.436	.452	.463
IOWA	1,315	1,570	1,610	1,645	1,660	.365	.436	.447	.456	.461
KANSAS	1,400	1,570	1,610	1,645	1,660	.389	.436	.447	.456	.461
KENTUCKY	1,150	1,400	1,570	1,630	1,670	.319	.389	.436	.452	.463
LOUISIANA	1,400	1,610	1,640	1,650	1,665	.389	.447	.455	.458	.462
MAINE	1,400	1,610	1,650	1,665	1,675	.389	.447	.458	.462	.465
MARYLAND	900	1,315	1,610	1,650	1,675	.25	.365	.447	.458	.465
MASSACHUSETTS	900	1,400	1,640	1,660	1,675	.25	.389	.455	.461	.465
MICHIGAN-NO.	1,400	1,610	1,630	1,640	1,670	.389	.447	.452	.455	.463
MICHIGAN-SO.	1,315	1,570	1,610	1,640	1,670	.365	.436	.447	.455	.463
MINNESOTA	1,315	1,570	1,640	1,650	1,660	.365	.436	.455	.458	.461
MISSISSIPPI	1,400	1,570	1,630	1,645	1,665	.389	.436	.452	.456	.462
MISSOURI	1,400	1,500	1,610	1,640	1,660	.389	.416	.447	.455	.461
MONTANA	1,570	1,630	1,645	1,660	1,670	.436	.452	.456	.461	.463
NEBRASKA	1,400	1,570	1,630	1,645	1,660	.389	.436	.452	.456	.461
NEVADA	1,315	1,610	1,650	1,670	1,675	.365	.447	.458	.463	.465
NEW HAMPSHIRE	1,075	1,500	1,640	1,660	1,675	.298	.416	.455	.461	.465
NEW JERSEY	900	1,150	1,630	1,655	1,675	.25	.319	.452	.459	.465
NEW MEXICO	1,500	1,610	1,640	1,655	1,670	.416	.447	.455	.459	.463
NEW YORK-NE	1,150	1,570	1,630	1,655	1,675	.319	.436	.452	.459	.465
NEW YORK-SE	900	1,500	1,630	1,655	1,675	.25	.416	.452	.459	.465
NEW YORK-W	1,150	1,400	1,630	1,655	1,675	.319	.389	.452	.459	.465
NORTH CAROLINA	1,315	1,500	1,610	1,645	1,675	.365	.416	.447	.456	.465
NORTH DAKOTA	1,400	1,630	1,645	1,655	1,665	.389	.452	.456	.459	.462
OHIO-NO.	1,150	1,400	1,570	1,630	1,670	.319	.389	.436	.452	.463
OHIO-SO.	1,150	1,400	1,570	1,630	1,670	.319	.389	.436	.452	.463
OKLAHOMA	1,400	1,570	1,630	1,645	1,660	.389	.436	.452	.456	.461
OREGON	1,400	1,630	1,660	1,670	1,675	.389	.452	.461	.463	.465
PENNSYLVANIA-E	900	1,315	1,610	1,645	1,675	.25	.365	.447	.456	.465
PENNSYLVANIA-W	1,150	1,315	1,610	1,645	1,675	.319	.365	.447	.456	.465
RHODE ISLAND	900	1,400	1,640	1,660	1,675	.25	.389	.455	.461	.465
SOUTH CAROLINA	1,315	1,570	1,630	1,645	1,670	.365	.436	.452	.456	.463
SOUTH DAKOTA	1,400	1,610	1,630	1,650	1,660	.389	.447	.452	.458	.461
TENNESSEE	1,400	1,500	1,610	1,640	1,670	.389	.416	.447	.455	.463
TEXAS-E	1,500	1,630	1,645	1,655	1,670	.416	.452	.456	.459	.463
TEXAS-S	1,610	1,640	1,645	1,655	1,670	.447	.455	.456	.459	.463
TEXAS-W	1,570	1,630	1,645	1,655	1,670	.436	.452	.456	.459	.463
UTAH	1,500	1,570	1,640	1,660	1,670	.416	.436	.455	.461	.463
VERMONT	1,075	1,500	1,640	1,660	1,675	.298	.416	.455	.461	.465
VIRGINIA	1,150	1,315	1,570	1,645	1,675	.319	.365	.436	.456	.465
WASHINGTON	1,610	1,645	1,660	1,670	1,675	.447	.456	.461	.463	.465
WEST VIRGINIA	1,075	1,315	1,570	1,640	1,670	.298	.365	.436	.455	.463
WISCONSIN	1,150	1,570	1,630	1,645	1,665	.319	.436	.452	.456	.462
WYOMING	1,400	1,610	1,640	1,650	1,670	.389	.447	.455	.458	.463

Fig. A-5. WATS Interstate Rate Guide (effective February 8, 1976)

MEASURED TIME

STATE	INITIAL PERIOD FIRST 10 HOURS SERVICE AREAS					EACH ADDITIONAL 1/10 HOUR SERVICE AREAS				
	1	2	3	4	5	1	2	3	4	5
ALABAMA	$219	$230	$236	$239	$244	$1.643	$1.725	$1.77`	$1.793	$1.831
ARIZONA	226	236	239	243	245	1.695	1.77`	1.793	1.823	1.838
ARKANSAS	219	230	236	239	242	1.643	1.725	1.77	1.793	1.815
CALIFORNIA-NO.	230	238	242	244	245	1.725	1.785	1.815	1.831	1.838
CALIFORNIA-SO.	234	239	242	244	245	1.755	1.793	1.815	1.831	1.838
COLORADO	230	234	236	239	244	1.725	1.755	1.77	1.793	1.831
CONNECTICUT	196	219	238	242	245	1.47	1.643	1.785	1.815	1.838
DELAWARE	196	219	234	240	245	1.47	1.643	1.755	1.80	1.838
DIST. OF COLUMBIA	196	219	230	239	245	1.47	1.643	1.725	1.793	1.838
FLORIDA	230	238	239	241	245	1.725	1.785	1.793	1.808	1.838
GEORGIA	219	230	236	239	244	1.643	1.725	1.77	1.793	1.831
IDAHO	224	234	239	243	245	1.68	1.725	1.755	1.793	1.823
ILLINOIS-NO.	214	224	234	238	242	1.605	1.68	1.755	1.785	1.815
ILLINOIS-SO.	214	226	234	238	242	1.605	1.695	1.755	1.785	1.815
INDIANA	214	224	230	236	244	1.605	1.68	1.725	1.77	1.831
IOWA	219	230	234	239	242	1.643	1.725	1.755	1.793	1.815
KANSAS	224	230	234	239	242	1.68	1.725	1.755	1.793	1.815
KENTUCKY	214	224	230	236	244	1.605	1.68	1.725	1.77	1.831
LOUISIANA	224	234	238	240	243	1.68	1.755	1.785	1.80	1.823
MAINE	224	234	240	243	245	1.68	1.755	1.80	1.823	1.838
MARYLAND	196	219	234	240	245	1.47.	1.643	1.755	1.80	1.838
MASSACHUSETTS	196	224	238	242	245	1.47¯	1.68.	1.785	1.815	1.838
MICHIGAN-NO.	224	234	236	238	244	1.68	1.755	1.77	1.785	1.831
MICHIGAN-SO.	219	230	234	238	244	1.643	1.725	1.755	1.785	1.831
MINNESOTA	219	230	238	240	242	1.643	1.725	1.785	1.80	1.815
MISSISSIPPI	224	230	236	239	243	1.68	1.725	1.77.	1.793	1.823
MISSOURI	224	226	234	238	242	1.68	1.695	1.755	1.785	1.815
MONTANA	230	236	239	242	244	1.725	1.77	1.793	1.815	1.831
NEBRASKA	224	230	236	239	242	1.68	1.725	1.77	1.793	1.815
NEVADA	219	234	240	244	245	1.643	1.755	1.80	1.831	1.838
NEW HAMPSHIRE	207	226	238	242	245	1.553	1.695	1.785	1.815	1.838
NEW JERSEY	196	214	236	241	245	1.47(	1.605	1.77	1.808	1.838
NEW MEXICO	226	234	238	241	244	1.695	1.755	1.785	1.808	1.831
NEW YORK-NE	214	230	236	241	245	1.605	1.725	1.77	1.808	1.838
NEW YORK-SE	196	226	236	241	245	1.47	1.695	1.77	1.808	1.838
NEW YORK-W	214	224	236	241	245	1.605	1.68	1.77	1.808	1.838
NORTH CAROLINA	219	226	234	239	245	1.643	1.695	1.755	1.793	1.838
NORTH DAKOTA	224	236	239	241	243	1.68	1.77	1.793	1.808	1.823
OHIO-NO.	214	224	230	236	244	1.605	1.68	1.725	1.77	1.831
OHIO-SO.	214	224	230	236	244	1.605	1.68	1.725	1.77	1.831
OKLAHOMA	224	230	236	239	242	1.68	1.725	1.77	1.793	1.815
OREGON	224	236	242	244	245	1.68	1.77	1.815	1.831	1.838
PENNSYLVANIA-E	196	219	234	239	245	1.47.	1.643	1.755	1.793	1.838
PENNSYLVANIA-W	214	219	234	239	245	1.605	1.643	1.755	1.793	1.838
RHODE ISLAND	196	224	238	242	245	1.47	1.68	1.785	1.815	1.838
SOUTH CAROLINA	219	230	236	239	244	1.643	1.725	1.77	1.793	1.831
SOUTH DAKOTA	224	234	236	240	242	1.68	1.755	1.77	1.80	1.815
TENNESSEE	224	226	234	238	244	1.68	1.695	1.755	1.785	1.831
TEXAS-E	226	236	239	241	244	1.695	1.77	1.793	1.808	1.831
TEXAS-S	234	238	239	241	244	1.755	1.785	1.793	1.808	1.831
TEXAS-W	230	236	239	241	244	1.725	1.77	1.793	1.808	1.831
UTAH	226	230	238	242	244	1.695	1.725	1.785	1.815	1.831
VERMONT	207	226	238	242	245	1.553	1.695	1.785	1.815	1.838
VIRGINIA	214	219	230	239	245	1.605	1.643	1.725	1.793	1.838
WASHINGTON	234	239	242	244	245	1.755	1.793	1.815	1.831	1.838
WEST VIRGINIA	207	219	230	238	244	1.553	1.643	1.725	1.785	1.831
WISCONSIN	214	230	236	239	243	1.605	1.725	1.77	1.793	1.823
WYOMING	224	234	238	240	244	1.68	1.755	1.785	1.80	1.831

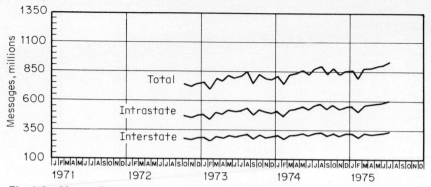

Fig. A-6. *Message Telecommunications Service (long distance)*

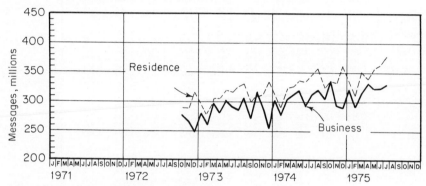

Fig. A-7. *Business and residence messages*

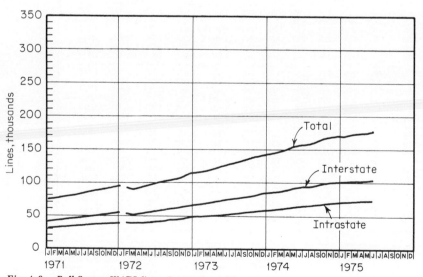

Fig. A-8. *Bell System WATS lines, intrastate and interstate*

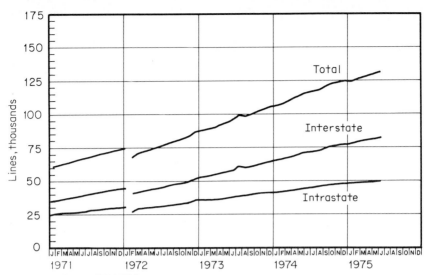

Fig. A-9.   Outward WATS lines

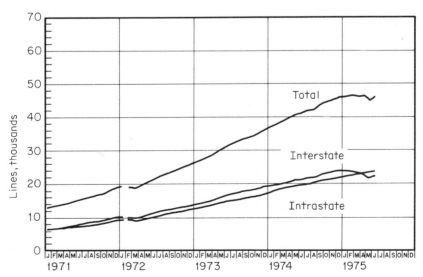

Fig. A-10.   Inward WATS lines

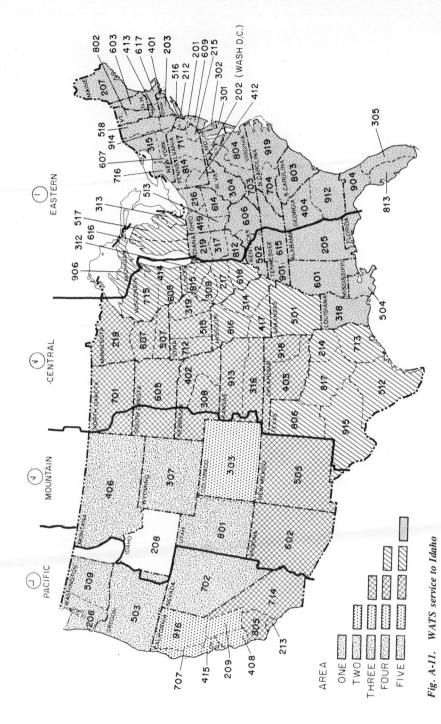

Fig. A-11. WATS service to Idaho

AREA
ONE
TWO
THREE
FOUR
FIVE

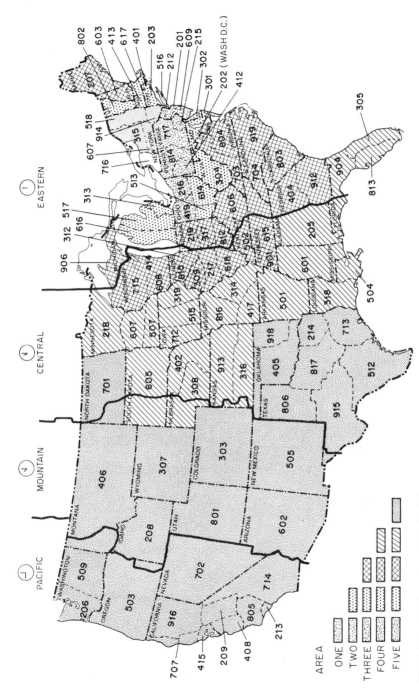

Fig. A-12.   WATS service to New York State area 716

AREA

ONE
TWO
THREE
FOUR
FIVE

TABLE A-1. Categories of Working Telephones by Operating Company

Company	Business *Main Telph.	Business †PBX	Business ‡Centrex	Residence *Main Telph.	Residence †PBX	TOTAL
New England	488,362	627,554	177,089	2,862,245	1,266	4,156,516
New York	1,108,414	1,072,322	833,294	5,423,000	4,284	8,441,314
New Jersey	455,700	499,964	153,976	2,413,596	270	3,523,506
Pennsylvania	515,035	572,499	290,830	3,011,025	565	4,389,954
Chesapeake and Potomac	543,541	641,428	584,836	3,102,488	13,067	4,885,360
Southern	787,250	818,318	282,465	4,094,599	340	5,982,972
South Central	649,425	583,995	260,697	3,880,388	605	5,375,110
Ohio	315,083	356,685	188,090	2,052,075	2,353	2,914,285
Michigan	400,428	374,975	237,973	2,421,465	2,110	3,436,051
Indiana	131,226	129,665	94,176	820,175	—	1,175,242
Wisconsin	157,095	198,435	98,220	964,062	38	1,417,850
Illinois	570,892	655,209	358,490	3,057,668	3,060	4,645,319
Northwestern	335,956	342,343	241,173	2,085,352	7,016	3,011,840
Southwestern	1,014,144	1,140,317	382,778	5,703,483	6,437	8,247,159
Mountain	489,698	460,330	242,324	2,564,775	38	3,757,165
Pacific Northwest	257,831	191,719	192,757	1,380,670	7	2,022,984
Pacific	1,274,847	1,135,219	618,421	5,694,801	2,376	8,725,664
Southern New England	169,022	208,737	89,863	1,008,292	414	1,476,328
Cincinnati	80,115	59,364	68,713	463,308	12	671,512
TOTAL	9,744,064	10,069,078	5,395,265	53,003,467	44,258	78,256,131

NOTES TO TABLE A-1

* Main Telephones (Business or Residence)   Only one telephone for each central office line is classified as main, subsidiary telephones connected to the same line being classified as extension, and not included in this data. In Key systems served exclusively by central office lines, all telephones up to the number of lines installed are classified as main, subsidiary telephones being classified as extention and not included in this data.

† *PBX Telephones (Business or Resident)*

A. Those telephones connected directly or through a Key system to Private Branch Exchange switchboards which in turn is connected to a central office or . . . .

B. Connected to subswitchboards which are subsidiaries of Private Branch switchboards or . . .

C. Connected as attendant telephones to order turrets, order-receiving tables, and similar answering and monitoring equipment which are subsidiaries of a PBX.

‡ *Centrex* Centrex telephones are those telephones working in a Centrex System and include both CO and CU.

175

TABLE A-2. *Total Accounts, by Selected Cities*
            (Percentage Classified as Business)

	Total Accounts	% Business Accounts
New England		
Boston	566,843	19.6
Springfield	120,755	12.0
New York		
Brooklyn-Queens	1,678,934	12.2
Manhattan-Bronx	1,369,093	16.9
New Jersey		
Newark	131,527	10.3
Pennsylvania		
Philadelphia	712,255	11.5
Pittsburgh	618,242	9.7
Diamond State	140,794	9.3
Chesapeake and Potomac		
Baltimore	280,264	9.0
Charleston	107,049	10.0
Norfolk	105,588	20.5
Richmond	194,858	10.3
Washington, D.C.	313,188	15.1
Southern		
Atlanta	312,205	16.8
Charlotte	142,203	15.3
Columbia	110,236	11.1
Jacksonville	205,170	13.6
Miami	536,535	14.7
South Central		
Birmingham	184,211	9.8
Jackson	101,120	13.2
Knoxville	103,725	11.8
Louisville	262,718	9.9
Memphis	264,140	10.6
Mobile	99,007	9.4
New Orleans	387,277	12.1
Shreveport	129,975	10.3
Ohio		
Akron	183,990	10.2
Canton	95,063	7.9

TABLE A-2. *Total Accounts, by Selected Cities* (*Continued*)
(Percentage Classified as Business)

	Total Accounts	% Business Accounts
Cleveland	696,496	13.9
Columbus	331,711	10.5
Dayton	219,352	9.0
Toledo	171,913	9.0
Youngstown	116,952	9.5
Michigan		
Detroit	680,965	7.6
Indiana		
Evansville	79,229	11.6
Indianapolis	339,679	10.5
South Bend	90,880	14.2
Wisconsin		
Madison	75,811	
Milwaukee	519,720	11.2
Illinois		
Chicago	1,140,200	11.9
Peoria	81,012	11.4
Rockford	77,920	10.5
Northwestern		
Des Moines	138,401	12.6
Minneapolis	403,327	11.3
Omaha	183,023	12.9
St. Paul	236,947	9.8
Southwestern		
Austin	148,751	13.6
Dallas	459,201	17.3
Fort Worth	280,388	12.9
Houston	691,301	16.0
Kansas City	268,554	10.2
Little Rock	114,615	14.0
Oklahoma City	226,832	16.8
St. Louis	634,969	9.4
San Antonio	284,827	13.2
Tulsa	174,864	16.5
Wichita	138,769	14.2
Mountain		
Albuquerque	129,417	12.2

TABLE A-2. *Total Accounts, by Selected Cities* *(Concluded)*
(Percentage Classified as Business)

	Total Accounts	% Business Accounts
Colorado Springs	125,632	14.1
Denver	489,720	13.8
El Paso	123,659	14.4
Phoenix	445,487	11.7
Salt Lake City	127,600	24.3
Tucson	161,684	13.8
Pacific Northwest Bell		
Fresno	129,575	12.2
Los Angeles Sector	2,007,067	17.9
Pasadena—Unit I	75,581	NA
Sacramento	263,052	11.0
San Francisco	472,522	19.3
Cincinnati		
Cincinnati	409,376	10.6
Covington	85,221	9.2

appendix fourteen/ *Alternative Telephone Marketing Systems*

IN ADDITION TO THE WIDE AREA TELECOMMUNICATIONS SERVICE (WATS) offered by the Bell System, other methods are available to marketers desirous of making individual calls to businesses and households in communities remote from the source of the call.

Foreign Exchange (FX)

An FX line can be thought of as a point-to-point, two-way phone line, since it is a local line in a specific city that is connected by rented trunk line to a distant community.

A Chicago firm, for example, can rent an FX line to Moline, Illinois. With this line there exists the capability of calling any and all Moline telephone subscribers from the point of origin in Chicago, while incurring only the local Moline rate for each call. Incoming calls to the Chicago headquarters can also be handled in the same manner.

Additionally, a toll call made from Chicago to a point near Moline is billed at the rate that would have been incurred had the call actually been initiated in Moline.

FX provides full 24-hour service and is cost-effective when a large volume of calls is planned to a specific city, on a regular or continuous basis, and when the overwhelming bulk of those calls are to be made within that city's local calling area. However, since FX lines are subject to a rental charge based on distance covered (plus a "local instrument" charge), this method is warranted, on a cost basis, only when the mileage between the two cities involved is not excessive; and total costs are considerably less than the cost of a WATS line which would reach into the "specific city" *but* also provide a far greater reach into the total geographic area.

Zenith/Enterprise Numbers

Known as "Enterprise" in some cities, and as "Zenith" in others, this Bell System availability provides the marketer with an ideal testing mechanism in targeted areas.

179

A special Enterprise/Zenith telephone number, listed in a specific city (or cities) telephone directory, or focused on through a solicitation via direct mail or local newspaper advertising, permits a prospect to initiate a long-distance call to the marketer at regular toll rates, paid for by the call recipient. In effect, it operates in much the same manner as the incoming "800" method, but avoids entirely the continual line rental charge which marks the "800" technique.

Each call is paid for separately, and is therefore billed at a higher per call figure than is incurred in "800" operations. However, when used as a marketing tool limited to highly restricted market segments, it can result in lower overall costs while furnishing a highly accurate testing mechanism.

In its total effect, the Zenith/Enterprise operation is equivalent to suggesting that the customer initiate a collect call to the marketer. However, its use generally results in greater volume of calls, since with this plan the customers or prospects are spared the psychological handicap of placing a "collect" call and of listening in while someone on the receiving end agrees to accept it. Callers simply ask for the Zenith or Enterprise operator and then ask for the listed number.

Zenith/Enterprise is available on a 90-day contract basis, during which time the marketer is committed to acceptance of all calls made to the special number. The separate call charge assessed for each such customer/prospect-initiated contact provides the marketer with a dependable test of his return call rate from the specific markets involved, and thus furnishes a guideline that can be used to project the feasibility of installing an incoming WATS operation for wider usage.

Microwave Communications

A number of private companies, designated by federal agencies as Specialized Common Carriers, provide services for long-distance communications, utilizing normal telephone equipment tied together by microwave channels rather than through conventional long lines.

Predominant in this group is MCI Telecommunications Corporation (1150 17th Street, NW, Washington, DC 20036, 202/782-1600), which offers a wide variety of services of which one, Execunet, is of primary interest to marketers.

Execunet reflects many of the fundamentals of the FX operation in that it permits a caller to establish telephone contact with any subscriber in a distant community while paying a local rate for each such call. At current writing, however, Execunet is available only in some 15 major cities within the continental United States.

There is a standard monthly charge, averaging around $75, plus an installation fee. MCI claims that, on average, its Execunet service can be maintained for about 30 percent less than equivalent FX service would cost.

Plans exist to extend Execunet to additional communities, but marketers are advised that the Federal Communications Commission is studying a challenge to the entire operation of microwave transmission tied to local phone equipment. Bell maintains that its significant investment in long-distance communications development is threatened by this newer approach and there are some authorities who foresee the possibility that denial of income to the nation's phone companies on this level might well result eventually in sharply increased local rates. Concurrently, however, Bell is working on development of its own microwave facility potentials as well.

Under the Execunet plan, marketers share the city-to-city microwave facility with other MCI customers, thus saving substantially on basic costs. Unlike most rented land line plans, each Execunet call is individually monitored and billed as a separate charge.

Several other organizations also offer nonlandline transmission services of a similar nature, but they are limited to statewide or regional areas. Among them are American Satellite Corporation (offering East-to-West-Coast service to large users), CIP Microwave, Inc. (serving Texas only), and Data Transmission Company (operating communications services between Chicago and Houston).

Communication via Satellite

For approximately $800 per month, a marketer located in, for example, San Francisco, can make an unlimited number of telephone calls to households and offices in, say, the Miami metropolitan area, seven days a week, 24 hours a day.

The instrumentality for this low-cost distant-communications technique is the fixed satellite, off which signals are bounced and transmitted between any two major communities in the Continental United States. Marketers can rent this service, on a monthly basis, from Western Union. Because of its great price advantage, it has been selected by Telecredit for use from its southern California base to selected communities across the nation in that firm's activities on behalf of credit card issuing organizations.

The cost, as indicated, is far less than would be the charge for an unrestricted WATS line, and thus usage of this method is beneficial where the marketer wishes to contact customers/prospects at a considerable distance from the calling area, but confined to a single concentrated community. Satellite does not offer the area coverage available through WATS, but it can in some cases be combined with, for example, FX lines at the point of reception to afford coverage of suburban areas at less cost than WATS would entail.

Since the satellite technique involves a rental payment of approximately the same $800 for each two-city hook-up, it is a method that is best restricted to a limited number of simultaneous target communities.

Additional advantages offered by the satellite method are its two-way communications availability, thus affording the marketer the benefits of the "800" technique for calls from a concentrated area, and its availability on a 24-hour basis without extra cost, allowing for the transmission of business data during hours when marketing activities are precluded. Negatives involve the "time lag" between the spoken word reaching and bouncing off a far-away satellite back to a customer or prospect listening on the phone; a 10- to 20-second difference can be frustrating for both marketer and client.

Tie Lines and "Hot" Lines

The tie line and the "hot" line are variations on the same theme: each is a rented line that runs from a specific remote point to a central switchboard.

The tie line, which is available from the Bell System, provides a means whereby a salesperson, sitting in a branch office, can make calls through his or her company's switchboard in a city other than the one in which he or she is located; thus, he or she can take advantage of the firm's rented WATS lines to make relatively low-cost long-distance calls to customers and prospects.

"Hot" lines, rented through arrangement with Western Union, perform a similar function.

Tie lines are most effectively employed by business organizations with switchboard installations in a large number of communities, since they then permit marketing operations based on the logistics of switching a calling operation's workload from one city to another without incurring substantial long-distance charges.

For example, a firm with installations in Boston, New York, and Philadelphia can set up tie lines interconnecting those cities; then, if personnel is available in Boston, calls can be made to the Philadelphia area—through the tie line and the Philadelphia switchboard—at local Philadelphia call rates. A concentration of marketing activity can thus be brought to bear in a given community, involving the use of personnel located in several other communities, through rented tie lines and the facilities of the company switchboard in the called community. FX lines can be brought into the circuit, of course, at the switchboard end, so that communicators sitting in Boston, New York, Newark, and Wilmington (as examples) might implement a series of calls to Lancaster or York or Harrisburg (through an FX line out of the firm's Philadelphia switchboard), all at the local rate for those communities.

Conference Calls

Essentially a "meeting via telephone," the conference call provides a means for simultaneous conversation and discussion with a group of individuals, each of whom is located at some geographical distance from all the others.

Agreements, which generally include prenotification to all participants of the date and time when the call will be set up, can be made through local telephone company representatives. While frequently used for administrative purposes within a given organization, the conference call does, in fact, have some marketing applications.

For example, it is an ideal tool for use by a corporate marketing or sales executive who wishes to discuss procedures, techniques, or even problems with any, some, or all of his or her subordinate marketing chiefs operating out of branch offices. In certain noncompetitive situations, the conference call can also serve as a dramatic method of stimulating interest in a home office announcement of a new product, an incentive program, or a new sales approach; such a procedure might well be invoked through arrangement of a conference call involving a manufacturer's distributors, located in different cities, all of whom can be approached and talked to at the same time through this procedure.

Costs will vary with such factors as the number of stations selected for the hook-up, the distances involved, and, of course, the time length involved in the call.

Telephone's Own ''Media Mix''

Marketing executives who are considering the use of any of these special availabilities should recognize that authoritative communications engineering opinion should be sought prior to making any final determinations.

Each of the above-noted services holds its own advantages and disadvantages in relation to the others, and cost factors represent a fundamental consideration in deciding which plan is best suited to the marketer's individual objectives. Accordingly, it is not unusual for a telephone marketing program to make use of a combination of plans, or even to switch from one available service to another at a specific point in the marketing operation's development.

Maximum cost-effectiveness might well lie, for example, in a judicious choice of FX service to some areas combined with measured WATS lines to other geographical market segments, or in testing restricted market areas with Zenith/Enterprise and then shifting to "800" operations on the basis of indicated results.

In any case, these special availabilities should be employed in direct relation to the marketer's specific and individual goals, and decisions should be made only after consultation with cost-conscious, qualified communications engineers.

Index

Costs (*Cont.*):
 supportive, 85–86
 telephone activity, 82–85
 ticket level and, 92
Courtesy, 114
Cousins, Norman, 4, 15, 48
 endpaper article: A Successful Case
  History, 202
Creative costs, 83
Credit handling, 24
Crisscross directories, 40
Cross-selling, 23, 25
Customer service, 23
Customers, 21, 24–25

Dartnell Corporation, 25
Data Transmission Company, 181
Day, Bob, 90
Day, Doris, 48, 49
Defining of market, 127
Demographic factors, 33–34, 139
Department of Commerce, U.S., 152
Description, lists of consumers by, 34
Dialing:
 automatic, 125
 direct, 84
Diction, 113–114
Direct dialing, 84
Direct mail, 3, 15
 costs of, 89–90
 irresponsible use of, 116
Direct-mail consultants, 159
Direct-marketing agencies, 157–158
 view point of, 203–204
Direct-marketing chronology, 210–211
Direct-marketing consultants, 159
Direct-response marketing, 2
Direct sales, 23
Directories, 165–166
 crisscross, 40
 REZIDE, 136–137, 142
DLA (Dreyfus Liquid Assets), 97–98
Door-to-door sales, 116
Dreyfus Liquid Assets (DLA), 97–98
Dual-contact technique, 89–90

Dun & Bradstreet, 42
Duplication on lists, 120–121

EDP system, 104
Educators, taped messages for, 149–150
Efficiency, mechanical basis for, 72
"800" operations, 93–104, 184
 business prospects and, 98–100
 communicators in, 101
 costs of, 93
 optimum response mechanism in,
  103–104
 restrictive regulations and, 97–98
 test program for, 99–100
Enterprise numbers, 179–180, 184
Equipment, revenues for, 133
Ethical standards, 129–130
Exchange of lists, 37
Execunet service, 180–181
Executives:
 marketing to, 199–200
 taped messages by, 50–51, 148–149
Expenditures for media, 132–134

Fairchild, John, 49
Federal Communications Commis-
 sion, 155, 181
Federal Insurance Contributions Act,
 153
Federal tax laws, 153
Federal Trade Commission, 117
Federal Unemployment Tax Act, 153
Fingerhut Company, 38
Foote, Emerson (endpaper article: An
 Advertising Tool), 200–201
Ford Foundation, 87
Ford Motor Company, 4, 12–14, 16
Foreign Exchange (FX) lines, 179, 180,
 182–184
Fund-raising, 217
Fund-raising consultants, 159
Furness, Betty, 48, 49, 51
FX lines [see Foreign Exchange (FX)
 lines]

Generation of leads, 23
Goldman, Sachs and Company, 49
Grossman, Gordon W. (endpaper article: Testing—Key to Success), 209–210
Guide to Directories, 165
Guralnik, David, 54–55

Hammond, William (endpaper article: An Advertising Executive's Testimonial), 208
Harvard Business Review, 10
Harvard Business School, 10
Hayes, James L. (endpaper article: Marketing to Business Executives), 199–200
Heston, Charlton, 48
Hoke, Henry R. "Pete," Jr. (endpaper article: Direct-Marketing Chronology), 210–211
"Hot" lines, 182–183
"How to Get More Business by Telephone" (Schwartz), 112
Hutchins, Robert, 49

IBM (International Business Machines Corporation), 50
Identification of market, 33–44, 127
Immediacy of impact, 2
Incentives for communicators, 67
Incoming WATS lines (see "800" operations; WATS lines)
Independent sales operations, 105–115
lists for, 106
verbal effectiveness in, 109–110
Industrial programs, 28
Inflection, 112
Information Management Workshop, 100
Input in training, 64
Inquiries, 21
trial sales to, 26
Institutional programs, 29
taped messages for, 149–150
Instruction of communicators, 62–64

Integrity, 116
Interdependency factor, 78–81
Internal Revenue Service, 153, 154
International Business Machines Corporation (IBM), 50
International commerce, telephone as instrument of, 215
International Telecommunications Union, 126
Interviews, for market research, 153–154

J. Walter Thompson Company, 12
Jay Norris Company, 38
Jones, David, 50
Josefowitz, Samuel (endpaper article: A Multimedia Tool), 204–205
Justice Department, U.S., 133

Klein, Bernard, 165
Knox, William T. (endpaper article: Tape Messages and Personal Communication), 206–207

Labor, telephone company expenditures for, 134
Labor-control techniques, 65
Lane Company, 95–97
Leads, generation of, 23
Legal aspects of telephone marketing, 152–156
restrictions in, 118, 119
Levitt, Theodore, 10–11, 65, 66
Levy, Gustave, 48, 49
Life-styles, changes in, 10
List brokers, 38–40, 143–145
List compilers, 145
Listening, 110–111
Listfax, 96
Lists:
brokers of, 38–40, 143–145
controlled circulation, 37
costs of, 41–42, 83
duplication on, 120–121

Lists (*Cont.*):
  effective usage of, 43–44
  exchange of, 37
  for independent sales operations, 106
  selection of, 33–34, 106, 127
  sources of, 35–41
  subscription, 36–38
Log sheet, 75, 78
Logical work flow procedure, 72
Long-distance telephone operations, 91
  (*See also* "800" operations; WATS lines)
Low-ticket items, 92

McGovern, George, 51
McGraw-Hill Information Systems Company, Sweet's Division, 26–27, 98–100
Mail-order consultants, 159
Mail-order houses, 38
Main telephones, 174
Mantle, Mickey, 49
Marginal accounts, sales to, 25
Market:
  definition of, 127
  identification of, 33–44
Market research, 23
  interviews for, 153–154
Market Research Association, 154
Market segments, optimum, 127, 142
Marketers, professional, informed insight from, quoted, 197–218
Marketivity, 213–214
Markewich, Daniel, 152
Markewich, Rosenhaus Markewich & Friedman, 152
Martin, William R., Jr., 95–97
Mass marketing operations, 68
Master log sheet, 75, 78
MCI Telecommunications Corporation, 180–181
Mechanical basis for efficiency, 72
Mechanized production techniques, 65
Media, total expenditures for, 132–134
Message Telecommunications Service, 170

Messages (*see* Promotional messages)
Metromail, 42
Microwave communications, 180–181
Miller, A. Edward (endpaper article: Marketivity), 213–214
Miscellaneous minor costs, 85
Monitoring operations, 73, 155
Motivation in training, 64
Multimedia mix, 2
Multimedia tool, telephone as, 204–205
Multiprogram operations, 92

National Association of Security Dealers (NASD), 97, 98
National Organization for Women (NOW), 49, 67
NCR Corporation, 50
Negative consumer reaction, 117–121
New City Directories, 165
New sales, 23–25
New York Affairs magazine, 49
New York State Association of Chiefs of Police, 155
New York State Public Service Commission, 155
New York Telephone, 122–123
New York Times, The, 97, 133
Newspaper advertising, 97
1972 SIC Basis, 138
Noncompetitive operations, obtaining lists from, 38
Numerical Listing of Manufactured Products in 1972, 138

Occupation, lists of businesses by, 34
On-approval sales, 23, 25
Oppenheimer, J., 48
Optimum market segment, 127, 142
Optimum response mechanism, 103–104
Optimum work conditions, 128–129
Order-taking, 23
Order-validation, 24
Outlook magazine, 48

Past customers, 21
Payment methods, 160–162
PBX (Private Branch Exchange) tele-
    phones, 174, 175
Performance objectives in training, 64
Periodicals, subscription lists of, 36–38
Personnel (*see* Communicators)
"Phone-Power," 66–67
Phone room, 71–74
"Piggyback" operations, 92
Political taped messages, 151
Prentice-Hall, Inc., College Division,
    53–55
Preprogrammed material, 16
Present customers, 21
    new sales to, 24–25
Previous orders, validation of, 24
Price & Lee Company, 165
Princess residence sets, 166
Private Branch Exchange (PBX) tele-
    phones, 174, 175
Production call cards, 75, 76
Production forms, 129
Production-line approach, 11
Production tally sheet, 75, 77
Profession, list of businesses by, 34
Program master log sheet, 75, 78
Promotional messages, 45–57
    script for, 55–57
    taped (*see* Taped promotional mes-
        sages)
Prospects, 21–22
    cold, 22, 25
    "800" operations and, 98–100
    new sales to, 25
Psychographics, 34, 139
Public Broadcasting System, 49, 87–90
Public image, 24

Questioning in training, 64

Radio commercials, 3
Range of applications, 20–32
    in establishing program, 27–31
    examples of, 24–27
    objectives and, 23–24

Range of applications (*Cont.*):
    preparing for operations and, 31–32
    targets in, 20–22
"Range of applications" cube, 21
Reactivations, 23
Referrals, 22
Reinforcement in training, 64
Related trade sources of lists, 36–41
Renewals, 23, 24
Repetition in training, 64
Residence telephones, revenues from,
    133
Restrictive legislation, 118, 119
REZIDE directories, 136–137, 142
Rooney, J. Patrick (endpaper article:
    The Combination Effect—Phone
    + Mail, 214–215

Salary for communicators, 67–68
Sales force, increasing effectiveness of,
    216
Sales magic, 212–213
Sales Management, 90
Satellite communications, 181–182
Saturday Review, 4, 15, 24, 91
Schwartz, Jack, 112
Scripts, 55–57
    for independent sales operations,
        106–107
    preparation of, 127–128
    for taped messages, 48–55
Securities and Exchange Commission,
    97
Selection of lists, 33–34, 127
    for independent sales operations, 106
Self-Employed Contributions Act, 153
"Service approach," 10–11
Service organizations for "800" opera-
    tions, 104
SIC (*see* Standard Industrial Classifica-
    tions)
Simulation techniques in training, 64
Smith, Margaret Chase, 49
Sollo, Eugene (endpaper article: In-
    creasing the Effectiveness of Sales
    Force), 216

Sources of lists, 35–41
Specialized Common Carriers, 180
Specialized press, 36–38
Speech, tempo of, 113
Sponsor benefits, 100
Standard Industrial Classification Manual 1972, 138
Standard Industrial Classifications (SIC), 34, 135–138
Standard & Poor's Corporation, 42, 48
Standard Rate & Data Service, 37
Standards, ethical, 129–130
Station Independence Project, 87–90
Steinem, Gloria, 48, 51
Stone, Robert (endpaper article: The Direct Marketing Agency Viewpoint), 203–204
Straight commissions, 160
Structured production-line approach, 11
Subscription lists, 36–38
Supervisory attention, 72–73
Supporting clerical activities, 73
Supportive costs, 85–86
Surveying, 23
Suskind, David, 49
Sweet's Division, of McGraw-Hill Information Systems Company, 26–27, 98–100

Tally sheet, 75, 77
Taped promotional messages, 48–55, 128
   attributes of, 51–52
   by business executives, 50–51, 148–149
   aimed at consumers, 150–151
   for educators, 149–150
   for institutions, 149–150
   and personal communication, 206–207
   political, 151
   script for, 55–57
   successful use of, 52–55
Technological innovations, 124–125
Telecredit, 181

Telephone-activity costs, 82–85
Telephone marketing, history of, as tool, 207
Telephone selling, art of, 218
Telephone workshop, 71–74
Tempo of speech, 113
Test program for "800" operations, 99–100
Test lists, 43–44
   for independent sales operations, 106
   selection of, 54
Testing, key to success, 209–210
Thomson, Sir William, 1
Ticket level:
   costs and, 92
   upgrading of, 23
Tie-in sales, 23–25
Tie lines, 182–183
Time magazine, 24
Time zones, 121
Tolls, revenues from, 133
"Tombstone" advertising, 97
Training:
   of communicators, 62–67, 128
   for independent sales operations, 107
Trial sales, 23
   to inquiries, 26
Trimline residence sets, 166
TV Guide, 24

United Nations, 126
United States Gypsum Company, 90
United States Steel Corporation, 50
University Microfilm, 91

Validation of previous orders, 24
Valley Industries, 17–18
Verbal effectiveness, 109–110
Volume, vocal, 113

Wall Street Journal, 97
WATS (*see* Wide Area Telephone Service)

WATS lines, 91, 101–102, 104, 182
  [*See also* "800" operations; Wide Area
    Telephone Service (WATS)]
WCBB television station, 49
Webster's New World Dictionary, 53–54
Weekend calls, 121
Westerfield, Putney (endpaper article:
    Instrument of International Com-
    merce), 215
Western Union, 181
Wide Area Telephone Service (WATS),
    84, 91–92, 133, 134, 167–173, 182,
    184
  incoming (*see* "800" operations)
  rate guide for, 167–169
WNET television station, 49
Women's Wear Daily, 49
Work conditions, 128–129

Work-control forms, 74–78
Work flow procedure, 72
Workshop, telephone, 71–74
World Magazine, 4, 14–16, 48

Xerox Corporation, 50, 91

Yellow Pages, 41, 134

Zeldin, Richard P. (endpaper article:
    Art of Telephone Selling), 218
Zenith numbers, 179–180, 184
Zip codes, 139–142
Zip sequence listings, 42

Endpaper

Endpaper

Other Views: Informed Insights from Professional Marketers

"Don't keep forever on the public road, going only where others have gone and following one after the other like a flock of sheep. Leave the beaten track occasionally and dive into the woods. Every time you do so you will be certain to find something you have never seen before."
ALEXANDER GRAHAM BELL, 1914

JUST A FEW OF THE "SOMETHINGS" we have "never seen before"—or not, at least, until very recently in the development of telephone technology—include electronic switching systems that permit direct overseas dialing; computer terminals for an extraordinary variety of business and educational applications; transmission of computer data by telephone circuits; the use of communications satellite systems, including coaxial cable, microwave towers, and the millimeter waveguide; the development of lightwave communications in which messages are transmitted by light pulses through cables of glass fibers—and much more.

With every technological advance in electronic communications, and they are coming at a dizzying pace, the ramifications for telephone marketing explode to new orders of magnitude.

But the outermost limits of possibility in every era must have a connection to past experience, and so it is with telephone marketing. There is a vanguard of marketers who, sooner than others and more than most, grasped the possibilities with which electronic communications technology has gifted us all, and seized upon them to make vital contributions to the marketing revolution that proceeds apace.

We have gone to some of these prescient and pragmatic marketers and asked them to share with our readers aspects of their professional relationship to the telephone. Our contributors come from the worlds of academia and advertising, publishing and insurance, banking and fund-raising, information systems and others. They are, all of them, familiar with and dedicated to the concept of *testing* as a way of life and primary tool of their professions. Each of them was provided with a copy of the manuscript of this book, and gently admonished to forsake panegyric for principle and examples of practice. This section, we told them, would be a kind of endpiece, but not an epitaph in which encomiums to the author would be forever engraved. The telephone is 100 years old; Murray Roman is somewhat younger and has a way to go before being mistaken for Alexander Graham Bell or Don Ameche—the few inferences to the contrary in what follows notwithstanding.

"Telephone marketing takes expertise!" is what the authors emphasize. Their contributions are an important part of the common effort that has made of telephone marketing a phenomenon to be reckoned with in the influencing of human behavior, as business strives to meet the expanding needs for goods and services of people everywhere.

JAMES L. HAYES
President, American Management Associations

Marketing to Business Executives

The cycle of the high cost of sales calls, with fewer sales, less work, lay-offs, and recession/depression appears to be a self-perpetuating series of events.

There seems to be a way to short-circuit these events through the use of tele-marketing. That is, using the telephone as a primary marketing tool.

On the surface this may seem like a very expensive proposition, but when compared to the cost of a personal sales call, which is currently averaging $60 per call, it is remarkably inexpensive and efficient, especially when handled by a staff of experts.

Telephone marketing successes I'm most familiar with are those achieved for American Management Associations over the last four years.

AMA, of course, has a highly specialized product. We design and produce courses, seminars, hardcover books, research studies, multimedia programs for in-company training, home-study courses, and a variety of other educational material. We count in our membership all types and levels of management.

Material as specific and varied as this appeals to many different audiences and our historical practice has been to target these markets with direct mail. This has been very successful for us. There are, however, certain circumstances under which we back up the mail campaign with telephone marketing.

Working in conjunction with CCI we identified a number of areas where we felt that tele-marketing could be used with a positive effect. Reinforcement is one of these areas. Those who have already received a mailing piece are called on the phone. This technique is usually used in connection with a topical meeting. The call is designed to help with information in addition to that which has already appeared in the mailing piece: information such as a new speaker added to the program or perhaps a new topic to be covered. In this area alone tele-marketing has produced a substantial average registration on the calls made.

Another area in which AMA uses tele-marketing is market expansion. If the program to be presented is highly specialized and the market, therefore, is too small for a mailing, CCI will produce a script aimed at the the particular market group, make the calls, answer questions, and send whatever literature is requested.

This is followed up with a second call. We have often been pleasantly surprised at the number of executives who will "sign up," over the phone.

AMA also uses tele-marketing for high-cost programs and developing qualified leads. Some of the higher-priced items have a high initial cost and a very low cost per person trained. To qualify the leads and attempt to get a company decision maker to attend a two-hour demonstration, a tape is used on the telephone; often this is followed with a second short testimonial tape.

Does this work? In our experience we have converted 13 percent of our qualified leads called to attend the demonstrations.

We pride ourselves on looking ahead for tools and techniques to aid the forward-looking manager. In an era of ever-rising costs every marketing person should certainly learn how tele-marketing can be helpful.

Interestingly enough, many marketing executives feel that potential customers resent being contacted by telephone rather than by a personal sales call. It has been our experience at AMA that this just isn't true. In fact, many people feel that the telephone takes less of their time than a personal sales call, yet enables them to get the same information.

EMERSON FOOTE
Co-Founder, Foote Cone & Belding

An Advertising Tool

As I reflect on telephone marketing, one word comes strongly to mind. That word is *leverage*. This book is capable of doing an enormous amount of good and helping prevent a great number of mistakes—as more and more marketers apply the power of the telephone to their selling requirements.

In my judgment, this book is completely scientific and completely practical with much that is quite new. There is perhaps a reason for this. While Alexander Graham Bell's invention is 100 years old, the use of the telephone as a tool for mass selling goes back less than two decades. And the greatest recorded achievements in telephone selling are *very* recent.

Telephone selling must increase markedly, though it is now a multi-billion dollar a year activity, because there is such a great need for it. And why is there this great need? Because of the decline—some say the decay—of face-to-face selling since World War II. It is my personal belief that one important reason we now have in America such a recession-prone economy is that man-to-man and woman-to-woman selling "ain't what it used to be." Advertising volume has greatly increased and has been, I am sure, a very positive factor in our economic development; but even the best advertising can never be completely personal—in the sense of one-to-one, two-way communication. Only the face-to-face sales representative or the telephone communicator can do that. And there are many indications that the telephone communicator can do it better!

I have often wondered why personal selling, once so vital to our national development, has declined in relative effectiveness. I do not know the answer. But it really doesn't make any difference, because its "replacement" has been found. It is selling by telephone.

In the case of a few businesses, the sales power of advertising alone is enough. Direct-response advertising, for instance. But generally advertising needs to be supplemented by selling effort at some level. I have no doubt that, increasingly, telephone selling will work *with* advertising to produce the best possible results—for marketers of all sizes. And this will not only be a happy marriage for the marketers, but will take some of the recession-proneness out of our economy. For some reason I do not understand, most economists all but ignore the role of selling effectiveness in keeping our economy healthy. I firmly believe that the increased use of sound telephone marketing will give them something that they *can* measure, a higher level of business activity.

In all marketing endeavors, the difference between success and failure can be devastating. This is bound to be especially true of telephone marketing because it is so new. The only serious threat to the glorious future of telephone marketing might arise from failure to curb unethical practices by some sellers—which could bring hampering regulations.

It is my belief that American business will be smart enough to prevent a reckless minority from dulling a marketing tool so vital to our national economic development.

NORMAN COUSINS,
Editor, "Saturday Review"

A Successful Case History

In 1971 I'd left *Saturday Review* magazine because of a respectful dis-
agreement with the new owners about their plans for the magazine. I
discussed the prospects of starting a new magazine with Murray Roman,
head of Campaign Communications Institute, who proposed a telephone
plan to bypass the whole promotional-literature jungle in starting a new
magazine. Soon thereafter, a battery of telephone solicitors began calling a list of prospects, asking whether they'd mind listening to a taped
message. The message talked about the new magazine and told of our
hope to develop a partnership with readers through long-time subscriptions to the new *World* magazine.

The telephone produced excellent results: Within a few months, 25,000
people had signed up—two-thirds of them for full three-year subscriptions at $25 each. Enormously heartened by this initial response, we went
ahead with our plans for launching *World*. In time, the new owners of
Saturday Review gave up on it, which enabled us to come home again.
After a brief period as *Saturday Review/World*, the magazine again became *Saturday Review*; things had come full-circle.

Throughout these changes, Campaign Communications maintains its
association with us—continuing its fine results.

ROBERT STONE
Chairman of the Board,
Rapp, Collins, Stone & Adler, Inc.

The Direct Marketing Agency Viewpoint

In my position as Chairman of Rapp, Collins, Stone & Adler, a direct-response advertising agency, I have seen, first-hand, remarkably successful telephone programs and dismal failures as well.

Sometimes we learn more from our failures than we do from our successes. Most campaigns I have seen fail have been of the "do-it-yourself" variety. The same marketing director who will settle for nothing less than the best advertising agency for print, broadcast, and direct-mail campaigns rationalizes that professional guidance isn't necessary for telephone marketing. "We'll put our best sales people on the phone. Any clerk can handle telephone selling." This is the type of fallacious thinking that stifles telephone marketing.

In this new day of multimedia, we are finding more and more that telephone is becoming an integral part of the media mix for our direct marketing clients. When telephone is first suggested to some clients, their immediate reaction is, "Too expensive." Our retort is, "Too expensive when compared to what?"

True, a telephone call is a more expensive *contact* than a contact by print, broadcast, or direct mail. But in direct marketing it isn't cost per contact that counts. What really counts is cost per order. And here telephone is often less expensive—particularly when used in combination with other media.

It is a truism that the telephone is the most personal of contacts outside of a personal call. And here, of course, with industrial sales calls being computed in excess of $60 each, the telephone compares very favorably. Industrial marketers have a vast, almost untapped opportunity to capitalize upon telephone marketing.

There is the case of a major RCS&A client who determined they no longer could afford to have their sales representatives call upon customers who were purchasing less than $200 worth of supplies a year. After-market business was going to local supply houses. A complete telephone program, including tape messages, was developed by CCI. Test markets were selected. Results were outstanding: 14 percent of all contacts were sold by telephone. After the test-marketing program, the client rolled out nationally.

We've seen other great successes through the medium of "800" numbers in catalog operations. It has been our experience that a professionally trained telephone order department will pay its way many times over.

Just to cite one example of the appeal of toll-free ordering privileges for a catalog operation, consider these figures. We urged a particular client to run a small squib in their catalog, offering toll-free ordering privileges. Twenty-six percent of all orders came in by phone. The average dollar amount of the phone orders was 19 percent greater than the average mail order. The next season, the convenience of toll-free telephone ordering was stressed throughout the catalog. Again the dollar amount of the phone orders was 19 percent greater than the average mail order. But the total number of phone orders leaped to 51 percent of all orders received.

In our opinion, to pass up the opportunities in telephone marketing, is to be blind to a proved marketing opportunity. Like all media, it can die aborning in the hands of the neophyte. Its potential demands the best of handling by a professional.

SAMUEL JOSEFOWITZ
International Direct Marketer

A Multimedia Tool

The telephone has emerged as a vital segment of the marketing media mix. Combined with strategically placed space advertising and mail follow-up, it provides a means for the marketer to construct a predictable, flexible, and measurable sales program whose profitability can be tested quickly and accurately.

For the advantages that the telephone offers in areas of testing, measuring, and projection of results can be maximized only when constant vigilance is applied day by day—indeed, hour by hour—to the analysis of properly designed, carefully kept individual call records.

A limited number of calls, completed within a very few hours, to split segments of a prospect list, can provide hard evidence as to the efficacy of each tested offer, copy approach, premium offer, and, in fact, to just about any factor the individual marketer wishes to explore. There is no long wait for the test mail returns plus analysis; the job can often be done within the limits of a *single* business day.

Precisely because of this, the telephone furnishes the marketer with a tool that facilitates the adjustment of marketing operations and the approach to the needs of the moment. The phone's immediate, person-to-person nature makes of it an ongoing test mechanism. Even after a supposedly "final" mass roll-out program has been decided upon, all the fundamental options of a continuing test operation remain open, since there is no commitment to a mass print run or a bulk mailing of fixed components. Constant vigilance over each day's results often reveals a new and changing trend to which one can react quickly—through a script change, a price change, a new offer—with almost instant feedback on the effect of the changes.

Within the media mix, telephone offers a further opportunity to increase the profitability of print advertising and mail efforts. Incisive questioning of those called can serve to reveal just why the prospect has not responded to the previous mailing. This knowledge can then be translated into improved mail approaches. And, through cold, previously unannounced calling of list segments, the telephone can give valid indications—within calculable bounds—regarding how responsive each proposed mailing list will be. In this manner a great number of lists can be quickly screened or pretested to enable the marketer to pinpoint prospective customers, to discard certain lists, and to concentrate mailings or calls only on those that have been demonstrated to yield profitable orders.

The above examples are just a few of the applications for which we, who are essentially in the direct-mail field, have found the telephone to be an effective marketing tool. But as with all new marketing techniques, the planning, the discipline of use, and the understanding of basic procedures is essential.

WILLIAM T. KNOX
Director, National Technical Information Service
of U.S. Department of Commerce

Tape Messages and Personal Communication

Before a sales transaction takes place between buyer and vendor, no matter how great the intervening physical or physiological distance, some kind of relationship between them must be created. That is why the primary marketing goal of any business organization must be to establish and continually reinforce customer relationships.

At the National Technical Information Service (NTIS) we have experimented with telephone marketing primarily to reach our regular customers in a direct, personal dialogue. This conversation further enhances an existing relationship, and even if a sale is not immediately gained, the quality of that relationship has been improved, and this strengthened customer relationship will help in future solicitations.

The unique advantage of the two-way communication between marketer and prospect made possible by telephone marketing is that NTIS can test new products or new markets for our current product line quickly. The feedback we receive from our sales calls has been invaluable to us in understanding our customers and the benefits and drawbacks our products hold for them.

Even though some observe that a recorded message is still impersonal for a mail-order organization such as mine, a telephone call with the ensuing dialogue can increase the personal and emotional satisfactions of a transaction.

Our consumers respond positively to this new sales medium. We recognize the consumer's critical attitude toward potential purchases, and that is why I want to give the NTIS message personally to as many of our users as possible. Today's electronic technology is the key to maximizing personal contact, strange and contradictory as that may seem. Through tape-recorded messages, I am able to "personally" talk to many of our customers about our common bond—NTIS products and services. Even though the professional communicators field the customers' questions, they are usually able to provide them with answers I have been a party to providing and move the prospect to make a decision to buy the item, request more information, or decide against purchases.

Our products and services are complex. The telephone makes it possible for us—without a field sales force—to engage the prospect and tell him our full story through the taped message and ensuing dialogue.

Today almost any product and service can be ordered by telephone. Like other telecommunication innovations, the telephone will be playing a larger role in marketing, and I predict, in actual delivery of our information products.

BLAINE COOKE
Frederick R. Kappel Professor
Graduate School of Business, University of Minnesota
Former Senior Vice President and Director TWA
   and Director Market Research, Ford Motor Company

Ford Started It

It seems longer ago than it was.

In fact it was in the early 1960s that telephone marketing came of age—came in fact to maturity as a sales tool. The event, of course, was the Ford Motor Company's massive commitment to the telephone as a precision marketing instrument.

The history of that program—in which I had a small part—is a history of success beyond anticipation. It produced solid, validated traffic across dealers' showroom floors at a more than satisfactory rate. It substantially increased sales efficiency by providing sales people with prospects known to be predisposed to buy. It proved that the telephone, intelligently and legitimately used, is a productive and cost-efficient tool.

WILLIAM HAMMOND
Senior Vice President, J. Walter Thompson Company

An Advertising Executive's Testimonial

Mass prospecting by phone seems a logical and obvious marketing option today. Fifteen years ago, however, Murray's proposal to phone twenty million households in pursuit of automotive sales moved the nervous needles off the scale. Participating in the most ambitious single commercial use of the telephone was a rare privilege indeed.

It is uncommon for most marketing mortals to witness, let alone participate, in the creation, development, and implementation of a truly big selling idea. We've all been experts in retrospect and we've all ruefully excused our timidity with something akin to, "I always knew it would work," after the fact.

In these times of instantaneous change the timid tend to cling to the security of familiarity. The history of successful business seems a litany of the reverse. The bold seem to survive with the simple and obvious idea. Like all success stories, there's an added special ingredient of hard work and no-quarter perfectionism. There are many in business who are convinced that success equates with innovativeness. This book certainly confirms the view by its detailed description of how to convert the telephone from a taken-for-granted home instrument to a supremely effective mass-communication vehicle.

GORDON W. GROSSMAN
Consultant; Former International Vice President and Director
Reader's Digest Association; President, Gordon Grossman
Associates, Inc.

Testing—Key to Success

The admirable case histories in this book describe many new facets of telephone marketing; yet I believe the most significant, lasting, and truly innovative feature lurks quietly (often invisibly) at the beginning of each success story:

"We tested this offer, and based on the results of our test . . ."

Perhaps only those of us who have grown up in direct mail could feel a tingling in the spine at such a throwaway line.

What's so special about testing? Doesn't everybody test? Aren't television commercials pretested, products market-tested, magazine ads Neilsened, T-G-I-ed, starched, pressed, rolled, and folded into computer printouts that contain more measurements than the Miss Universe quarter-finals?

Yes, of course, everybody *measures*. But very few *test*, directly and simply, with projectable results. In many cases, there are too many factors involved in the tortuous route from manufacturer to consumer to isolate any one variable without distorting others. Telephone marketing has the virtue of relative simplicity.

But old-fashioned telephone marketing had one significant variable which prohibited accurate projections from test quantities. The delivery of the message was largely in the hands of the communicator. The star telephone salesperson could *make* the program—or at least make the program look good, until it was expanded to involve a dozen or a hundred or a thousand other not-so-star communicators.

Uniformity of message is a basic theme in this book. Taped messages are often featured—as they should be—but uniformity of delivery can be achieved with or without tape.

Adequate controls assure a uniform delivery. Uniform delivery produces a (statistically) uniform response. This response can be projected with confidence—and telephone marketing has come of age as a direct-response medium.

Testing with projectable results is the key to the future in this lively medium. Not *everything* can be sold by telephone, not every sensible thing can be sold by telephone, but *every* sensible thing can be tested. Through testing, alert marketers will continue to discover effective means of selling new products and services.

HENRY R. "PETE" HOKE, JR.
Publisher, **"Direct Marketing"** *Magazine*

Direct Marketing Chronology

It was in 1966 at the relaunch of Direct Mail Days in New York that luncheon speaker Robert Burke of the New York Telephone Company stunned some 800 direct mail users and producers with a closed-circuit presentation on a large screen from N.Y. Telco's studios. This presentation speculated that consumers would one day phone their orders to a store or mail-order firm, that would never be closed . . . the customers having seen an ad in a newspaper or magazine, on TV, a piece of direct mail, or a catalog. It was the first hint that an alternative would exist to clipping a coupon and mailing it via the U.S. Postal Service. The push-button telephone would be the ordering device for not only dialing a toll-free number, but entering the number into the phone to an awaiting voice-response computer . . . 24 hours a day, seven days a week!

Several years later, Simpson Sears, a department store in Toronto, Canada, announced the first live application of this explosive idea. Murray Roman was early in detecting the importance of the telephone as an important new tool in the marketing process. In 1970, he made the first presentation at Direct Marketing Day in New York, describing a voice-selling system to augment the mails. Also in 1970 an imaginative advertising agency executive was offering an "In-WATS" service to any marketer who would use Win Roll's (Listfax) unique "800" number in his ads. Customers would reach a Connecticut facility filled with operators to take orders or inquiries.

In 1971, Direct Marketing Day in New York ran a full-page, couponed ad in *The New York Times*, including Listfax's number which boosted attendance by 500 to 1,850.

A similar system is offered now by Western Union. It will take orders on toll-free lines from customers perusing media, and can transmit orders over telephone lines at the end of the day or on demand to mini-terminals on the advertiser's premises.

Information Management, Inc. takes "800" inquiries from national network television (including prime time) for Canadian Olympic Coins, Franklin Mint, and the Philadelphia Bicentennial.

Lawrence G. Chait, the direct-marketing consultant, was apparently the first to explore In-WATS for a mail-order firm, Alden's, a division of Gamble Skogmo. He inserted in the September 23, 1967 issue of *The Saturday Evening Post*, a 16-page catalog section, which bore Alden's "800" number.

Today we talk of linking this activity to Electronic Funds Transfer Systems, by which the customer authorizes direct withdrawal from his bank account to the seller's bank account over the telephone lines.

Murray Roman's major contribution has been in organizing the selling function. In many cases, sales success has been cost-efficient, fast, and a viable auxiliary to direct-mail and advertising media.

It is in this area, however, that much needs to be done to set up guidelines of appropriateness.

A call from a so-called "boiler room," "hard-selling" sporting event tickets to business executives does not qualify, nor do many senseless calls from insurance and stock brokerage houses hoping to find a "pigeon." Well-recognized guidelines will make restrictive regulations unnecessary in this fascinating marketing area. Professional marketers should jealously guard their franchise into electronics which can provide inestimable service to the public and lower the cost of marketing.

LAWRENCE G. CHAIT
Direct Marketer and Mail-Order Counselor

It was in the mid-sixties that Murray Roman and I began to talk, in rather primitive terms, about what has since been labeled the "multimedia" approach to achieving acceptance in the marketplace for goods or services. It took us many years and many hours of conversation to come to a joint understanding of the ways in which both classic "media" and more subtle influences of a less well-defined nature combined to assault the eyes, the ears, the brain, and the psyche as a measurable force in the distribution process.

Marketing communicators whose vision is all-encompassing and who enjoy mature and senior status are increasingly hard to find in a business world which has skewed off in the direction of training highly structured specialists rather than all-around generalists.

There is nothing wrong with specialization in the field of "persuasion for profit" so long as the specialist remembers that an attempt to produce conviction on a mass scale is a multifaceted kind of thing. Thus, in this book on telephone selling, Murray talks as that kind of a specialist.

The telephone may indeed be found in the millions everywhere on earth, but as a machine to be employed in selling, Murray brings to it the same sense of awe that must once have been felt by Alexander Graham Bell.

What follows is taken from our original report from the *Reporter of Direct Mail* magazine of September 1965. It holds up well today. . . .

Sales Magic: Combine One Stamp, One Phone, Two Well-worn Shoes

Among all the available methods of advertising and sales communication, three convey a feeling of me-to-you intimacy: a letter, a telephone call, and a face-to-face meeting.

We would like to suggest that you take this nice old-fashioned "troika" and put it to work making money for you . . . in a big, carefully organized, adequately budgeted way.

Now obviously, there is nothing new in suggesting that a direct-mail program be used to secure inquiries and qualified leads for the sales force; nor in suggesting that sales reps use the telephone to supplement their sales calls. Thousands of firms do this every day.

A somewhat astonishing thing in this situation is, however, how few firms use these three truck-horse sales methods *in planned combination*.

The telephone conversation refers directly to the prospects' recent receipt of the mailing, and encourages immediate over-the-phone placement of orders "while stocks are complete and still available at the prices quoted."

You would be surprised at the number of people who say, in effect, "Glad you called—and intended to send the order in but have been so busy, etc.".

One recent effort along these lines produced an 18 percent conversion-to-sale among nonrespondents to the mail effort. But it must be emphasized that the advance mailing educated the prospect as to the product line and softened resistance for this product. In the course of our telephone effort, as well as through examination of the initial mail response, it is possible to determine which prospect is qualified for intensive attention by the relatively high-cost sales force . . . based on the size or complexity of the customer's need.

In the event your product line is a broad one, your pricing structured in the "big ticket" range, or your product technically involved . . . then you shall certainly find the advanced preparation by mail and telephone of great value in reducing wasted sales time and thus making your live sales team far more efficient and effective.

A. EDWARD MILLER
President, Downe Communications

Marketivity

The fabulous American industrial system, the envy of much of the world, had its roots in the Industrial Revolution. Since then, our ability to produce goods efficiently has been a function of capital investment, which has in turn produced more and more products with greater efficiency in the use of labor. As long as the process continued, we were safe from the ravages of inflation.

Several years ago that continuing process of improved productivity suddenly and mysteriously stopped. It has functioned on a more sporadic basis in recent years—a fundamental reason, I feel, for the economic ailments which have troubled our country and the world.

It is unlikely we will ever again enjoy the increasing productivity which nourished our economy for such a long time.

Our next source of economic nutrition may be found in creating marketing efficiency to match the production efficiency which sustained us for so long. Perhaps, we need to apply to marketing the same kind of research and study which blended the use of machines and labor to achieve ever-greater goals of production. I might go so far as to suggest that we name this new scientific approach to more effective marketing "marketivity" to match the meaning which the term "productivity" has taken on in industry.

As we seek to improve the marketivity of our economy, I think we will find that one of the key tools is the telephone, which has efficiently linked together 125 million homes in the United States.

My own experiences with the use of the telephone go back to its more primitive beginnings. Some fifteen years ago, I was concerned with the efficient sale of subscriptions for *Life* Magazine. Two basic sales techniques were direct mail and door-to-door selling. After a few days in the field with a door-to-door selling crew, I urged *Life* to find a new and better way to sell subscriptions; it was by telephone. After much testing and experimental work, techniques were developed which sold subscriptions effectively. A bonus developed, since it was found that the telephone was an excellent means for renewing subscriptions after normal means of renewal by mail were exhausted.

I suspect that the developments in the next decade will dwarf all that has gone before. As postal expenses increase, as store distribution fails to achieve increasing efficiency, as our economy becomes more competitive, we will find a new business climate in which the telephone—with its infinite possibilities for immediate, personal and responsive marketing—will achieve full recognition and utilization.

J. PATRICK ROONEY
Chief Executive Officer, Golden Rule and Congressional
Life Insurance Companies

The Combination Effect—Phone + Mail

Our company's most exciting use of the telephone in our marketing efforts has been in relation to the agricultural and cattle market. Here, sheer distance and widely scattered locations of our audience make traditional face-to-face sales calls impractical.

Our initial step to this market is direct mail designed to generate a qualified lead. We reply to inquiries with a fulfillment package, then phone those who, after a certain time interval, have not bought.

Our key products to this market are a major medical policy and estate insurance. The need for the latter has arisen as a result of the extraordinary appreciation in farm property values over the last decade.

We have found that the selective use of the telephone, in conjunction with our direct-mail promotion, has substantially increased policyholder acquisition.

PUTNEY WESTERFIELD
President, Chase World Information Corporation,
Former Publisher, "Fortune" Magazine

Instrument of International Commerce

The telephone today projects into the future a number of provocative insights of vital interest to anyone engaged in international commerce.

In the period immediately on the horizon, the development of satellite communications, the broadening of direct dialing connections overseas, and other technological advances will make every foreign business prospect as close to you as your own telephone. The purchasing agent in Zurich, the housewife in Lyons, the business executive in London, the retail merchant in Milan, the magazine subscriber in Tokyo—all will be available for personal conversation with the individuals on your mass-marketing, direct-response communicator staff.

Within the United States, the telephone has amply proved its attributes as a cost-effective medium of sales, inquiries, prospect screening, credit jogging, surveying—indeed, as a marketing tool attaining dozens of normal objectives.

Effective users of the telephone have learned that its successful employment encompasses a good deal more than just sitting an experienced salesperson at the instrument; it requires sound planning, professional creativity, control of personnel selection and training, accurate and knowledgeable record keeping, sensitive interpretation and projection of results and, above all, management level supervision and control.

These lessons—learned in some instances only after difficult and painful experience—can now be applied to the profitable use of the telephone as an instrument of international commerce.

EUGENE SOLLO
President, Carlyle Marketing

Increasing the Effectiveness of Sales Force

In this age of rising sales costs, of need for greater coverage, of better market penetration, and the increasing demand to be aware of customer and consumer problems, no business executive really needs an excuse to improve sales efficiency.

It is no wonder, then, that the telephone has become a critical way of life for all of us in sales and marketing. What is so amazing is that so many companies have not yet found that this is true. How then can the telephone become the vital peg on which we hang our sales and marketing plans?

My own experience, both professionally when I was Executive Vice President of *Encyclopaedia Britannica*, and as a most interested consumer who responds to lead-producing space ads, is that thousands of leads generated at great cost are never followed up.

The telephone can certainly be vital in this role. For instance, many companies have developed criteria to determine which customers should be seen by a sales representative face-to-face, and which can be handled through a highly organized telephone marketing operation.

JOAN AND ROBERT BLUM
Partners, Blum Associates

Fund-Raising by Phone

The telephone has added an extraordinary dimension to fund-raising when it is used in a framework of ethical responsibility and professionalism. It has earned for itself a definite place in annual giving, along with personal visits and direct mail.

Specifically, in renewals of previous gifts, the phone is an excellent follow-up to direct-mail solicitation, preserving the all-important continuity of giving.

In upgrading previous gifts, the phone communicator can suggest increased amounts, working downward as necessary to assure regularity. This two-way communication often provides the opportunity for immediate revision of individual goals and can be vital for continuation and upgrading. The phone can be used, too, for inviting givers to special events for "special" donors.

Lapsed donors can be successfully reinstated by phone. Here again, it is the two-way communication capability that can ferret out concealed reasons for not giving, and answer questions in the policy area, for instance, if it is this that is troubling the lapsed donor. The phone communicator can apply more, and more subtle, pressure on the donor than a mail piece which can be safely ignored.

RICHARD P. ZELDIN
President, Xerox College Publishing

Art of Telephone Selling

If effective communication is the keystone of successful marketing, then the art of telephone selling demands careful study and understanding. The future success of companies in most industries will be affected by how well they understand the environment, the market, and how to reach it most effectively. As a result many innovative marketing people are turning to telephone selling as one way of getting an edge on the competition. The telephone makes it possible to approach every potential customer with a prepared, predetermined, uniformly presented message copy, while at the same time permitting reasonable flexibility in response to each individual prospect's requirements.

Whether the product being offered is a book, a magazine subscription, a department store sale, a credit-screening call or a car rental, telephone selling today requires more than the personal selling techniques used in face-to-face selling. Significant advances have been made in the development of the telephone as a sales medium. The "production line" concept of using the phone opens an entire new era of solving marketing problems by objective and scientific means.

Telephone selling is an increasingly important factor in any total marketing effort. In many marketing plans it is the major element.